Social Work in a Turbulent World

Seventh NASW Symposium

Selected Papers

Seventh NASW Professional Symposium on Social Work
November 18–21, 1981, Philadelphia, Pennsylvania

Miriam Dinerman, Editor

National Association of Social Workers, Inc.
7981 Eastern Avenue
Silver Spring, Maryland

Library of Congress Cataloging in Publication Data

NASW Professional Symposium on Social Work (7th :
    1981 : Philadelphia, Pa.)
    Social work in a turbulent world.

    Includes bibliographical references.
    1. Social service—United States—Congresses.
2. United States—Social policy—Congresses. I. Diner-
man, Miriam,1925–   . II. National Association of
Social Workers. III. Title. [DNLM: 1. Social work—
Trends—United States—Congresses. W3 NA254 7th 1981s / HV 85
N269 1981s]
HN53.N28   1981   361'.973   83-8216
ISBN 0-87101-108-5

Printed in the U.S.A.

Professional Symposium Planning Committee

Positions are those held at the time of the symposium (November 1981).

JAMES R. DUMPSON (Chairperson), New York Committee Trust, New York, New York

MIRIAM DINERMAN, School of Social Work, Rutgers—The State University of New Jersey, New Brunswick

SUZANNE DWORAK-PECK, Malibu, California

E. DANIEL EDWARDS, Graduate School of Social Work, University of Utah, Salt Lake City

RICHARD L. EDWARDS, School of Social Welfare, State University of New York–Albany

FRANK FERRO, Administration for Children, Youth, and Families, U.S. Department of Health and Human Services, Washington, D.C.

SUSANNE E. HEPLER, Graduate School of Social Work, University of Houston, Houston, Texas

LAWRENCE HERLICK, Jenkintown, Pennsylvania

ARABELLA MARTINEZ, Washington, D.C.

GEORGIA L. McMURRAY, Community Service Society, New York, New York

JULIA WATKINS, University of Maine, Orono

Symposium Book Committee

Positions are those held at the time of the symposium (November 1981).

MIRIAM DINERMAN (Chairperson), Professor, Graduate School of Social Work, Rutgers—The State University of New Jersey, New Brunswick

E. DANIEL EDWARDS, Associate Professor, Graduate School of Social Work, University of Utah, Salt Lake City

CAREL B. GERMAIN, Professor, School of Social Work, University of Connecticut, West Hartford

PAUL A. KURZMAN, Professor, School of Social Work, Hunter College, New York, New York

ELAINE PINDERHUGHES, Associate Professor, School of Social Work, Boston College, Boston, Massachusetts

JACQUELINE MARX ATKINS (staff), Director of Publications, National Association of Social Workers, New York, New York

Contributors

Positions are those held at the time of the symposium (November 1981).

SHEILA H. AKABAS, Ph.D., Professor and Director, Industrial Social Welfare Center, School of Social Work, Columbia University, New York, New York

GARY ASKEROOTH, MSW, Director, Westside Neighborhood Housing Center, St. Paul., Minnesota

JULIUS R. BALLEW, MSW, Project Coordinator, Special Family Services Project, Michigan Department of Social Services, Lansing

RITA BECK BLACK, DSW, Assistant Professor, School of Social Work, Columbia University, New York, New York

WILLIAM H. BLAU, Ph.D., Licensed Psychologist, Pasadena, California

EDWARD A. BRAWLEY, DSW, Associate Professor, Department of Sociology, Pennsylvania State University, University Park

LESLIE G. BRODY, MSW, Executive Director, Eliot Community Mental Health Center, Concord, Massachusetts

BARBARA DITZHAZY, MSW, Program Manager, Preventive Services for Families, Michigan Department of Social Services, Lansing

MARGARET GIBELMAN, DSW, Senior Staff Associate, National Conference on Social Welfare, Washington, D.C.

CATHEY A. GRAHAM, MSW, Clinical Social Work Specialist, Huntington Memorial Hospital, Pasadena, California

DIANNE F. HARRISON, Ph.D., Associate Professor, School of Social Work, Florida State University, Tallahassee

CYNTHIA J. HAWKINS, MSW, Clinical Social Worker, Huntington Memorial Hospital, Pasadena, California

ALLIE C. KILPATRICK, MSW, Assistant Professor, School of Social Work, University of Georgia, Athens

JORDAN I. KOSBERG, Ph.D., Professor, Department of Gerontology and Department of Social Work, University of South Florida, Tampa

MARY LYNCH, Ph.D., Research Analyst, Ramsey County Community Corrections Department, St. Paul, Minnesota

RUFUS SYLVESTER LYNCH, DSW, Executive Director, Center for Studying Social Welfare and Community Development, Philadelphia, Pennsylvania

EDWARD J. MULLEN, DSW, Professor, School of Social Service Administration, University of Chicago, Chicago, Illinois

JOHN POERTNER, DSW, Assistant Professor, Legal Studies Program, Sangamon State University, Springfield, Illinois

SHELDON L. RAHN, DSW, Associate Professor, Faculty of Social Work, Wilfrid Laurier University, Waterloo, Ontario, Canada

CHARLES A. RAPP, DSW, Assistant Professor, School of Social Welfare, University of Kansas, Lawrence

WILLARD C. RICHAN, DSW, Professor, School of Social Administration, Temple University, Philadelphia, Pennsylvania

BETTY RIVARD, MSW, Social Services Coordinator, West Virginia Department of Welfare, Charleston

MARIO TONTI, DSW, Director of Social Services, The Benjamin Rose Institute, Cleveland, Ohio

PATRICIA V. VANCE, MSW, Associate Dean, School of Social Work, Florida State University, Tallahassee

THOMAS H. WALZ, Ph.D., Professor, School of Social Work, University of Iowa, Iowa City

DEBORAH K. ZINN, MSW, doctoral candidate, Social Work and Social Science, University of Michigan, Ann Arbor

Contents

Editor's Introduction

The Seventh Professional Symposium of the National Association of Social Workers (NASW), held in Philadelphia in 1981, was charged with a special, electric excitement. It was one of the largest gatherings of social workers ever. More important, it was held as the full impact of a major reversal of American social policy was becoming visible to the professional community. The budget of the Reagan Administration for fiscal year 1982 was in place, and the ramifications were becoming clear. Federal funds were being drastically cut from what Budget Director David Stockman called the "entitlement" programs. The existing array of regulatory protections were being systematically reduced. The governmental role that had been slowly built up since the Progressive Era and that was designed to limit the excesses of private enterprise, protect the vulnerable, and correct the deficiencies of state and local governments was now being dismantled.

When the Symposium Planning Committee began making plans at its first meeting in April 1980, it chose "Social Work Practice in a Turbulent World" as a theme for the symposium. It is ironic that the turbulence the committee had in mind was that caused by major technological and economic changes and changes in resources that are revolutionizing the relationship of one nation to another, the relationship of individuals to work, the role of the family, and relations among family members. The committee was thinking of computerization, the use of robots, and the growth of multinational corporations and cartels as these affect individuals in American society. It talked of the stresses caused by the reorganization and relocation of the workplace and similar consequences. At a more general level, these pressures and dislocation due to large-scale changes would be played out on the disadvantaged, the frail, and other consumers of social work services as well as bring to us new populations, damaged by these changes in ways that could be only partly guessed at this time.

By the time the symposium took place, however, different sources of turbulence were uppermost in everyone's mind. The president who was in the White House was claiming to have a mandate to reduce government intervention in every sector of American life.

For those future readers who will perhaps only dimly remember this era of turbulence, President Reagan tried to do four things in the first budget during his term of office entirely of his own making: increase spending on defense, decrease taxes, reduce government regulation, and lower the overall level of government spending. These were all assumed to be beneficial, the last three being specifically intended to address the severe economic woes of the United States in the early 1980s. These economic troubles consisted of recalcitrant inflation, stagnant economic growth with attendant high and rising unemployment, and the loss to foreign competition of significant sectors of the markets formerly dominated by American industry. In light of the planned sizable increases in defense spending, the large reduction in government spending was to come mainly from the social sector of the federal budget. All this was complicated further by a three-year tax reduction plan intended to provide investment capital to upgrade and modernize American industries so that they could once again compete successfully against foreign industry. The final factor affecting budgetary efforts was that a very large proportion of the federal budget represented long-term commitments not easily subject to change, such as charges for the interest paid on high and rising federal debts, social security payments, especially when indexed to the cost of living, and long-term procurements and construction projects. Although some of these trends had been foreshadowed in earlier administrations, the location, direction, and magnitude of the Reagan initiatives made them in truth a new phenomenon.

As part of his proclaimed commitment to "getting the government off the backs" of the people, the president made three broad proposals. One involved lumping a number of separate categorical programs together into single block grants and turning the money, the decision making, and the administration concerning them over to the states. The catch was that projected funding was initially set at about 25 percent less than prior levels, and a further phase-down was planned. Although the states' governors were pleased to have the money and the discretion over its spending, many soon added up the costs and backed away. They could foresee being blamed by angry citizens as services and programs were cut, even if the federal government was the source of the cutbacks. The president did not push further for this plan.

The second proposal was a swap, billed as an even exchange, in which the federal government would assume all the costs and administration relating to Medicaid while the states would assume all the costs and administration relating to Aid to Families with Dependent Children (AFDC), food stamps, and certain other programs that aid the poor. Again, the states' governors totted up the figures and foresaw both increased costs and increased trouble in running programs no one liked. They also saw the difficulties involved in making cutbacks that could not be implemented without political penalty and in losing their ability to pass the buck. So proposals for the "new federalism" disappeared from view. All these activities hardly made for a climate of peaceful planning or for clarity in service delivery, however.

The third part of the Reagan plan was a huge tax reduction, with the greatest part of the benefits going to the wealthy and to business on the assumption that this would provide the needed economic stimulus to expand, improve, and modernize American industry. This in turn was to boost the number of jobs available and cure the prevailing economic woes of high inflation, low economic growth, and high unemployment. However, when coupled with the largest rise ever in military expenditures, the tax cuts resulted in huge and increasing deficits in the federal budget. In an effort to bring down these deficits, which were projected to grow to a staggering size, further cuts in social programs were both enacted and planned for future budgets.

A variety of related issues also claimed the nation's attention. There had been a steady growth in federal expenditures for all purposes, especially after the end of World War II, whether measured as a percentage of the gross national product in constant or in current dollars. From 1965 on, the rate of this growth accelerated, doubling (in 1981 dollars) from 1965 to 1981.[1] This trend can be accounted for in part by a growth in the number of people in the country, in part by the federal takeover of functions previously carried out by states, local governments, or the philanthropic sector, and in part by the expansion of new programs and services and by inflation. There was, in addition, a major expansion of government activity. During this time, the priorities of different sectors within the federal budget changed. In spite of the Vietnam War, from 1965 to 1981 spending on the armed forces in general gave way to spending on social programs.[2] This coincided with national concern about reducing poverty and making access to health care, education, and opportunity more equal.

The rhetoric of the early eighties stated over and over that "throwing money at problems" did not solve them and that government programs in the social sector had not only failed, they had made things worse, since they were now judged to be the cause of many of our economic troubles. Certain facts—that poverty had declined substantially, especially among the aged, since the declaration of the War on Poverty, that access to health services was made almost equal for the poor and the nonpoor, that minorities and women began to make progress toward equal opportunity

---

[1] See Ann K. Bixby, "Social Welfare Expenditures, 1979," *Social Security Bulletin,* 44, (November 1981); Ida C. Merriam and Alfred M. Skolnick, *Social Welfare Expenditures under Public Programs, 1929–1966,* Social Security Administration Office of Research and Statistics Report #25 (Washington, D.C.: U.S. Government Printing Office, 1968), and Sheldon Danziger and Robert Haveman, "The Reagan Budget: A Sharp Break with the Past," *Challenge* (May June 1981), p. 513.

[2] Danziger and Haveman, op. cit.

in the areas of higher education, pay, and promotion, and that other social gains had taken place—were ignored.

With the budget for fiscal year 1981 in place and the budget for fiscal year 1982 under discussion, the pattern was becoming clear. At least some of those hurt by the cuts in benefits and services had complained effectively to Congress. Questions were being raised about the value of some military expenditures and especially about our nuclear policies. Questions were being presented even more clearly regarding the enormous deficits projected by an administration that had campaigned on the theme of a balanced budget by 1984. Most relevant to social work, the promised safety net for those judged "truly needy" was found to be flawed, and was being cut to ribbons besides.

This safety net was a peculiar contraption. It was composed of programs like Medicare, social security, and veteran's programs, whose benefits go primarily to the nonpoor and, in fact, often go to the well-to-do; it also contained income-tested programs like AFDC and Supplemental Security Income (SSI) as well as Head Start. It became clear that the safety net was no longer immune to cutbacks as the regulations governing eligibility for disability payments under both SSI and social security were changed, making thousands of recipients no longer able to receive benefits. Other changes in rules and regulations made additional thousands of AFDC recipients either totally ineligible for benefits or able to receive only sharply reduced benefits. In one county in New Jersey alone, 1,600 families were removed from the AFDC rolls due to these changes, and many more received smaller checks. It should be remembered that the loss of AFDC often means a simultaneous loss of Medicaid—the only form of protection against health costs available to most of the very poor—as well as the loss of an array of other interrelated program benefits. These cuts primarily affected women who were the heads of a household, were single parents with small children, were working, perhaps part time and perhaps at low-paying jobs, and whose welfare benefits served to supplement earnings up to a not-very-generous state standard of need. These standards varied from a low of $187 a month in Texas to a high of $629 in Vermont for a family of four.[3] At the same time, virtually every other social program was also being cut. Some cuts were direct, and some were more hidden, as when a number of programs were combined into a single block grant that was funded at a significantly lower level than the original programs had been. Programs relating to women,

---

[3] *AFDC Standards of Need: An Evaluation of Current Practices, Alternative Approaches, and Policy Options, Appendix A,* Social Security Administration Office of Research and Statistics SSA #13-11742 (Washington, D.C.: U.S. Government Printing Office, 1981).

infants, and children's nutrition, college student loans, Title XX, child-hood immunizations, community development, and day care were only some of those that were reduced. It was not clear that the average American citizen was ready to oppose these general policies, although there was clear and strong opposition by some to particular decisions.

By the time of NASW's symposium, the nation had entered a serious recession. Large areas of the country were reporting unemployment as high as 20 and even 40 percent. The same newspapers that carried headlines about these events also reported stories of fiscal crises from many statehouses and city halls, clearly presaging that neither state nor local government could be expected to fill the vacuum caused by the federal government's actions. The president called on the philanthropic sector and business to step into the breach, believing that these could do a far better job than the government in any case. Members of both sectors pointed out early and often that even if each doubled its present efforts, they could provide only a tiny fraction of the resources needed.

In a climate like this, social workers and social work were under attack. They were accused of being both ineffective and bleeding hearts. In this atmosphere, social work professionals gathered in unprecedented numbers in Philadelphia and took courage from the sheer number of colleagues present. They found renewal in the sharing of ideas, innovations, and practice developments and in the rousing call to action that enjoined them to enter the political arena to fight and to bear witness to the injustice and inhumanity of the new policies and the pain they inflicted on the old, the very young, minorities, the working poor, and the disabled. This call came from outside the profession from Carl Rowan, nationally syndicated columnist, and from inside the profession from Nancy Humphreys, past president of NASW. And the over 4,100 social workers present went away renewed, restored, determined, and prepared to fight for social justice in behalf of those who suffered the brunt of these program and policy changes.

The symposium was also the scene of a special tribute to Chauncey Alexander on the occasion of his retirement as executive director of NASW. The very size of the symposium was a testimony to the tremendous growth of the association under Chauncey's leadership. In addition, the symposium reflected another aspect of the growth of the profession during Chauncey's tenure—the increase in both scholarly work of high caliber and in the variety of roles and techniques that social workers have developed. Three hundred and fifty papers were selected for presentation from many hundreds submitted for consideration. Topics representing every letter of the alphabet were covered, from abortion and accountability to visual impairment and women. The criteria used to select papers for inclusion in the present volume were quality, wide applicability, and incorporation of sufficient supporting evidence. Many fine papers were not submitted for consideration to the Symposium Book Committee, and many others could not be accepted for publication because of lack of space. We offer this volume as one of enduring interest, but it cannot be judged an accurate reflection of the Symposium itself in all its variety and richness or of the array of forms and places of social work practice in 1981. Many of the articles reflect the turmoil created by the massive reversals in American social policies. They reflect too the historic concerns of the profession and the desires of social workers to attend to the needs of individuals and families in trouble and victimized by forces beyond their control and to work for social reform and social action to ameliorate the impact of those forces. Fifteen articles cannot adequately represent either the full diversity of the symposium's twenty-two invitational speakers nor the range of papers chosen from the more than three hundred workshops. In their different ways all reflect the profession's historic concern with bettering the social functioning of members of society, addressed as always in the traditional bifocal vision of social work, which concentrates on the person-in-situation.

The articles in this volume are divided into three sections. The first documents the extent of the turbulence now characterizing American social policy and the impact of the changes in government policy being carried out. The second deals with ways to improve social services and practice in a world thrown into turmoil by those changes. The last suggests innovative and creative responses to cope with a turbulent world and enhance the growing edge of practice.

MIRIAM DINERMAN

November 1982

Part One
Confronting a Turbulent World

Editor's Comments

Four articles that examine the impact of Reagan's policies on the shape of the "welfare state" and its organizations and that describe some efforts to oppose these developments comprise Part One. The first, by Walz, Askerooth, and Lynch, looks at the peculiar way in which the welfare state in the United States developed and predicts the likely results of supply side economic theories on its next phase. It is likely that most Americans believe that we have a well-developed welfare state and that it provides substantial benefits to the poor at the expense of almost everyone else. Walz, Askerooth, and Lynch argue that instead the bulk of the benefits have gone to the middle class. Indeed, there is considerable evidence that the middle class, in fact, have been the primary users of such openly available services as public higher education, subsidized mortgages, and tax benefits for home owners, and have indeed gotten greater benefits from the elementary and secondary school system than their poorer fellow citizens.[1] Walz, Askerooth, and Lynch also say that although the middle class gain more, the poor receive a large amount of social control with the services they do get. Moreover, the authors predict that the current revival of social Darwinism will result in an increase in social control for the poor and more social ameliorative services for the middle class. In other words, they state that the Reagan policies will disperse both welfare and "dyswelfare" in ways that suit the wisher but not in ways that conform to the image that Americans have of their welfare state.

In the second chapter, Richan offers two case histories in an effort to help us learn some of the techniques for effective obstructive tactics in an antiwelfare time. Both techniques registered considerable success, and this fact should encourage social workers to join together at local, state, or national levels to exert their political muscle. As a further encouragement, it should be noted that our American system of government with its dispersion and division of power, its checks and balances, makes it far easier for all organized effort to block than to initiate and carry through a program. Let us as social workers read the lessons of these two examples carefully!

---

[1] W. Lee Hansen and Burton A. Weisbrod, *Benefits, Costs, and Finance of Public Higher Education* (Chicago: Markham Publishing Co., 1969).

The third chapter, by Zinn and Rivard is also designed to help social workers develop tactical skills for an antiwelfare time. Zinn and Rivard analyze social work's experience with the allocation decisions of block grants to help the profession improve its techniques in dealing with the new sources of funding for many social programs. In addition, many of the procedural requirements of old block grant programs such as Title XX have been eliminated, with consequences that can only be guessed at now. The tactic of combining multiple sources of funding is suggested to gain one coordinated, locally delivered program. The authors offer ways for workers to locate successful and unsuccessful contenders in the battle for funds so that they can be prepared for their own battles. Zinn and Rivard also point out the consequences of some of the different ways in which states may handle crucial allocation and priority decisions as well as some of the devices open to social workers who oppose those decisions. The new arena of critical action for social work will be state capitols, which are much closer to home than the old arena in Washington, D.C. If the profession fails to move into funding debates at state levels, decisions will be made in its absence, ones that may not be liked. It is, thus, important for social workers to take the time and energy to roll up their sleeves and help get decisions more to their liking. But they will have to watch carefully so that they do not fight one another but rather look for the interconnections, the alliances, and the coalitions among social workers from different agencies and from others outside the profession who share common goals.

The last chapter in Part One, by Brody, brings the prevalent issues to the level of a single human service organization. The environment of such an organization is now more complex. This creates the need for organizations to be more flexible not only in regard to reductions in funding and legislation such as Proposition 13, but also in regard to conflicts among the goals of the various levels of govenment, distrust of financing for social services generally (especially when compared to concrete ways on which to spend public money), demands for greater accountability, and other stressful attitudes. Brody uses concepts from organizational theory specific to mental health agencies. The extrapolation to any social welfare organization should not be hard to make, however. Brody sees these times as an era when the concern is survival and the tasks are defensive ones that promote survival. The specific tactics he suggests are based on principles that should be applicable to the particular circumstances of any organization.

The New Upside-Down Welfare State

Thomas H. Walz
Gary Askerooth
Mary Lynch

It has been nearly a decade since we, the authors, put forth the argument that the welfare system in this country is "upside down"—that the nation's social policies and programs are benefiting most those who are in the least need of public support.[1] At that time, we were concerned about the growing backlash against the War on Poverty. We documented the inverse benefits of housing, tax, and welfare policies that had been ostensibly designed to benefit the poor. We return now, in 1983, to restate the "upside-down welfare" argument that it is not the poor who benefit most from governmental social policy. At this time, the historic American "tension between the humanistic goals of the modern welfare state and the requirements of the free market" is especially weak.[2] It is important to pay heed to the messages of the past about the "Other America" of the poor, about the risks to the common good of this nation of targeting governmental economic and social programs to the rich at the expense of the poor. This article will briefly recall the concerns of Michael Harrington, will recast the upside-down welfare argument, and will present evidence of progress against poverty in the 1970s. It will then examine the overtly upside-down welfare orientation of the current administration, as articulated by George Gilder and David Stockman, critique their positions, and lay out the risk involved in implementing current economic and social policies.

Liberal Economic Agenda

In *The Other America: Poverty in the United States*, Harrington argued that because the poor had become a minority in an affluent society,

11

their poverty was more devastating than ever before.[3] He also pointed out that the poorest of the poor were the least likely to be assisted by public programs and were becoming "invisible" to the new middle-class majority. For a brief period, until the war in Vietnam diverted the federal budget and fueled inflation, the conscience of the middle class was pricked enough to support an abundance of legislation aimed at eradicating the social "disease" of poverty.

In the 1960s and 1970s, a liberal economic agenda dominated politics in this country. Social legislation provided for transfer payments, in-kind provisions, and improved status rights that reached growing numbers of the poor and the minorities. Although the social disease of poverty was not eliminated during that period, it was mitigated. A new social rhetoric emerged with such resounding declarations as the "War on Poverty" and "maximum feasible participation" of the poor. What happened in that era? Social security insurance was improved by anchoring it to the cost-of-living index to lessen the impact of inflation on the retired; unemployment, although allowed to float somewhat, was nonetheless confronted with a variety of public employment programs and the extension of un-employment benefits; and the housing shortage was challenged by a range of new public housing strategies and a new rental assistance provision. Furthermore, inflationary health costs were met with new amendments to the Social Security Act—Title XVIII (Medicare) and Title XIX (Medicaid). Another controversial amendment was Title XX, which, at least for a time, opened the purse strings in support of expanded social services. In addition, equal opportunities for racial minorities and women were extended through equal rights and affirmative action legislation.

Harrington noted that the pool of poor people was growing smaller and thus the poor had become invisible. And, indeed, the real and relative numbers of the poor continued to decrease dramatically. Between 1959 and 1969, the number of poor individuals decreased from 40 million (22 percent of the total population) to 24 million (12 percent of the total population). That trend remained basically constant until 1977, when the poor numbered 25 million, or 12 percent of the population.[4]

Other, more ambitious social programs had a much less measurable impact on reducing poverty, especially if the original goal of restoring everyone to productive, independent, dignified lives is the measure. The Aid to Parents with Dependent Children (AFDC)–Work Incentive Program (WIN) produced victories as Pyrrhic as did former President Ford's WIN on the inflationary battlefield. Female-headed households are still much more likely to be poor than are male-headed households. And the employment prospects of minority youths (and adults) never were boosted perceptibly despite years of the Comprehensive Employment and Training Act and its various permutations. Only the civil rights and women's rights movements seem to have had a lasting socioeconomic effect on American public life, and even these movements are under direct attack by the Reagan Administration, which sees itself as the defender of the embattled upper middle class.

Throughout the period of expanded governmental initiatives, there was an uneasy feeling that the liberal agenda could easily be sidetracked. The years of the Nixon Administration increased that feeling as the victims of a stagnating economy and unwinnable domestic and foreign wars were publicly blamed for the general ills of the society. Thus, it should be remembered that the attack on the unproductive poor did not recently resurface after decades of liberal goodwill. In 1973, former Secretary of Housing and Urban Development Romney had this to say of the problems of single mothers: "We have had a long time of encouraging people to think they are going to get something for nothing in this country, and consequently it is beginning to affect a lot of the problems that we have."[5] The increasing costs of social programs have rankled the middle class and distressed social planners. In 1960, social welfare expenditures represented 11 percent of the gross national product (GNP) and 33 percent of the total governmental expenditures. By 1978, 19 percent of the GNP and 58 percent of the government's expenditures were devoted to social programs.[6] There is a residue of belief that these expenditures go to the "undeserving" and the able bodied, despite repeated explanations that the vast majority of funds go to children, the very old, and the disabled. It is also believed that these expenditures are an intolerable addition to energy costs and inflation.

The sudden rise in fuel costs and in inflation stemming from the long-deferred costs of the Vietnam war produced fresh concerns among this country's newly defined "real majority." Heilbroner described this new selfishness as "civilization malaise"—a loss of faith in the inevitable progress of high technology.[7] Whether the visible effects represent a dramatic change in the public philosophy about welfare is questionable. John F. Kennedy's "liberal" victory was a narrow one over the same Richard Nixon who eight years later was elected to dismantle all social experimentation. It is interesting to note that it was the Carter Administration which began reversing the trend of increased social welfare. From 1978 to 1982, the growth in nondefense spending was only 0.3 percent after a decade of dramatic increases—the greatest one being 13 percent in 1975.[8]

Supply Side Economics

In 1982—twenty years after the "other America"—"another America" is taking shape, one built on the theory and philosophy of "supply side" economics. In its simplest form, supply side economics argues for reduced governmental spending (particularly in the realm of social programs) and added incentives for encouraging industrial production (as a means of increasing the supply of goods). The assumption is that if the government feeds the corporations well, they will, in turn, be better able to feed people. The previous governmental strategies of improving demand by bolstering incomes and increasing credit and borrowing while including some redistribution of income through improved transfer payments have been rejected. Supply side economics shifts transfer payments from one constituency (the poor) to another constituency (the nonpoor and the corporations), thus reducing the impact of redistribution. Note that it does not eliminate transfer payments. In lieu of welfare subsidies, the government shifts to a greater use of subsidies to the middle and upper, classes through tax exemptions and loopholes; both are clear forms of public welfare but they are aimed at different publics. For people at the zero-tax level, a tax cut has little meaning except that it further increases the gap between their income and that of others. In 1982, Congress unanimously passed an unprecedented three-year tax-interest program skewed heavily toward the upper-income brackets.

The new upside-down welfare state is being shaped by the economic theorists of supply side economics, guided by David Stockman, director of the Office of Management and Budget, and intellectually inspired by Arthur Laffer. Laffer argues that lower tax rates can stimulate business by shifting income from tax shelters to taxable activities.[9] Such a shift, he believes, will result in higher tax revenues that can allow for the continued support of activities in the public sector. This is a theory that proposes giving special economic rewards to the economically privileged.

Gilder popularizes this conservative economic approach in *Wealth and Poverty*. He turns around the previously covert upside-down orientation and argues aggressively that

> . . . an effort to take income from the rich, thus diminishing their investment, and to give it to the poor, thus reducing their work incentives, is sure to cut American productivity, limit job opportunities and perpetuate poverty.[10]

Gilder admits that supply side economics will add to upside-down welfarism; as he puts it, "the poor will be asked to pay for the recovery of prosperity on the faith that they too may eventually benefit from the new economics."[11] To get a grip on the problems of poverty, Gilder offers the following:

> . . . one should also forget the idea of overcoming inequality by redistribution. Inequality may even grow at first as poverty declines. To lift the income of the poor, it will be necessary to increase the rates of invest-

ment, which in turn would tend to enlarge the wealth, if not the consumption, of the rich. The poor if they move into the work force and acquire promotions, will raise their income by a greater percentage than the rich; but the upper class will gain by greater absolute amounts, and the gap between the rich and the poor may grow.[12]

In a more specific prescription for escaping poverty in a supply side economy, Gilder outlines the only "dependable" route: work, family, and faith. Accordingly, he states:

> The first principle is that in order to move up, the poor must not only work, they must work harder than the classes above them. The second principle of upward mobility is the maintenance of monogynous marriage and family.[13]

Faith is the third principle of upward mobility:

> Faith in man, faith in the future, faith in the rising returns of giving, faith in the mutual benefits of trade, faith in the providence of God are all essential to successful capitalism.[14]

The new assumption is not that the defects in the poor are necessarily the cause of their impoverishment, but that liberal redistributive and social support programs are to blame. In Gilder's view, these programs rob the poor of the need to work as cheap labor and make it economically possible for families to tolerate divorce and the abandonment by men of the household.

Modern social Darwinism had been quietly regaining its position in American mythology until the Reagan victory removed all restraint on its proponents. David Stockman's aggressive budget cutting was foreshadowed by Earl Butz's efforts in 1976 to cut food stamps to their 1962 level. Long before he became secretary of defense, Caspar Weinberger proposed the elimination of AFDC, food stamps, and Supplemental Security Income (SSI).[15] Weinberger also called for some other measures, including making the income tax less progressive and adding a strict work requirement to all transfer payments.

High-Technology Society

Liberal alternatives were, of course, not true solutions to the growth of a permanent underclass of "unusable" human resources. The public assistance programs never raised a significant number of people beyond a near-poor level of dependence. As Cloward and Piven noted, these programs were used to control the supply of surplus labor in conjunction with the economic cycles of capitalism.[16]

Cloward and Piven's observation needs updating in this postindustrial age. First, there is no critical need for cheap labor in a high-technology society and, similarly, racism no longer serves a real economic purpose.

The new purpose of social welfare as an appendage to the economy is to exploit the poor in an attempt to cope with the economic instability of the society. The liberals' solution was Keynesian interventions aimed at "stimulating" demand and a concern for redistributive values; the conservatives' solution is to cut governmental spending while affording new incentives to business and industry. The liberals advocated using the government as the employer of last resort. The conservatives believe in less government; they assume that employment opportunities will grow from increased private investments. It is little wonder that Gilder calls for an act of faith in the working of the new economics.

The poor and the vulnerable are no longer categorized as a "social indicator" but as a "macroeconomic statistic," which falls on the "cost" side of the equation. The goal is to reduce that cost to the maximum, while building up the supply side of the economy. The poor are once again "invisible" because they are being dealt with as statistical abstractions, not as human beings who have been caught up in the exigencies of a high-technology world. It is the economist, not the social worker, whose voice is heard and listened to. The conscience of this country has become dulled by the fears and mass insecurities produced by lingering inflation. There is a widespread belief that the standard of living is being eroded by inflation—a belief that is not supported by the high levels of consumption enjoyed by middle America. Inflation does produce economic hardships and insecurity, but principally for those who are being subjected to the biggest governmental budget cuts—the poor and the near poor.

The poor are increasingly vulnerable to the current upside-down philosophy of welfare. For example, studies of the displacement of persons from apartments that have been converted to condominiums show that a large proportion of these persons are low-income, elderly, and minority tenants. The government offers greatly improved tax benefits to the converters of older buildings through accelerated depreciation schedules but Section 8 certificates for the displaced are cut back drastically.[17] Furthermore, migrant workers and other illegal aliens contribute more in taxes than they receive in cash and services from all governmental sources. Employers accept illegal social security numbers from aliens and submit contributions that the aliens never will be able to collect.

When interest rates rise drastically because of energy-company profits and years of deficit financing of a military economy and drive home ownership out of the reach of 90 percent of the people, the government authorizes versions of mortgage loans that may result in buyers having less equity in five years than at the time of purchase. Although middle-income homeowners receive tax credit for installing energy-saving equipment, the poor get the benefit of indignities heaped on them free of charge. During the coldest winter months of 1980, Community Action Programs in northern Minnesota were distributing pamphlets showing poor people how to wrap themselves in newspapers if their heat was shut off![18]

Even though the Bureau of Labor Statistics and the Environmental Protection Agency concluded that about one million jobs would be created by a $15 billion investment in pollution control, the government decided to cut pollution control programs.[19] This loosening of regulations against pollution directly benefits the corporate sector, which is within the supply side orientation. The disadvantages fall on those workers who would be hired for the new pollution-control jobs and to the public at large, which lives in a less healthy environment.

Upside-down welfare measures that were only threats in the 1970s are now grim realities. The following is a preview of potential subtractions from the years of slow social progress that the authors see as emanating from the supply side orientation:

1. Raise the minimum retirement age and limits for earned income for recipients of social security. This proposal will hurt most those who die young (e.g., minorities) and the unskilled who cannot "moonlight."

2. Reduce early retirement benefits, which also will hit the unskilled and unhealthy.

3. Eliminate the minimum floor on benefits. This proposal is aimed at double public pensioners—those who retire from governmental service, go into the labor market, and then receive both federal pensions and social security. However, it will hurt those whose benefits fall to the point where they will be shifted to the SSI program because SSI will be identified as "welfare," not insurance.

4. Tighten eligibility for disability, which will move many persons either into SSI or into the unemployment lines.

5. Reduce the length of unemployment benefits, which will shift unemployable or noncompetitive workers into a welfare status.

6. Index social security to annual wage levels rather than to the cost of living. This cost saving has been sought for many years because the cost of living has been rising faster than wages.

AFDC has always been the favorite scapegoat of reformers of all persuasions. Between 1965 and 1972, the welfare rolls rose from 4 million to 10 million.[20] Welfare cheating became a useful political issue, which eventually resulted in the establishment of the National Welfare Fraud Association. What the investigations of this association have revealed is open to serious debate. However, even if its highest claims of fraud (30–40 percent) are true, the number of ineligible recipients is vastly lower than that of those who are eligible but never apply for assistance. Evidence of this can be seen when the unemployment rates go up suddenly, as in 1975, and more people apply for assistance.

With the new Gilder-Reaganomics in vogue, AFDC is in for further attacks. Large urban states, especially in the North and Northeast, provide greater benefits and have more liberal eligibility requirements. Perhaps some of these states will not institute punishment of women who make the mistake of owning the wrong property or living with the wrong man. However, if the Moral Majority campaigns continue to focus on the so-called traditional family, it is certain that unemployment insurance for male-headed households will be valued over support for AFDC, whose recipients are less-skilled women of childbearing age.

In-kind Supports

The relative improvement in the lot of the welfare class has been the result of the increased availability of a mix of in-kind supports, such as food stamps, voucher-paid health care, and rental assistance. These supports are the major targets for reductions in spending. Before any such actions are taken, however, it should be remembered that two of three eligible persons, who are among the most vulnerable in society, have yet to take advantage of their eligibility for such supports because of ignorance, intimidation, or apathy. Moreover, the government has done little to educate the public about who is entitled to these governmental supports, which itself is a statement of the limited commitment of the government to reach the neediest of the needy with these programs.

The very existence of in-kind supports raises the question of whom these programs are designed to serve. The Food Stamps program serves the food industries as readily as it serves the poor, health-care vouchers add to the income of physicians and hospitals as assuredly as they provide for the health needs of the poor, and rental assistance helps landlords as well as it does low-income tenants. It will be interesting to observe the difference in the impact of the cuts in governmental spending on providers and consumers. Most providers can pass on the cuts to consumers through price control—a factor that will add to the upside-down impact of any reductions in governmental spending for social programs.

Public-supported social services present a different challenge to the conservatives, and the moral flavor of Gilder's theory makes it unlikely that there will be a direct attack on such services. Social-control services (such as work and training), except perhaps aggressive abortion and family planning services, may well be given public support. Gilder's argument that the breakdown of the family is a principal cause of poverty must typically force his followers to stand behind those support services that bolster the position of the man as the head of the household.

A number of personal social services are popularly supported by the middle and upper classes. Day care, community mental health, and family counseling services are frequently used by these classes. Therefore, cuts in these areas will not have the same broad-based support as cuts in services whose recipients primarily are poor.

Furthermore, cuts in social services are more apt to be directed toward Title XX services, which are aimed at the poor, than to Title III services, which are vociferously supported by organized groups of the elderly. The politics of social services operates as vigorously in a conservative administration as it does in a liberal administration and with the same structural impact. Thus, the poor will continue to get social-control services designed to keep them from becoming more expensive public dependents, and the middle class will get a disproportionate share of personal social services.

Conclusion

The Reagan Administration's stance is remarkable in its consistency. Stockman, Gilder, and Martin Anderson (Reagan's chief domestic aide) articulate a consistent approach to social policy. Leonard Silk summarizes this approach as follows:

> Thesis One: The war on poverty has been won.
> Thesis Two: The vertical elimination of poverty has costly side effects. It has made indignant bums of us.
> Thesis Three: We have to continue to hold some sort of safety net for people who are collapsing, but we've got to ban welfare for everybody else who can take care of themselves if they're properly kicked into it.
> Thesis Four: . . . radical political reform is out and . . . it belongs to idealogues.[21]

An overt attack on the redistribution of income is coming. As Aaron Wildavsky stated: "The people's real income is going down . . . and when people's incomes are going down they're less disposed to give it away."[22] It is in such a constrained economic situation that the most vulnerable among us must struggle for a fair share.

The television series "M.A.S.H." has made most Americans aware of the medical concept of triage as it is used during war to conserve scarce resources. According to triage, those who can survive without help are left to their own resources, and those who are too weak to be given care to survive are left to die mercifully. The precious medical assistance is then concentrated on those in the middle—those who can be salvaged with treatment. Perhaps the War on Poverty will finally be won now that middle America has learned that triage is both economical and socially acceptable.

Notes and References

1. Thomas H. Walz and Gary Askerooth, *The Upside Down Welfare State* (Minneapolis, Minn.: Advocate Services, 1973).

2. Mary Bryna Songer, *Welfare of the Poor* (New York: Academic Press, 1979), p. 155.

3. Michael Harrington, *The Other America: Poverty in the United States* (New York: Macmillan Publishing Co., 1962).

4. *Social Security Bulletin, Annual Statistical Supplement, 1977–79* (Washington, D.C.: U.S. Government Printing Office, 1980), Table 1, p. 1.

5. George Romney, "Interim Report on HUD Investigation of Low and Moderate Income Housing Programs," Committee on Banking and Currency, House of Representatives, March 31, 1971, p. 46.

6. *Social Security Bulletin, Annual Statistical Supplement, 1977–79*, Table 10, p. 60.

7. Robert L. Heilbroner, *An Inquiry into the Human Prospect* (rev. ed.; New York: W.W. Norton & Co., 1980).

8. "Debating the Welfare State—Its Forms, Its Functions," *New York Times*, September 13, 1981, p. E3.

9. See George Gilder, *Wealth and Poverty* (New York: Basic Books, 1981), p. 180.

10. Ibid., p. 67.

11. Ibid., p. 67.

12. Ibid., p. 68.

13. Ibid., p. 69.

14. Ibid., p. 73.

15. Walz and Askerooth, op. cit., p. 49.

16. Richard A. Cloward and Frances Fox Piven, *Regulating the Poor* (New York: Pantheon Books, 1971).

17. Dennis Keating, Richard LeGates, and Chester Hartman, *Displacement: How to Fight it* (Berkeley, Calif.: Legal Services Anti-Displacement Project, National Housing Law Project, 1981).

18. *CAP Newsletter* (Duluth, Minnesota), Winter 1980; and *No More Heat? A Self-Help Booklet* (rev. ed.; Washington, D.C.: Community Services Administration, 1981), Pamphlet No. 6143-16.

19. National Research Council, *Manpower for Environmental Pollution Control* (Washington, D.C.: National Academy of Sciences, 1977).

20. See the various issues of *Public Assistance Statistics Monthly* (Washington, D.C.: Social and Rehabilitation Service, U.S. Department of Health, Education & Welfare, 1971), esp. tables on social insurance and welfare services.

21. "Debating the Welfare State."

22. Ibid.

Obstructive Politics for an Antiwelfare Era

Willard C. Richan

Throughout American history, the politics of social welfare has generally consisted of attempts to expand the people's collective responsibility for one another against resistance of varying intensity. In fact, the pattern of humanitarian initiative has become so deeply imbedded in the culture that terms like "reformer" and "change agent" are automatically tied to specific political orientations. Now the nation is faced with an inversion of this traditional pattern, with the initiatives coming from those who would dismember the social welfare system. Every step backward represents a basic change that will not soon be repaired. Thus, it is urgent that the fallback be held to a minimum. So human service professionals must learn a new type of politics: the politics of obstruction. If this message sounds defensive, so be it. The profession is in a period of defensive warfare.

But social workers should by no means be defeatists. Mr. Reagan's impressive achievements to the contrary notwithstanding, our system of government is inherently resistant to change. The sheer complexity of the process of making policy gives a natural advantage to the obstructionist, and social workers, despite their reputation of being well-meaning but politically impotent, have demonstrated a capacity for effective political action.[1]

This article examines two cases in which social welfare advocates were able to abort serious attacks on human services against formidable odds. One case involves the attempt by the Nixon Administration at the height of its power in early 1973 to curtail sharply the federal support for social services. The second case concerns a proposal by the governor of Pennsylvania to eliminate 81,000 so-called "employables" from the roles of public assistance.

Latent Constituencies

The power to make policy, in a formal sense, is usually vested in a few individuals. Even taking into account those actively involved in trying to influence decisions, there are still relatively small numbers of policy-makers. Analysts generally agree that the American political system is characterized by a relatively low level of participation by the citizenry.[2]

"Conflicts are frequently won or lost," says Schattschneider, "by the success the contestants have in getting the audience involved in the fighting or in excluding it, as the case may be."[3] Such intrusion by "outside forces" is especially important to groups that lack political resources. According to Lipsky, "The 'problem of the powerless' in protest activity is to activate 'third parties' to enter the implicit or explicit bargaining arena in ways favorable to the protestors. This is one of the few ways in which they can 'create' bargaining resources."[4]

"Audience," as used in this context, is best thought of as a set of shifting constituencies with varying potential for being drawn into any particular contest. (By "constituency" is meant an identifiable segment of the population, organized or unorganized, with a common stake in a political issue.)[5]

Three factors that determine the readiness of a latent constituency to become politically involved are organization, self-interest, and legitimacy. Organization provides the structure through which policy issues can be interpreted to members and through which appropriate responses or action can be defined. Constituencies are moved to invest energy in an issue when their self-interest is at stake. Policy proposals may be viewed as beneficial or threatening, and the cost of political involvement itself (such as the threat of retaliation) weighs heavily in decisions of whether to get involved or not. Finally, a constituency must define its activity as legitimate. For example, a professional community must be able to justify its political role according to its ethical code.

Among constituencies that do become activated, the power to affect policy decisions varies greatly. Three key factors are size, position, and information. The importance of size seems self-evident, yet the evidence regarding this factor is mixed.[6] For example, intensely committed minor-ities have been able to win out against adverse sentiment in the public opinion polls, as in the case of abortion and gun control.[7] The concept of position may refer to formal authority to make decisions or access to those vested with such authority. Information, as a source of political influence, can be thought of in two senses: (1) evidence for use in swaying opinions and (2) strategic intelligence regarding political actors and the decision-making process itself.

Two other factors that are important as means of gaining access to or utilizing these resources are organization, as described previously, and money. This latter factor is translated into staff time, mailings to members, and access to information. Direct campaign contributions may also affect policy decisions, although their impact on specific policy questions may be exaggerated in the popular mind. The application of this framework is illustrated in the following two case histories.

Battle of the Social Service Regulations

The first of these two illustrative cases began with the 1962 amendments to the Social Security Act, in which the federal government committed itself to match state funds on a three-to-one basis for designated social services.[8] The formula was open-ended; that is, states were free to increase their expenditures with a guarantee that the federal share would be paid. Liberalization of this scheme in 1967 was followed in subsequent years by a rapid escalation of state claims, and the federal share rose by more than 13 percent in the space of one year (fiscal 1972). Alarmed, Congress placed a $2.5 billion ceiling on these social service expenditures in the fall of 1972.

Meanwhile, the Nixon Administration, buoyed by its landslide reelection victory, moved ahead with more drastic medicine. In February 1973, the Department of Health, Education, and Welfare (HEW) announced stringent new regulations to govern the three-to-one grant-in-aid formula. Services were to be geared, directly or indirectly, to the single purpose of making welfare recipients self-supporting. The number of services covered was drastically reduced, and the number of nonrecipients allowed to become eligible for social services was sharply cut. The proposed rules would go into effect in ninety days. Comments were invited, but the decision to modify the rules or leave them intact was up to HEW.

The new regulations posed a serious threat to consumers of services, to social agency programs, and to the careers of many social workers and other human service workers. The reaction was swift. Within a few months, HEW was deluged with over 200,000 negative comments. In cities and counties across the country, agencies, professional organizations, and consumer groups formed action coalitions. At the national level, a Social Services Coalition was organized, spearheaded by the National Association of Social Workers (NASW) and including representatives of national agencies, labor unions, community action projects, the National Governors' Conference, and staff aides of Senator Walter Mondale and a Michigan congressman.

The formal power to modify the language of the regulations lay solely with HEW, but Congress had the authority to delay the implementation. This it did on two occasions in order to buy time to fashion totally new legislation that would render the regulations null and void. Threatened with being bypassed completely, HEW officials made overtures to the social service advocates. The legislation finally enacted was a compromise that reflected the views of the administration, the Social Services Coalition, and state governors and welfare directors. This was the Social Services Amendments of 1974, or Title XX of the Social Security Act. Far from being the restrictive policy of the original HEW regulations, it was a commitment by the federal government to support social services for a diverse population and not just for welfare recipients. However, it remained consistent with President Nixon's "new federalism" by leaving wide areas of discretion to the states.

What can be learned from the battle of the social service regulations? First, it seems clear that in issuing the new regulations, HEW officials misinterpreted the Nixon Administration's electoral "mandate" as well as the potential strength of the opposition. The appeal of the restrictive policy was to a broad range of constituencies that were amorphous and had little awareness of or investment in social services. "Middle America" could respond to the sloganized messages of an election campaign in which the choices were stark and global, but it is doubtful that the average voter was ever more than dimly aware of the social service controversy at any point.

In contrast, the opposition constituencies were organized, and they faced a palpable threat to their vital interests. Here we see the concept of position (the administration's authority to write regulations) pitted against that of size (the demonstrated involvement of a number of interests at the national, state, and local levels). This was an important factor in enlisting Congress, which is ever alert to the importance of numbers—and it was Congress that tipped the scales by taking the initiative away from the administration.

On the surface, it might appear that Congress—both houses of which were controlled by the Democrats—would be a natural bulwark against administration action. It is true that partisanship entered into the struggle. But most of the membership of that Congress was also there in the previous session, when a ceiling of $2.5 billion was placed on social service spending. Influential senators and representatives were sympathetic with what the Nixon forces were trying to do to social services. Added to this was the natural hesitancy of politicians to get involved in unnecessary controversies. It would have been all too easy for the Democratic leadership to have taken no action and then used HEW's heartlessness as a campaign issue later on. The active involvement of social service constituencies helped to prevent this from happening.

Also of critical importance in the battle of the social service regulations was the factor of information. Ordinarily, the administration has a built-in advantage over both Congress and outside groups, whose data sources are generally more limited. But the human service professionals outside the system had expertise and well-developed pipelines and thus could break the information monopoly of HEW. In addition, the Social Services Coalition and allied groups were led by sophisticated Washington lobbyists who knew the decision machinery and those who made it run.

General Assistance in Pennsylvania

The second case is similar to the first in that an administrative initiative was opposed by pro-welfare constituencies on the outside.[9] But the task of the social welfare advocates was more formidable because the administration's party controlled one legislative chamber, the opposition was less well organized, and the focus of the contest was the emotion-laden subject of able-bodied welfare recipients.

General assistance (GA) is the catchall category of public assistance in which the federal government has no role. In Pennsylvania, the program has been liberal both in budgetary standards and administration. Administered by the state's Department of Public Welfare, it is a cash-assistance program that uses the same budgetary standard as Aid to Families with Dependent Children (AFDC). The·$172-per-month grant in 1978 was by no means generous, but as of the end of that year, Pennsylvania's average GA grant was exceeded only by those in the District of Columbia, Hawaii, and New York.[10] Since the severe 1974 recession, the GA rolls in Pennsylvania had been growing rapidly. In the eyes of some, the program was out of control.

Consequently, reform of the public assistance program was high on the agendas of the new governor and the State Legislature (the General Assembly) at the beginning of 1979. The 1978 elections had returned control of both Pennsylvania's executive branch and its House of Representatives to the Republicans—in the latter by a razor-thin margin—and the Democratic majority in the State Senate was weakened. In the background was a national political climate that was growing increasingly conservative.

Among a dozen or so welfare reform bills that went into the hopper of the House of Representatives in the early months of 1979, the major one concerned "workfare," a plan to require GA "employables" to work off their grants in unpaid jobs. The notion that able-bodied recipients should have to work for what they get is a popular one, and the bill·had sixty cosponsors representing both parties.

Beset by financial problems, the administration of Governor Richard L. Thornburgh was not enthusiastic about workfare, an approach that in some states had produced administrative costs five times larger than the savings from reduced caseloads. Meanwhile, a task force drawn from the executive office and the Department of Public Welfare was evolving the notion of simply eliminating employables from the GA rolls. This was in essence the plan that the governor unveiled in a speech to both houses of the General Assembly in October 1979. So-called "transitionally needy" (that is, employable) persons would be given GA for one month a year and would then be ineligible the rest of the time. To make the program more attractive, the governor proposed to use part of the savings to augment grant levels in both GA and AFDC and to use the rest in new employment and training programs. Immediately, the workfare proponents in the house embraced the governor's plan, which became House Bill (HB) 2044.

Meanwhile, the opposition was not idle. Constituencies that had already begun to mobilize against workfare quickly turned their guns on the governor's proposal. Prominent among the antagonists were groups that saw their own vital interests threatened: organizations of welfare clients; welfare workers' unions; and organized labor in general, which did not want the job market saturated with low-skilled workers. Allied with these was an array of church-related and other public interest organizations and individuals. The Pennsylvania chapter of NASW took an active role, although its rank and file membership was never significantly involved. On the other side, there was virtually no organized support for HB 2044 outside of the administration itself. However, it was clear from the news media and from legislators' informal soundings in their home districts that the governor's plan had hit a responsive chord.

To a large extent, the battle over HB 2044 was a war of words. In his original announcement of the plan, the governor declared, "The classified section of any daily newspaper is full of jobs. . . . It makes no sense for us to subsidize those who are unemployed simply because they choose to be so."[11] This writer scanned the want ads in the newspaper in which that statement was quoted and found that out of the first one thousand ads, only twenty-seven fitted the qualifications of the average GA employable as specified in state officials' own statistics. By constantly hammering away at this and other weaknesses in the administration's case, it was possible to raise doubts in the public's mind regarding the proposal and the credibility of its sponsors. The opposition was aided in this endeavor by the fact that the administration had not done its homework thoroughly.

HB 2044 soon earned a nickname—"Thornfare"—derived from the name of the bill's chief proponent, Governor Thornburgh. The nickname and its negative connotation were picked up by the news media, and eventually even members of the administration were using the term. But the major focus of the opponents was the bleak employment picture in Pennsylvania. The state had lost 219,000 jobs in a ten-year period. Although Philadelphia had been hardest hit, the problem affected many areas. "Where are the jobs?" became the battle cry. The administration was never able to answer the question effectively.

But nicknames and data on joblessness were of little interest to the leadership in the state's House of Representatives, which pressed for early action on HB 2044. The House Health and Welfare Committee and Appropriations Committee both rammed the bill through in a matter of minutes, without debate. This kind of heavy-handedness would come back to haunt the Republicans later on. On March 5, 1980, HB 2044 was passed by a resounding 142–37 margin in the house, with many Democratic members crossing over to be recorded in favor of "welfare reform." Last-minute parliamentary maneuvers by the black caucus and other Philadelphia Democrats to stall action were thwarted, and as the juggernaut rolled over the opposition, a group of angry welfare rights activists surged onto the floor of the house, creating a sense of chaos.

These events, widely reported in the news media, helped reinforce the belief that the typical opponent of Thornfare was black, strident, and a resident of Philadelphia. This was also the popular stereotype of GA employables in many parts of the state, despite the fact that the majority of recipients were white and resided outside of Philadelphia. In Pennsylvania politics, issues are frequently defined in terms of Philadelphia versus the rest of the state. The racial issue, though unstated, is also potent. Unless someone changed the public perception of what kinds of people supported and opposed Thornfare, these stereotypes could help to assure the passage of the bill.

The action then shifted to the Senate Public Health and Welfare Committee, chaired by W. Louis Coppersmith, a respected moderate from west-central Pennsylvania. Coppersmith kept his counsel on Thornfare, but he let it be known that the measure would be given a thorough airing, in contrast with the rubber-stamp action by the House committees. Not only would public hearings be held, but Coppersmith and the committee's ranking Republican agreed to hire outside consultants to analyze the bill's potential impact.

The hearings proved to be more significant in the ongoing propaganda battle in the news media than they were in influencing committee members' views directly. Given the paucity of hard information from the administration and the use of careful documentation and analysis by the opponents, many newspapers around the state began treating Thornfare as an arguable issue.

The hearings also demonstrated a basic difference between the two sides: So many speakers wanted to be heard in opposition to Thornfare that committee staff had difficulty scheduling them all, but the proponents had trouble finding any speakers outside of the administration. Even the Pennsylvania Chamber of Commerce, known to favor welfare reform, turned down the invitation to testify, saying it was too involved in other things.

The administration then unveiled what was to be its decisive blow. Governor Michael Dukakis of Massachusetts, who had pushed through a Thornfare-type measure, was to appear before the Senate Public Health and Welfare Committee. It was assumed he would make a convincing case for HB 2044. Instead, he equivocated and was unable to supply some of the information asked of him by senators. For the Thornburgh Administration, it was, in the opinion of some observers, a disaster.

The fight was still very much in doubt, however. As committee action neared, Chairman Coppersmith began sounding more and more sympathetic to the core concept of Thornfare—the denial of general assistance to employables. But he was losing control of other Democrats on the committee. Eventually, they caucused in the chairman's absence and endorsed a proposal by freshman Senator James Lloyd of Philadelphia that would effectively nullify the Thornfare concept.

There followed a bewildering series of parliamentary maneuvers, including an effort to tie Thornfare to an antiabortion measure and a much-needed funding appropriation for child welfare services. The intent was to force legislators and the governor to accept unwanted items in order to obtain what they were after. In a succession of extremely close votes, these efforts were defeated, and the Senate approved an emasculated version of HB 2044. Before further action could take place to reconcile the two versions of the bill, the legislative session died, and with it, HB 2044.

Given the intricate maneuvering inside the General Assembly on Thornfare, it is easy to miss the significance of the role played by outside constituencies. But clearly, if there had been no outside pressure, HB 2044 would have been enacted into law in rapid order. Both the number of constituencies and their range were important, although behind some of the field commanders the ranks were rather thin. Fortunately for the opponents, they were never required to rally their forces to back up a threat or a promise. The Thornfare supporters were never able to stir up wide interest in "welfare reform." For the average Pennsylvania voter, Thornfare remained an abstraction, whereas to the opponents it was a critical issue.

Information proved to be an important factor in this struggle. The constant barrage of material from the opposition kept the administration off balance and created doubts in the minds of the public about such issues as the availability of jobs, the ripple effect of Thornfare on local economies, the threat of crime and civil disorder, and the administrative costs of the program.

Social Workers in the Political Arena

The preceding two case histories demonstrate the importance of the factors discussed at the beginning of this article. Organization and self-interest were at work in mobilizing certain constituencies as opposed to others. The fights against cutbacks in social programs were consistent with the ideologies of the opponents and thus furnished a legitimate occasion for political action. Size, position, organization, and information helped to determine the effectiveness of the antagonists in the political arena. Money was important mainly in providing staff resources and communication with rank-and-file membership.

The role of social workers in these two cases is instructive. In the first case—the struggle over the HEW regulations—a majority of NASW members could see a direct stake for themselves and their clients in the outcome. They readily threw themselves into the fight. In the case of Thornfare, the plight of GA employables was somewhat more remote. A concern for the downtrodden was not enough, in and of itself, to muster the Pennsylvania NASW membership in depth. Ironically, while anti-Thornfare activists were decrying the lack of involvement of social workers, NASW members were taking steps to form a human services coalition to fight the attack on social services by the Reagan Administration.

This author has discussed elsewhere social work's "mixed agenda," that is, the combination of public interest and self-interest that moves social workers to engage in political action.[12] Issues that do not involve the vital interests of the social work community itself fail to mobilize the kind of energy needed for intensive and sustained involvement. On the other hand, matters of pure self-interest are viewed as inconsistent with the service mission of social work. It is the combination of public interest and self-interest that leads to political activism by social workers. And social workers have the capacity to influence policy significantly, especially when allied with other groups concerned about human services.

Epilogue

Contrary to most fictional versions of life, actual political contests often lack real endings—let alone happy ones. The initial defeat of Thornfare is a case in point.

In January 1981, Republicans took control of the Pennsylvania State Senate and thus dominated both houses of the General Assembly as well as the governorship. A series of bills encompassing the governor's welfare reform plan went through the House of Representatives, though not without difficulty. The proposal was later coupled with provisions for bringing the state into line with the new federal guidelines for AFDC, and a workfare provision was added. However, the proposal remained stalled in the Senate for months despite Republican control of that chamber. After more parliamentary maneuvering, the bill was finally adopted in March 1982, 2½ years after it was originally proposed.

Did the opposition achieve anything other than a delay in passage of the measure? Aside from assuring that GA employables continued to be eligible for benefits in the intervening thirty months—a significant plus in view of the state's high and worsening unemployment during that time—the opponents were able to get the eligibility period for "transitionally needy" in the measure extended from one month to three.

But in politics, as in skeet shooting, a miss is as good as a mile. Paperthin margins of victory in elections are taken as vindication by "the people," whereas defeat by a handful of votes is proof that a candidate is "out of step with the times." If one or two anti-Thornfare senators had not defected or absented themselves on critical procedural votes (the kind that do not show up on voting records), Thornfare might have been dead once again. There were indications that the governor would not have brought it up a third time. But now it is law.

Yet, in view of the general popularity of "welfare reform," the opponents of Thornfare scored an impressive achievement in holding the line for 2½ years, and the lessons regarding the potential ability of social workers and their allies to influence social policy are just as valid as if they had won.

In the second go-round on Thornfare, the Pennsylvania Chapter of NASW assumed a front-line position in the coalition. This demonstrated that opposition was not limited to the welfare clients themselves and also allowed politically vulnerable coalition members to work behind the scenes. Yet at no point did the rank and file of NASW members become actively involved in the welfare reform issue. This was not surprising, perhaps, in view of the growing threat to their own social service programs. Had the membership become involved, they might have tipped the balance against Thornfare, considering the measure's perilous and prolonged course through the legislative process.

Notes and References

1. See L.W. Milbrath, "Lobbyists Approach Government," in R.H. Salisbury, ed., *Interest Group Politics in America* (New York: Harper & Row, 1970), p. 423; and R.L. Presthus, *Elites in the Policy Process* (London, England: Cambridge University Press, 1974).

2. See, for example, T.R. Dye and L.H. Zeigler, *The Irony of Democracy: An Uncommon Introduction to American Politics* (3d ed.; North Scituate, Mass.: Duxbury Press, 1975), pp. 236, 266; L.W. Milbrath, *Political Participation: How and Why Do People Get Involved in Politics?* (Chicago: Rand McNally & Co., 1965), pp. 142–143; and V.O. Key, *Public Opinion and American Democracy* (New York: Alfred A. Knopf, 1961), pp. 535–543.

3. E.E. Schattschneider, *The Semi-Sovereign People, A Realist's View of Democracy in America* (New York: Holt, Rinehart & Winston, 1960), p. 4.

4. M. Lipsky, "Protest as a Political Resource," *American Political Science Review*, 62 (December 1968). See also W.A. Gamson, *The Strategy of Social Protest* (Homewood, Ill.: Dorsey Press, 1975), p. 140.

5. Ibid., pp. 9–10.

6. Ibid., pp. 52–53.

7. See, for example, H. Schuman and S. Presser, "Attitude Measurement and the Gun Control Paradox," *Public Opinion Quarterly*, 41 (Winter 1977–78), pp. 427–438.

8. The material in this section is based on W.C. Richan, *Social Service Politics in the United States and Britain* (Philadelphia: Temple University Press, 1981), pp. 151–179. See also P.E. Mott, *Meeting Human Needs: The Social and Political History of Title XX* (Columbus, Ohio: National Conference on Social Welfare, 1976); and J. Havemann, "Welfare Report: Impasse Over Social Services Regulations Appears Broken," *National Journal Reports*, 6 (December 7, 1974), pp. 1840–1844.

9. The material in this section is based on uncataloged documents, news clippings, interviews, and the author's personal experience.

10. *Social Security Bulletin*, 42 (June 1979), p. 62.

11. Pennsylvania, General Assembly, *Legislative Journal*, 1 (October 2, 1979), p. 1899.

12. See Richan, op. cit., pp. 237–248.

Who Owns Title XX?

Deborah K. Zinn
Betty Rivard

As a result of the establishment of a social service block grant by the Reagan Administration, funding that has come through Title XX of the Social Security Act since October 1981 has been funneled to the states at a reduced level and has been subject to fewer federal regulations and greater discretion on the part of the states. These changes have resulted in substantial shifts in the location of decision making regarding the use of funds and in the mix of factors that affect the planning and implementation of social service delivery. The reduction of funds has required immediate adjustments, while the increased regulatory discretion of the states has permitted a more gradual transition to a state-defined system. These developments have heightened the interdependence of agencies, clients, and citizens who are affected by the expenditure of federal social service funds.

The changes occurring in the wake of the recent implementation of block grants have a profound impact on the answers to the questions of who owns Title XX and what we can do about influencing the decisions made in regard to social service funding. The answers that were appropriate for the 1975-to-1981 version of Title XX may not be appropriate for today's version, otherwise known as the Social Services Block Grant (SSBG). However, past experience with Title XX as well as with other block grants, such as the Community Development Block Grant, that were in existence prior to the current spate of grants will be the best guide for action in the future. Therefore, this article will analyze the past as a basis for understanding the future of social service funding in this country. In addition, it will develop a series of guidelines to enable social workers as well as other concerned citizens and professionals to analyze how funding decisions under Title XX have been determined in their states.

Title XX Before and After

This article is based on a firm conviction that delivery systems can be redesigned and improved to provide more efficient and effective services for the benefit of clients. Improvements will require redefinitions of boundaries, job responsibilities, and special interests and can only be made if the people affected are willing to look beyond their present situations to the creation of a new whole. Before guidelines for analysis and action are presented in this discussion, an overview of the similarities and differences between Title XX as it was passed by Congress and implemented by the states in 1975 and SSBG established by Congress in 1981 will be useful.

Before Title XX was added to the Social Security Act, most of the social services provided by state welfare departments were directed toward people receiving public assistance and had the goal of helping individuals become self-supporting. Funding for these services came primarily from Title IV-A of the Social Security Act, which is the law providing funds for welfare in the form of Aid to Families with Dependent Children (AFDC). Title XX changed this. It reflected the recognition that clients' financial independence was only one goal of social services and incorporated this recognition into a set of five goals: self-support, self-sufficiency, the protection of children and adults from neglect or abuse, the delivery of community-based care whenever possible, and the provision of institutional care when necessary. Under Title XX, social services continued to be provided to poor people but were also extended to working people and others in need of service, and a range of services to families and children as well as to aged and disabled people were funded. These services could be provided directly by the public welfare agency or by other private or public agencies with which it concluded purchase-of-service contracts authorizing the agencies to provide certain services to segments of the community.

These aspects of Title XX as it was implemented in 1975 remain unchanged under SSBG. However, as noted earlier, the regulations governing the administration of programs and the level of funding have changed. Title XX as added to the Social Security Act in 1975 consolidated into a modified block grant federal social service grants that were formerly separate. SSBG is a full-fledged block grant and has five basic characteristics possessed by block grants in general: (1) federal aid is authorized for a wide range of activities within a broadly defined functional area, (2) recipients of funds have substantial discretion in identifying problems and in designing programs and allocating resources to deal with them, (3) federally imposed requirements concerning such areas as planning and administrative and fiscal reporting are kept to the minimum necessary to ensure that national goals are being accomplished, (4) federal aid is distributed on the basis of a statutory formula, and this limits the discretion of federal administrators and provides recipients with a sense of fiscal certainty, and (5) eligibility provisions are statutorily specific and favor general-purpose governmental units as recipients and elected officials and administrative generalists as decision makers.[1]

The change from Title XX to SSBG has primarily involved the elimination of regulations. For example, the following have been done away with: the requirement that half the money provided for services be spent on the poorest people (those receiving AFDC or Supplemental Security Income); the mandate for preventive programs in the areas of information and referral, family planning, and protective services; the stipulation that provision be made for public input into the planning process; and the necessity for a single state agency to administer and coordinate all services funded by Title XX. Overall, the intent and goals of the Title XX legislation remain unchanged, but the ways in which these goals are to be achieved have been made more flexible by the elimination of regulatory restrictions on the states. This relates to a key issue in the debate regarding block grants, namely, the decentralization of control from the federal to the state level. One outcome has become certain as a result of recent changes: the administration of social service programs will become more variable.

In addition to regulatory changes, profound cuts were made in the levels of funding under SSBG. Funding was reduced by 25 percent from the Title XX ceiling of 2.5 billion dollars. Also, in the past, states had to match each seventy-five cents of federal money received with twenty-five cents of state money. This is no longer required. Therefore, many state legislatures have chosen to take state funds formerly earmarked for social services and use them for other public services. The net result is that only about half the funds available for social services in fiscal year 1981 are assured of being available in future years.

The effects of these changes on the recipients of services have been observable. Needed services such as day care, home-based care, and child protective programs are being cut, if not totally eliminated. Decreases in funding for services that do remain have necessitated tightened eligibility requirements. This has resulted in people in need of service having to do without and in a decline in the quality of care because of increased caseloads and decreased travel budgets for social service staff. The media have documented the impact of reduced services on children in day care centers, older persons in nursing homes, and children who are at risk of suffering neglect or abuse. Systematic research is now being conducted to assess the full extent of the suffering and harm that have taken place as a result of the funding cuts.[2]

Given the upheaval that has occurred in social service funding, how can someone interested in shaping the changes that are now taking place in a state's social service system become an effective participant in important decision-making processes? The first series of guidelines to be discussed in this article suggest that one should begin by identifying the individual actors and groups that have exerted power over Title XX and that continue to influence decisions on how SSBG funds are spent within the state. This portion of the analysis to be conducted is political in nature, for the interplay of those with varying degrees of power can be observed and analyzed as the basis for future action. In general, power determines the efficacy of action. It can come from political mandate, as in the case of state legislators, from numerical superiority, as in the case of service recipients, from economic power, as in the case of a state's powerful business interests, or from institutional authority, as in the case of those controlling a state's major departments.

Actors and Interests

The first step toward being able to understand and influence the implementation of SSBG is to identify the primary individuals, groups, and organizations that have historically controlled and presently control decisions concerning social service funding. Interests may be defined along several different lines: public versus private, professional versus consumer, broad-based versus special interest, statewide versus local, and permanent versus *ad hoc*. One method for identifying influential actors is to conceptualize Title XX and SSBG, along with those immediately affected by funds derived from them, as a social service system. The next step would be to think of the individuals, agencies, organizations, or organized interests that furnish resources to the system or who in turn receive resources from the system. Resources include clients, staff, money, services, and authority.[3] Because the "raw materials" of social service agencies are people, clients are an essential resource. They can in turn be shared with or referred to other agencies outside the system. Money is another important resource. It comes into the system from various sources, is funneled to different parts of the system, and may even produce financial benefits for those not immediately involved with the block grant. For example, local businesses may save money if the productivity of their workers who are alcoholics improves as a result of counseling services. Authority is equally important as other resources, although less tangible. For example, it is authority, or the force of law, that allows the investigation of reports of child abuse. Authority can also be shared with those delegated to carry out responsibilities derived from the SSBG legislation. A case in point is the influence wielded by agencies with purchase-of-service contracts that have been designated to provide services funded by SSBG.

Different actors are concerned with different sets of resources. They may be observed to influence the distribution of resources of interest to them by advocating particular social service policies and procedures. In addition, the set of actors who have an impact on decisions concerning social service funding is dynamic, for the actors change as interests and the political climate change. In many states new coalitions have been formed in the hope of shaping the nature of the block grants as they are being implemented. To the extent that these groups are broadly representative, their members' familiarity with a variety of different services and programs may contribute to a more comprehensive knowledge of the service system. One such group is the Michigan Coalition for Fair Implementation of Block Grants, whose main purpose is "to advocate for the needy and vulnerable citizens [of Michigan] by assuring that the needs of the poor, children and youth, the elderly, the mentally impaired, the handicappers and other groups at risk are being met as block grants and federal budget cuts are implemented in Michigan."[4] This coalition includes over one hundred statewide and umbrella organizations, such as the Michigan League for Human Services, the International United Automobile Workers, the Michigan Chapter of the National Association of Social Workers, and the Michigan Catholic Conference.

The identification of those who seek to influence social service policy is just the first step for someone interested in shaping the implementation of SSBG. Some individuals or groups are more effective than others, and attention should be directed toward those who are more powerful. Once these groups have been identified, it may be possible to determine what their agendas have been and how successful they have been in attaining their goals. For example, a task force of foster parents may have been organized in an attempt to get payments to foster parents increased, but did it succeed? A coalition of senior citizens' organizations may have lobbied for more money for in-home care providers, but what effect did this have? An alternative approach might be to look at major changes in social service funding and to trace back who influenced the changes and why they were made. For instance, if a sudden infusion of funds was channeled into programs dealing with domestic violence, what actors or groups were responsible? What strategies were effective in bringing about this change?

Although a wide variety of groups have an impact on social service policy, special attention must be directed to the agency responsible for administering SSBG. Under Title XX, a state's governor designated a single state agency, such as the welfare department or the department of social services, to be responsible for the implementation of all Title XX programs. Because of this, the administering agency gained power over the state's social service system by controlling the flow of funds to other public and private agencies. In such a situation, agencies with purchase-of-service contracts, for example, were forced to conform to reporting requirements and other policies prescribed by the administering agency in order to continue to receive funds.

However, under the new block grant requirements, it is not necessary for governors to appoint a single agency to administer the block grant funds, although such an arrangement is one possible option. Consistent with the move to greater generalist control, a governor might designate the state's fiscal agency, equivalent to the federal Office of Management and Budget, to control the block grant funds. A third option would be the use of a cabinet for decision making or the distribution of funds through several agencies. Although most states have left the administration of SSBG with the agency that was responsible for Title XX, in those cases in which the state agency did change, new power balances would be established. In general, the agency in charge of SSBG is the direct and indirect target of attempts by individual actors and groups to influence decisions affecting the block grant. Therefore, a knowledge of this agency's personnel, decision-making policies, and past funding patterns is an important basis for the development of strategies to effect change.

Public participation can also influence policy decisions. Under Title XX, regulations called for the publication of a proposed plan for spending priorities and for the plan's advertisement and availability for public review and comment for forty-five days throughout the state. At the end of this period, a final plan was prepared. To comply with these regulations, the states chose from a variety of optional mechanisms for public input, including the use of regional hearings, advisory committees, and postcard surveys. However, requirements for public participation were reduced with the passage of SSBG. The rhetoric accompanying this change argued that increased state control and a heightened involvement of state and local officials in SSBG would provide alternative opportunities for public input. This remains to be seen. Nevertheless, the public must continue to be informed of opportunities for such input. Some citizens may use political connections to influence funding decisions, but others may only be able to gain access to these decisions through formal mechanisms. Those responsible for administering SSBG should ensure that this access continues to be available.

The social service system is political in nature, both in the partisan and more general sense of the term. Various groups are vying for benefits from the system and use a variety of strategies to achieve their ends. The preceding discussion focused on some of the major actors involved in social service decision making. The next guidelines to be discussed shift from an emphasis on the individual and organizational actors involved in social service policymaking to a look at the "economy" of the social service system by examining how resources are distributed. They outline key decision points that govern the amount of funds available for social services as well as how these funds are distributed.

Distribution of Resources

In the past, state and local and public and private funds were used to match the federal Title XX funds that were received by a state. Sources of matching funds varied from state to state. However, as already indicated, with the elimination of SSBG matching requirements, some state legislatures are withdrawing funds originally earmarked as matching funds for federal social service money from their budgets, thus changing both the amount and mix of funds available. Nevertheless, social service programs funded by SSBG may also receive funds from a variety of other sources. For example, senior citizens' centers and mental health centers are often funded through a combination of federal funding titles, state taxes, general revenue sharing, and private sources. A knowledge of past and present funding levels and sources is necessary in fighting recision; advocates must have some basis by which to judge proposed levels of funding.

In general, sources of funding used in the past are drying up. Therefore, it is necessary to consider what alternative resources can be developed for programs dependent on SSBG. Advocates have begun to lobby for increases in state and local revenues as federal taxes are lowered. Although achieving success in this area is difficult, proponents of such increases may have little choice but to adopt this strategy. If they are successful, they must simultaneously develop the political clout necessary to bargain for a chance to have some input into the use of the increased tax revenues.

The operation in a state of the community services block grant, the low-income energy assistance block grant, and the alcohol and drug abuse and mental health services block grant can affect social services funded by SSBG in several ways. On one hand, funding for social services may be reduced because of provisions in SSBG that allow for the transfer of up to 10 percent of the federal funds received by a state to either the low-income energy assistance or health block grant. On the other hand, funds from the low-income energy assistance block grant may be transferred into SSBG. Finally, in the community services block grant, a state may, after the first year, use the block grant funds for services that may not have traditionally been provided through community action programs. This may open up this funding for use for other social service programs.

The exchange of funds between block grants illustrates the use of intertitle transfers. The budgets of social services funded by SSBG can also be supplemented by other federal programs. One example of this is family planning services, which can be a part of SSBG or can be funded under Title X of the Public Health Services Act. Therefore, states can explore the combination of federal funds that results in the greatest amount of social service funding and flexibility.

Private charity is an alternative source of funds. The role of the United Way and related agencies is becoming increasingly important. However, recent changes in the federal tax law have reduced the tax benefits to businesses and individuals who make charitable contributions, and a recent study undertaken by the Urban Institute predicts that charitable giving will decline because of these changes.[5] Agencies often require user fees from their clients, who in turn rely on third-party payments from insurance to offset service costs whenever possible. Historically, third-party payments have been available for counseling services in highly unionized or wealthier states; the poor are penalized because these benefits are usually connected to past or present employment. Nevertheless, if citizens who are better off financially can have their service needs paid for by insurance, some of the pressure on the public system may be relieved.

Although the absolute amount of available funds in a state is important, the distribution and use of funds are crucial as well. In most states the allocation of SSBG money from the state to the local level takes place through two channels. First, funds are spent for services provided directly by the local offices of the SSBG agency. Second, money is funneled to agencies with purchase-of-service contracts. The allocation of funds among public and private agencies for purchase-of-service contracts is a political process. Potential purchase-of-service providers submit proposals to the agency administering SSBG, and proposals are then selected according to criteria established by the agency. Many states reserve a substantial portion of their available funds to support state-delivered services, a large number of which are mandated by state law. This causes consternation among the private agencies that have increasingly relied on public funds and have, in effect, become quasi-public agencies. Organizations of provider agencies usually try to increase the amount of funding allocated for purchased services.

With SSBG the allocation of block grant funds becomes more closely tied to a partisan political process than was the case with Title XX. For example, as states are given more discretion in the use of funds, many state legislatures are asking that block grants be channeled through the legislative allocation process so they can decide which services and agencies to fund. At the same time, governors and representatives of the executive branch advocate the continued control of funding by state agencies. The criteria that are used by a state government's legislative or executive branch to determine the portion of funds assigned to each county or region need to ensure that assistance is targeted to those most in need. Factors in each locality that may be taken into consideration in making allocation decisions include population size, income levels of residents, previous levels of support, needs of special populations, and level of unemployment.

History can play an important role in policymaking. Therefore, past patterns of service allocation can provide insight into current practices. One can go back to pre-Title XX days when social service funding of the Title XX type was primarily designed for former, current, and potential welfare recipients or for those in need of child welfare services. In most states, the advent of Title XX (and increased funding levels) did not mean the discontinuance of any traditional services but instead resulted in an expansion of services focused on meeting newly identified needs, such as in the area of spouse abuse or protective services for the aged, blind, and disabled. However, as states reached their Title XX ceilings, they began to retrench and, of necessity, to limit the growth of services.

With the advent of SSBG and the other block grants, the 1975-to-1981 version of Title XX became the relevant past. Although initially the continuation of the status quo so that constituencies would not be angered had tremendous political appeal, this was not possible because the block grants incorporated severe budget cuts. Therefore, services have been eliminated and groups of clients ruled ineligible for services. But where have cuts been made? One mechanism to use in determining the programs that have most recently been funded is to examine the Title XX plan for fiscal years 1981 and 1982. These plans represent the services and levels of funding mapped out before and after cuts necessitated by the lower funding levels of SSBG. Therefore, cuts can be identified and this knowledge used as the basis for future strategies.

Documents similar to the Title XX plan may be available for other social service funding sources. It would be useful to involve experts in various service programs in a joint analysis of the overall funding picture. Links like this will become increasingly important if funding continues to decline. To some extent, coordination will be forced by the nature of the block grants, but there is also the chance of any impetus toward cooperation that is facilitated by the block grant legislation being more than offset by the competition engendered by decreased funding levels.

In the current era of cutbacks, the policies that guide the termination, continuation, expansion, or addition of programs and services become controversial. Is it possible to determine neutral bases for decision making and to avoid pitting programs and target populations against each other? This is obviously difficult to do, especially because it is virtually impossible to find people who are interested in social services without their being affected by these services in some way. Yet this is the issue that must be addressed if divisiveness and conflict are to be avoided. Cooperation will increase in importance as regulations become more open-ended and decision making falls more into the realm of partisan politics.

Some general considerations might be acceptable to all involved. Foremost among these is that each change in services or funding levels be seen as affecting the whole service delivery system. In many cases this will require that existing connections be made evident. Many inter-relationships may be found, such as that between day care funding and the size of the AFDC caseload or between home repair programs for senior citizens and the possibility of placing foster children with their grandparents. The identification of interdependencies may foster communication and stretch current funding levels as much as possible until such time as increased funding is again available.

Directions for the Future

Who owns Title XX and the federal funding to come? We all do. What can we do to influence social service funding? The answer is, study what has been done, determine future strategies, and keep the following points in mind: no plan of action can be developed in a vacuum, and the qualities most needed in the coming times are adaptability and flexibility. It is important to understand the past but disastrous to cling to it; it is necessary at every point to seize the day.

The agencies and programs that give structure to what social workers do and what clients receive are all dispensable. There are many ways to meet an individual's needs. New combinations of services can be developed without jeopardy to those who are vulnerable. If people pull together, not separately, responsibilities for caring can be dispersed and shared in such a way that everyone benefits and both gives and receives.

Great change will occur in the lives of professionals who grew up during the expansion of social service delivery. The crumbling of walls that were once thought to be solid will be witnessed. Somehow, the ability to affect systems and the faith in positive change that inform professionals' service to clients must not be lost. Social workers must find ways to act on their beliefs and support the meeting of human needs even if the structures they are used to must be changed.

When the main arena for social service decision making was in Washington, social workers could contribute to organizations that would advocate for their interests; advocacy itself could remain remote from their day-to-day work. But now this arena is shifting to the states, and the separation of advocacy from daily concerns is no longer possible. Social workers will need to come to terms with the differences among themselves as well as with the citizens—including friends, co-workers, neighbors, and relatives—with whom they will, in effect, be negotiating arrangements concerning their priorities.

A serious professional is able to move past his or her limitations and preferences in order to develop and expand the skills that will best meet the needs of clients, whether they be individuals, groups, organizations, or communities. This same ability to learn will be required in dealing with social service planning and decision making in the states. A person with experience in and a taste for confrontation may need to realize that in some cases a softer approach can be more effective. Someone who has shunned the political arena in favor of casework on a one-to-one basis may find that it becomes necessary to join with others in locally organized groups. The individual who has chosen to engage in community organization with the poor may need to step forward and mingle with local politicians and business leaders in order to help raise awareness about community needs.

This is a professional challenge. The times demand it. The commonality and caring displayed by social workers themselves can pave the way for a better society. This has always been part of social work's mission, and it has never been as clear as in this country at this time. What each person does can have an impact far beyond himself or herself. Collective work within the profession can pave the way for positive changes that address human needs.

Notes and References

1. *Block Grants: A Comparative Analysis* (Washington, D.C.: Advisory Committee on Intergovernmental Relations, 1977), p. 6. For details of block grant regulations, see U.S. House of Representatives, *Omnibus Budget Reconciliation Act of 1981 (Conference Report)* (Washington, D.C.: U.S. Government Printing Office, July 29, 1981), pp. 135–174; 191–266; 422–434; 518–552; and 573–582.

2. "Cutting the Strings on Title XX—Social Services Undercut by Federal Retreat," *NASW News*, 27 (November 1982), p. 3.

3. For a discussion of the importance of resources to organizations, see David Jacobs, "Dependency and Vulnerability: An Exchange Approach to the Control of Organizations," *Administrative Science Quarterly*, 19 (1974), pp. 48–59; and Yeheskel Hasenfeld, *Human Service Organizations* (Englewood Cliffs, N.J.: Prentice Hall, 1983), pp. 66–83.

4. Michigan Coalition for Fair Implementation of Block Grants, "Statement of Purpose," Lansing, Michigan, August 18, 1981, p. 1.

5. John Palmer and Isabel Sawhill, *The Reagan Experiment* (Washington, D.C.: Urban Institute Press, 1982).

New Initiatives for Human Services Programs

Leslie G. Brody

In the 1980s, human services programs face a serious peril—the possibility that in meeting the need to specify procedures and coordinate resources, they will lose the flexibility needed to adapt in a rapidly changing environment. According to Becker and Gordon, the complexity and diversity of environmental interactions and the need for rapid responses are critical variables that must be addressed in analyzing the dilemma facing human services programs.[1] Since the inception of the initiatives for property tax relief at the local and state levels, as well as the Reagan Administration's block grants that reduced categorical funding, the environment surrounding local organizations has become increasingly complex, diverse, and turbulent, creating the need for agencies to be more responsive to fluctuations in funding, requirements for accountability, and demands for services.

Today, local human services programs must be concerned with specific environmental factors that affect their operations. During the time when many of these programs developed, the thrust was to provide direct services to clients. Major funding sources, which were largely the federal and state governments, expected that local programs would develop community funding and become less dependent on government resources. The bureaucrats and legislators who drafted and enacted these programs did not anticipate the impact of inflation and decreased funding on the maintenance of existing programs. Also, little funding was provided for the development of new programs as needs and demands changed. In the past few years, government at all levels has tightened up on measures of both fiscal and service accountability, yet new measures are not accompanied by the funding needed to hire staff and evaluate services. In

43

addition, federal and state funds are often granted to accomplish institutional goals—such as deinstitutionalization and increased services to special needs populations (the elderly, minorities, the handicapped, abused children, and so forth)—that are not necessarily the goals of local agencies. In essence, local human services programs operate in the 1980s with increased demands for services, less federal and state money, and increased standards of accountability.

The preceding issues—taken in conjunction with the "Proposition 13 mentality" that pervades the decision-making process in local government—create major concerns for human services programs. It is crucial for these programs to confront the reality that cities and towns are more interested in property tax relief, reduced operating costs, and "hardware services" (roads, septic systems, and fire and police personnel) than in human services. Local government's recognition of mental health and other social services needs and its allocation of resources to meet those needs usually take a backseat now to the provision of more tangible services.

Furthermore, the bureaucratic push for increased accountability in general and for deinstitutionalization of the chronically mentally ill in particular often pressures local mental health programs to take on this extremely difficult clientele as a means to obtain operating capital. The dilemma this creates is that the local programs may not have stabilized their current funding base and existing clinical services. Creating community programs to support deinstitutionalized mental patients often deters local agencies from developing the fiscal and staff flexibility needed to deal effectively with demands from their larger constituencies. How, then, can community human services programs stabilize their fiscal bases in environments that are constantly changing?

Thompson argued that organizations must maintain a viable technology and have the capacity to satisfy the changing demands of those parts of the environment that are relevant to the accomplishment of goals.[2] Survival of human services programs in the 1980s will depend largely on the organizations' abilities to maintain core clinical technologies, stabilize present services, and stake out new program territories that offer a higher return than the resources needed to develop and maintain them.[3] This article (1) examines specific concepts in the organizational literature that are relevant to how human services programs can adapt to changing environments, (2) presents a model delineating three program initiatives (fundraising, employee assistance, and training) that have a reasonable potential for providing financial resources for human services programs in the 1980s, and (3) provides some suggestions for implementation of these three initiatives.

Organizational Concepts for
Reducing Environmental Fluctuations

In the context of human services, examples of "input" into an organization would be requests for information and clients enrolling for services; examples of the organization's "technology" would be the testing, diagnosis, and therapy or other services provided to clients; and examples of "output" from an organization would be provision of services to clients, the referral of clients to other agencies, and written reports. Thompson discusses the notions of buffering, smoothing, forecasting, and rationing as they relate to input, technological, and output activities of organizations.[4] These notions are of particular importance to the adaptability required of human services programs.

According to Thompson, buffering enables organizations to absorb environmental fluctuations and convert them into steady conditions. Buffering on the input side for human services organizations could take the form at peak times of giving priority to clients with more serious problems. Training, staff development, and maintaining a multidisciplinary staff are other "input buffers." On the output side, buffering might include extending time in treatment for certain clients. In essence, the primary buffering problem for human services programs in a turbulent environment is how to maintain a diversified staff who can meet changing needs such as clients' use of drugs and their work-related problems.[5]

Smoothing or leveling makes an attempt to reduce fluctuations via inducements, prevention, early detection, or scheduling. Sliding-fee scales are an example of an inducement to clients. Intensification of community education and consultation services during slack periods is another example of smoothing. Through prevention and early detection, the demand for services can be kept to manageable proportions; however, because demand cannot be kept completely level, organizations must rely on forecasting techniques to anticipate environmental changes. For human services organizations, seasonal fluctuations in the number of clients can be anticipated and staffing can be adjusted for enhanced efficiency and cost-effectiveness. Finally, through rationing, a process by which priorities are determined for the allocation of organizational resources under adverse conditions, the ratio of staff members to clients, the types of cases admitted, and the kinds of treatment techniques to be used can be determined to protect the organization's core technology.[6]

In further applying Thompson's notions to human services programs in mental health, it appears that the deinstitutionalization of chronic patients from state hospitals is removing a buffer that in the past kept many patients from being served by local mental health programs. More attention should be paid to smoothing strategies through the development of prevention programs and better scheduling of clients. Development of forecasting methods to anticipate service demands and funding shifts more accurately will become a necessity. Also, rationing plans that establish priorities for clients to be served and the types of new programs to be developed should be integrated into current planning strategies.

The degree of centralization or decentralization of the service area and of the authority for decision making are important considerations for human services programs. In times of declining resources, centralization of programs and decentralization of decision making should be reinforced. Centralization of programs can reduce operating expenses and free precious resources for reallocation. However, decision making should be decentralized to facilitate rapid responses to changing conditions.

It is critical to know what the desired organizational outcomes and the degree of environmental stability are before determining the level of centralization or decentralization that would be most effective. For example, Hall analyzed the effects of centralization on the organization as a whole, on coordination, and on the speed of decision making in organizations. This analysis indicated that centralization considers the whole organization, facilitates coordination, and enhances the speed of decision making in times of crisis. The costs of centralization are that it does not take into account the degree to which local conditions vary, ignores special features of problems, and overloads key personnel.[7]

Rosner's discussion of administrative controls and innovation adds another dimension to the consideration of centralization and decentralization of human services in the 1980s. According to Rosner, the control of activity reduces the search for new programs and the individual's incentive and capacity to innovate, whereas observable consequences allow organizations to evaluate the effect of innovation on the attainment of goals, thus rewarding and encouraging successful innovations.[8] Human services programs must weigh carefully the extent of administrative control needed to manage their organizations in times of declining resources and the need for innovative programs that will keep pace with inflation and offset deficits in programs that do not break even.

Hage and Aiken found that ". . . a high degree of participation in agency-wide decisions, a low degree of job codification, and a high rate of job satisfaction were most highly associated with a high rate of program change."[9] Again, weighing the extent of centralization and administrative controls needed versus the degree of decentralization necessary for innovation and ultimately for survival is seen as critical.

The discussion of the preceding concepts has emphasized their usefulness to human services programs struggling to survive. One can conclude from this discussion that (1) minimal activity control, decentralized systems of decision making, and observable consequences can encourage innovation and (2) adaptability to environmental fluctuations is essential to the survival of organizations.

Examining the Program Initiatives

The model found in Table 1 delineates the initiatives of fundraising, employee assistance, and training programs that should be considered by human services agencies as they confront this turbulent decade. The author has found that these programs offer resource alternatives to

Table 1. New Initiative Model for Human Services Programs

Elements of Organizations	Initiatives		
	Fundraising	Employee Assistance	Training
Action system	Development committee with appropriate subcommittees (membership, special gifts, corporate gifts, benefits)	Industrial team	Training committee with subcommittees on special topics
Participants	Individuals representing social and economic interests or providing relevant functions locally	Executive director and director(s) of consultation and community education, mental health professionals	Technical experts, trainers, interested staff
Targets	Individuals, business and industry, foundations	Industry	Schools, human services and mental health programs, industry
Values orientation	Individuals and businesses are socially concerned Contributions are often made based on who is soliciting them Human services programs need and have a right to expect local support	Businesses and industry are concerned about employees and are interested in productivity Businesses and industry are part of the mental health delivery system	Human services programs have talented staff with expertise worth sharing at competitive costs Other agencies' staff will attend training workshops of their interests

(continued)

Table 1. Continued

Elements of Organizations	Initiatives		
	Fundraising	Employee Assistance	Training
Conflict			
Agency	Board, clinical subsystems	Board, clinical subsystems	Direct service subsystems
Community	Community chests, other human services agencies	Private entrepreneurs, industry subsystems, other human services agencies	Other human services agencies, private entrepreneurs, federal and state training consortiums, colleges, universities
Empowerment	Influence, expertise, income	Legitimation, influence, expertise, income	Expertise, income, influence
Goals			
Short-term	Capital improvements, new programs	Contracts for employee assistance programs, stress management programs	Semiannual seminars
Long-term	Endowment, community action system for needs assessment, program planning, legislative alert, and "resource pool" of individuals for fundraising and board development	Consortium, corporate donations for fundraising, major profitable programming to offset deficit programming	Annual symposium

strengthen fiscal support. In putting forth these initiatives, the author has adopted the following premises:

• Human services programs must develop local resources to survive.

• No single funding source should be allowed to supply too large a part of the organization's income.

• Agencies must guard against the displacement of goals resulting from the acquisition of specified program funds that can direct their efforts inadvertently toward programs not included in their short- or long-term plans.

• Knowledge of advertising, marketing, and sales techniques should prove more beneficial to developing new funding sources than reliance on traditional low-key human services approaches to program development.

In examining each of the three program initiatives, the following elements will be used: action systems, participants, targets, values orientation, conflict, empowerment, and goals. These elements are defined as follows:

Action System: a formal group, committee, team, or task force of an organization.

Participants: the individuals constituting the action system.

Target: the individual, group, agency, or organization that is the focus of a particular initiative.

Values Orientation: the participants' and the targets' beliefs and opinions that are germane to the implementation of a specific initiative.

Conflict: the clash of differing points of view within or between the organization's subsystems: the action system and the targets.

Empowerment: the acquisition of power in the forms of money, knowledge, information, and influence.

Goal: the desired short- and long-term results.

For an outline of how the three initiatives may be carried out within organizations and have effect on them, see Table 1.

Action System

Action systems for all three initiatives entail the formation of a committee or team. In fundraising, a development committee should be formed with appropriate subcommittees (for example, membership, special gifts, corporate gifts, and benefits). The team approach appears to be the most useful in initiating employee assistance programs because it tends to broaden the capacity for delivery. In starting a training program, the formation of a training committee would be the most appropriate. Regardless of the particular type of action system selected, the operation of that system will become a critical factor in the ability of the organization to accomplish its stated goals. Action systems should be integrated into the operation of the host organization: for example, the development committee should become a standing committee of the board of directors, and employee assistance programs and training committees should become organizational subdivisions or special programs of the agency.

Participants

In initiating fundraising committees, two models are particularly useful for selecting participants. Individuals should be identified from agencies or organizations that provide the locally relevant functions Warren described—production, distribution, and consumption; socialization; social control; social participation; and mutual support—to form a strong development committee.[10] This would involve local human services programs with access to all levels of the community. A second alternative would be to select persons representing only socially prominent and economic interests. Although this latter option might not provide as diverse a participant group, it could hasten the start of fundraising activities. Either option must bring together people who have access to individuals and organizations that have the potential to make financial contributions to human services programs in the community.

Action systems for employee assistance should include the executive director, the director(s) of consultation and community education, and one or two other clinically trained social workers or psychologists of a given human services program to constitute the industrial relations team. Involvement of the executive director and director(s) of consultation and community education can assist the team in gaining entry to local companies, because corporate officers and managers will often take time from their schedules to meet with another executive. Inclusion of clinical staff develops the team's legitimacy with medical, nursing, and personnel representatives of corporations. This diversified team approach permits multilevel entry points to various companies, thus enhancing the potential for success. It is also important to remain flexible in selecting team members so that the team can be responsive to corporate needs.[11]

In forming action systems to initiate training seminars or workshops, a training committee should include technical experts, trainers, and interested staff. This committee should plan to deliver a variety of programs that increase the potential to attract various professional and community markets.

It is critical that the search for participants for action systems in all three initiatives be exhaustive and that qualities such as leadership, interest, expertise, and know-how be considered. Participants will need diverse skills, and a reasonable degree of harmony must be maintained among members to enhance the potential for success.

Targets

A target represents the available market for a program initiative. Industry, for example, offers a potential market for fundraising, development of employee assistance programs, and delivery of training programs to various supervisory, managerial, and employee groups. Traditionally, human services programs have restricted their efforts to working with individuals, local school systems, and a limited number of human services agencies. Given the potential of industry as a major market for mental health services, it is critical that the traditional focus of social services be expanded to include industry lest the market be lost to private mental health entrepreneurs.

Industry is also a reasonable target for substantial contributions to local mental health programs. Most companies have relatively informal application procedures for requesting support, and many companies have funds managed by executives or employee groups who consider the requests. It should be noted that an organization can increase its chances of obtaining corporate support when the company's employees live in the same geographical area served by the local mental health program and are eligible for the program's services.[12] It also helps when participants on the development (fundraising) committee have relationships with the specific companies being solicited. Human services personnel may also solicit local businesses to donate advertising or merchandise for selected agency programs.

The Conference Board and the American Association of Fundraising Counsel ". . . put the total of corporate giving in 1981 at approximately $3 billion. This amounts to a 5 percent share of total private-sector giving—about the same as that of private foundations."[13] This can be compared to individual contributions of $44.5 billion.[14] Contributions also occur through the voluntary services of millions of individuals. It is extremely important to identify and solicit help from these persons so that human services programs can obtain their fair share of philanthropic resources and volunteered services.

Clients of human services programs may also be a potential target group for fundraising activities. The issue of confidentiality and concerns regarding exploitation and coercion, however, should be examined carefully before engaging this population.

The last targets of fundraising efforts are local, state, and national foundations, most of which have specified application procedures and trustees to review all requests. In addition, foundations tend to specify the types of programs funded, the dollar amounts granted, and the geographic area to be served. It is helpful to identify individuals who are trustees or administrators of foundations and to try to link persons involved with the agency with those individuals. This can often increase chances of obtaining funds.

Employee assistance programs have industry as a primary target. Industry is now recognizing the need for mental health intervention with troubled employees. Community human services programs can assist industry in developing employee assistance policies and can provide training, consultation, referral linkages, and treatment resources.[15] It should be noted that productivity is of major importance to industry, and therefore the matching of local mental health programs' resources with industry's needs is essential. The need to be and to remain responsive cannot be overstated. The development, maintenance, and expansion of employee assistance programs will rest largely on timely and responsive action.

Besides industry, targets for training programs also include other human services agencies and schools. Knowledge of the target group's training needs and the level of fees they are able to pay, coupled with well-advertised programs conducted in pleasant surroundings, should provide the impetus to begin capturing these markets.

Values Orientation

To implement successfully any of the initiatives discussed in this article, traditional program development postures must be abandoned and more aggressive, competitive marketing be adopted. Traditionally, human services programs used low-key approaches to seek state or federal funds for new program development, relying on their credibility with the funding source. As state and federal funding becomes more limited, these traditional approaches must be reevaluated.

Successful fundraising campaigns cannot be implemented unless human services programs adopt values consistent with soliciting philanthropic support. These values often include the firm beliefs (1) that local contributions can be realized, (2) that a community agency has the right of access to these funds, (3) that the relationship of the person soliciting the funds to the funding sources can be the major factor in what individuals and businesses contribute and how much is realized, and (4) that some capital outlay will be needed to run a successful fundraising campaign.

In developing employee assistance initiatives, human services programs must first recognize that industry is a potential and legitimate target for mental health services and that providing such services can legitimate mental health as a proper concern of industry. Recognition must also be given to industry's concern with employees' productivity. Outcomes desired by the company—for example, reduced absenteeism—must be acknowledged as a means to build in reasonable expectations and specified evaluation procedures when an employee assistance program is implemented.[16]

Development of training programs involves recognizing the value of an organization's existing staff by giving them the opportunity to share their expertise. The belief that other agencies will pay to have their staff attend training seminars offered by other human services programs must also be adopted before launching this initiative.

Conflict

In assessing the potential difficulties that could arise in implementing fundraising, employee assistance programs, and training, consideration needs to be given to conflict within the organization and between the organization and other agencies. Boards of human services programs could be a potential source of conflict in fundraising and in program development for employee assistance because board members may not see these endeavors as germane to the agency's mission. For all three initiatives, a conflict could arise if the program's direct service practitioners view services as properly being directed only to disadvantaged populations. Thus, the initiatives might be perceived as draining scarce resources and energy.

According to Hall, Katz identifies three bases of organizational conflict: (1) functional conflict induced by various organizational subsystems, (2) competition between units with similar functions, and (3) hierarchical conflict stemming from struggles among interest groups over rewards.[17] It is in these three areas that conflict could arise within the organization when new initiatives are undertaken. Perrow views conflict in organizations as a struggle among people who do not share the same values or goals.[18] He argues that goals can be pursued in sequence or simultaneously with relatively minimal conflict if the environment poses few threats to the organization. However, when resources are inadequate and the environment is not "benign," goals within an organization may conflict. This latter point highlights conflict over the goals in an agency as a primary source of contention in establishing the three initiatives in the 1980s. However, the potential for new programs that are based on these initiatives to attract resources could stave off any major clash within the agency or between the agency and its board.

Conflict can also develop between human services agencies and other local organizations. In fundraising, community chests may be a source of potential conflict regarding competition for contributions. Other human services agencies may also be competing for contributions and for participants in employee assistance programs and training workshops. Of particular note is the potential conflict that can occur in departments or divisions of companies when employee assistance programs are implemented by outside organizations. Conflict in a turbulent, competitive environment is inevitable, and it is of critical importance for conflict to be anticipated and confronted constructively.

Empowerment

Understanding the concept of power and empowerment—the process of acquiring power—can facilitate the implementation of the initiatives under discussion. Hall reports that French and Raven delineate five bases of interpersonal power: reward, coercive, legitimate, referent, and expert.[19] Etzioni identifies three forms of power: coercive, remunerative, and normative.[20]

Although all these forms of power will not necessarily derive from the implementation of each initiative, the author believes that successful programs based on the three initiatives can enhance the influence, expertise, and income of human services agencies. Through empowerment, human services programs may further their ability to survive in a rapidly changing environment.

Goals

Short- and long-term goals provide the final element in the analysis of new initiatives. A major short-term goal for fundraising could include obtaining funds for capital improvements and new program development. It should be noted, however, that the use of contributions to offset general operating expenses is a dangerous precedent that can lead to major financial distress when fundraising goals are not reached. Long-term fundraising goals could include the development of an endowment fund and the creation of a community action system that can assist in planning, needs assessment, and program development and can provide a source of prospective board members.

Short-term goals for employee assistance programs could include the securing of industrial contracts for mental health services and the delivery of stress management programs. Long-term goals should include the development of a consortium for employee assistance programs in industry and the establishment of campaigns for sustained corporate giving.

Primary short-term goals of the training initiatives could be to offer spring and fall seminars within industries or other organizations. A long-term goal could be to provide an annual symposium.

Suggestions for Implementation

The three initiatives discussed in this article—fundraising, employee assistance programs, and training—have to a major extent been implemented successfully by the Eliot Community Mental Health Center, which serves nine towns in the Concord, Massachusetts, area. The center's fundraising has grown since 1979 from a nonexistent base to a $25,000 annual campaign that includes corporate and individual gifts, special projects, and benefits. In addition, an endowment fund has been established. The employee assistance program (also initiated in 1979) brings in an annual income of approximately $40,000. This program includes program development for employee assistance, and seminars and consultations for good health and stress management.

The following suggestions are put forth for human services programs to consider when implementing the initiatives discussed in this article:

• Take stock of the agency's resources in the forms of capital available for development and expertise of the staff and board of directors.

• Determine the level of activity of other community agencies and organizations in the initiatives the agency is interested in undertaking.

• Identify and overcome organizational constraints—such as lack of resources, resistance, negativism, apathy—that could impede successful implementation.

• Segment the potential markets in the community for the initiatives the agency is considering; be certain that a match exists between each initiative and an existing or potential market.

• Design and market new programs.

• Try not to overestimate or underestimate potential revenues; remember that new initiatives have start-up costs, and when successful, they have continued long-term returns.

• Avoid dependence on any single revenue source and diversify.

Conclusion

This article discussed the organizational dilemma facing human services programs in the 1980s. A review of organizational concepts examined (1) the necessity for flexibility in coordination, (2) the effect of centralization and decentralization on decision making and coordination, (3) administrative controls and innovation, and (4) factors effecting change in programs. This review highlighted the need for community human services programs to confront the turbulent 1980s by maintaining centralized systems that have a decentralized control of activity to encourage innovation.

The initiatives of fundraising, employee assistance programs, and training were outlined. It is anticipated that these programs offer a potential for increased revenues that can strengthen waning fiscal bases of local human services organizations.

The model used in analyzing these proposed initiatives included the following elements: action systems, participants, targets, values orientation, conflict, empowerment, and goals. Analysis of the model focused on congruent and divergent factors and attempted to highlight the importance of various conditions that affect initiation of new programs. Some suggestions for implementation were presented.

This article aimed to integrate research on organizations with practical operating experience. The author does not attempt to provide a cookbook approach to new program development but intends to inspire the administrative imagination at a critical time in the chronology of human services programming.

Notes and References

1. Selwyn W. Becker and Gerald Gordon, "An Entrepreneurial Theory of Formal Organizations; Part I: Patterns of Formal Organizations," *Administrative Science Quarterly,* 2 (December 1966), p. 335.

2. James D. Thompson, *Organizations in Action* (New York: McGraw-Hill Book Co., 1967), p. 145.

3. Ibid., p. 26.

4. Ibid., p. 19.

5. Ibid., pp. 19–21.

6. Ibid., pp. 21–23.

7. Richard H. Hall, *Organizations: Structure and Process* (2d ed.; Englewood Cliffs, N.J.: Prentice-Hall, 1977), p. 192.

8. Martin M. Rosner, "Administrative Controls and Innovations," *Behavioral Science,* 13 (1968), pp. 36–43.

9. J. Hage and M. Aiken, "Program Change and Organizational Properties: A Comparative Analysis," *American Journal of Sociology,* 72 (March 1967), p. 503.

10. Roland Warren, *The Community in America* (Chicago: Rand McNally & Co., 1972), p. 167.

11. See Paul R. Brooks, "Industry-Agency Program for Employee Counseling," *Social Casework,* 56 (July 1975), pp. 404–410; Francis M. Moynihan, "Closing the Gap between Family Service and Private Industry," *Social Casework,* 52 (February 1971), pp. 67–73; and Sheila H. Akabas and Susan Bellinger, "Programming Mental Health Care for the World of Work," *Mental Health,* 61 (Spring 1977), pp. 4–8.

12. See Sheila H. Akabas and Paul A. Kurzman, eds., *Work, Workers, and Work Organizations: A View from Social Work* (Englewood Cliffs, N.J.: Prentice-Hall, 1982), chap. 9.; and Allan R. Cutting and Frank J. Prosser, "Family Oriented Mental Health Consultation to a Naval Research Group," *Social Casework,* 60 (April 1979), pp. 236–242.

13. *Grantsmanship Center News,* 9 (May–June 1982), p. 57.

14. Ibid.

15. See Paul A. Kurzman and Sheila H. Akabas, "Industrial Social Work as an Arena for Practice," *Social Work,* 26 (January 1981), pp. 52–60.

16. See Bradley Googins, "Employee Assistance Programs," *Social Work,* 20 (November 1975), pp. 464–473; Sheila H. Akabas, Paul A. Kurzman, and Nancy S. Kolben, eds., *Labor and Industrial Settings: Sites for Social Work Practice,* proceedings of a national conference, June 7–9, 1978, comp. Diana de Vegh (New York: Council on Social Work Education, 1979); and David C. Blomquist, Daniel D. Gray, and Larry L. Smith, "Social Work in Business and Industry," *Social Casework,* 60 (October 1979), pp. 457–470.

17. Daniel Katz, "Approaches to Managing Conflict," in Robert L. Kahn and Elise Boulding, eds., *Power and Conflict in Organizations* (New York: Basic Books, 1964), p. 105, as cited in Hall, op. cit., p. 230.

18. Charles B. Perrow, *Complex Organizations: A Critical Essay* (Glenview, Ill.: Scott, Foresman & Co., 1972), pp. 160–162, 202–203.

19. John R. P. French and Bertram Raven, "The Bases of Social Power," in Dorwin Cartwright and Alvin Zander, eds., *Group Dynamics* (3d ed.; New York: Harper & Row, 1968), pp. 259–269, as cited in Hall, op. cit., p. 202.

20. Amitai Etzioni, *A Comparative Analysis of Complex Organizations* (rev. ed.; New York: Free Press, 1975), p. 5.

Part Two
Improving Services in a Turbulent World

Editor's Comments

Part One moved from the societal to the political and finally to the organizational level in charting the new problems social work faces under supply side economics and ways in which the profession can respond; Part Two examines a number of broad concerns that affect the delivery of social services in these antiwelfare times.

In the first chapter, Mullen offers a useful service to the profession by reviewing the existing literature on evaluating the effectiveness of direct practice. Given the limits of evaluative studies, the frequent lack of specific goals, the complexity of the problems and phenomena with which social work struggles, and the small investment of the profession, it is heartening for one to note that social work has come this far. Mullen names the following four broad areas in which social workers can speak with some confidence: (1) multilevel and ecologically designed interventions work better than single-mode approaches, (2) specific and planned interventions work better than nonspecific, but a variety of technologies, modes, professional affiliations, and ideologies all seem equally effective, (3) a mutual, shared expectation between worker and consumer is critical to a successful outcome, and (4) interpersonal technologies are as effective as a credible placebo would be to a successful outcome, but the success rate is far better if the criterion is engagement. Given the attacks on social work's effectiveness, it is clear that to survive the profession must invest more of its scarce resources in carefully designed tests of its reservoir of practice wisdom. It needs the kinds of studies that say that this particular approach works with this particular kind of client who has this particular problem(s). Further, social work needs to alter its curricula so that it offers interventive models based on evidence (or lacking that, based on explicitly acknowledged practice wisdom) and not on models based on explanatory theory, effort, or dogma. The critical task is finding a way to combine a scientific bent with a commitment to social work's goals and values at the same time as attending to the demands for efficiency as well as efficacy.

Next, Rapp and Poertner tackle the dual dilemma of social work's need to cope—in an era of fewer resources—with pressures to tighten eligibility requirements and with accountability so as to survive in the short run and its need to give attention to providing high-quality services and assuring program effectiveness in the long run. In their effort to reconcile these two horns of the dilemma, the authors examine a number of data collection schemes that will help the decision maker organize information in ways that will locate problems and that will indicate some of the uses and limits of various solutions. In a field of vague goals and techniques, of unobservable processes and poor traditions of accountability, it is a true contribution to find a number of performance measures, let alone the illustrations and examples to show the limits and advantages of each.

The third chapter, by Rahn, continues in this same line by examining how agencies must think about costs, effectiveness, and, that transplant from the business world, cost-effectiveness measures, which are being increasingly applied to the now profit-oriented world of social services, at times with disastrous results. The profession could learn to manipulate cost-effectiveness measures as judgmentally as any economist or it could use the measures to extract the maximum of service for every community dollar in its search for the goals of better service. Cost-effectiveness, however, is clearly a two-edged sword. It can be used illegitimately to reduce costs by selecting only "easy" or "quick-service" clients or by hiring only untrained social workers. Or it can be used to locate efficiencies that do not affect the quality of the service or the kind of client social work serves. Social workers must know how to use this weapon so that it is not turned against them.

Gibelman reports on a study of the consequences of purchase-of-service agreements for who is served and what service they get. Purchase of service was a growing phenomenon in Title XX and child welfare services. It is likely to increase in importance given the current ideology that the philanthropic sector and the private for-profit market can do any job better than the public sector. The consequences of the government's delegating responsibility for social service delivery to an array of voluntary and for-profit agencies are serious and at times unexpected. Although this is a study of one part of one state-wide agency, it is suggestive—and surprising. It may be that the existing three-tier system of social services—the poor served by the public agency, the middle class by the voluntary agency, and the wealthy by the market sector—may be blurred by purchase of service. It may also be that social work's belief that public agencies provide concrete services and private agencies offer "soft" services only is erroneous. In this study, the private agencies had the capacity for a far wider range of services. The growth of purchase-of-service arrangements will necessitate attention to issues of monitoring, perverse incentives, overall planning in a more complex, political environment, and ultimately the kinds of training the staff of both public and voluntary agencies need to have.

The last chapter in Part Two, by Lynch and Brawley, reports on an effort to bring both expertise and commitment to the needs of minority populations. A group of minority professionals developed a model to offer not only an advocacy planning capacity to their community but also advocacy research, policy studies, and other aids to improve service delivery, community development, and empowerment. Although this report covers only the start-up of this effort, it is offered as a model that others might adopt to serve other vulnerable communities.

Evaluating Social Work's Effectiveness

Edward J. Mullen

The profession has undergone two decades of critical self-evaluation. Many of its traditional practice models have been systematically evaluated. New practice technologies have emerged in response to changing conditions, and to some extent these more recently developed approaches have been evaluated. Although the profession now has available to it an information base regarding the relative effectiveness and efficiency of many of its technologies, the utility of this information in a rapidly changing world is problematic. Questions of technological effectiveness can only be meaningfully addressed within the context of values, goals, and, most fundamentally, the changing nature of human need.

Practice Effectiveness

The effectiveness of social work practice is critical to the future of the profession. Societal conditions largely responsible for the present emphasis on effectiveness and efficiency will become more pronounced. As the world's population expands, as its societal arrangements become increasingly complex, and as resources dwindle, social workers will be challenged increasingly to do more with less. During the 1980s, effectiveness and efficiency will become pivotal issues for the profession. Within this context, a serious assessment of the current effectiveness of practice becomes particularly relevant: Where is the social work profession now and what is the challenge for tomorrow?

Given the critical importance of the subject and the attention it has received during the last twenty years, relatively little is known about the effectiveness of social work practice, which is disheartening. Moreover, this author and his colleagues reached essentially the same conclusion

63

eleven years ago when they assessed the experimental evaluations of social work effectiveness available then.[1]

Why has so little progress been made? At least four factors pertain. First, questions of effectiveness hinge on the explication of specific practice objectives. Herzog and more recently Wholey have identified goal specification as an essential precondition for evaluating effectiveness.[2] But the precise specification of practice objectives has been difficult.

A second factor is the complexity of the phenomena dealt with in social work practice. To a large extent, practice depends on knowledge made available through research in the social and behavioral sciences to elucidate social work concerns. However, because of the complexity of some phenomena involved in practice, available knowledge may be insufficient to clarify those concerns. The Atlantic Street Center experiment in Seattle, Washington, which sought to prevent juvenile delinquency, illustrates what can happen if such elucidating knowledge is not available.[3] In spite of an attempt to design an intervention program derived from current theories of delinquency, workers found no theory adequate to guide planning for intervention. Consequently, the intervention proceeded with the acknowledged absence of a model or theory of delinquency, and, indeed, of a rationale for intervention.

Complexity also figures in the effectiveness of social work practice at the micro level as compared with the effectiveness of psychotherapy and behavioral modification. Research on social work micro-level practice has generally produced less evidence of effectiveness than has parallel research in the areas of psychotherapy and behavioral change. What accounts for this difference in effectiveness? The findings of Smith and Glass in their analysis of outcomes suggest a possible explanation.[4] As part of their review, they examined success by type of problem and reported major differences in success rates for various problem areas. For example, a greater degree of success was reported for interventions that addressed circumscribed problems such as anxiety or fear than for interventions with chronic or pervasive problems such as alcoholism, delinquency, and general social adjustment. It may well be that social workers generally focus on problems of the latter type, which are more resistant to change. This may be a partial explanation for the differences in success rates between social work and psychotherapy interventions.

A third factor limiting knowledge about effectiveness has to do with the reactivity of the social work profession to shifts in society's priorities. Inasmuch as the study of effectiveness is complex, it requires an investment of evaluation activity in specific areas of intervention over a substantial period. However, social work's responsiveness to and dependence on societal interests and priorities have mitigated against this long-term investment. Instead, the profession's attempts at innovation and evaluation have been sporadic, driven by funding opportunities that reflect the shifting interests of federal agencies and foundation boards.

A final factor is that social work has invested little in the development of an evaluation capability. This dearth is reflected in the low level of funding for evaluation activities focused on practice, the failure to prepare investigators to conduct evaluation studies, and the incidental attention given to development of evaluation methods and techniques.

Promising Findings

Although relatively little is known about the effectiveness of social work practice, social workers do seem to have learned something about it during the last twenty years of research. It now seems reasonably clear, for instance, that multilevel interventions hold the greatest promise of effectiveness for certain disadvantaged groups. This conclusion is based on studies evaluating the effectiveness of social work practice with such disadvantaged groups as the poor and the aged, in which the practice focused on problems and needs whose remedy greatly depended on the availability of community resources. However, much of the evidence supporting this conclusion is indirect and based on intervention failures rather than on successful demonstrations of multilevel interventions. For example, in studies reported by Brown and by Mullen and associates, workers dealt with economically disadvantaged populations but failed to intervene on an institutional or community level.[5] Similarly, Blenkner and her colleagues reported that caseworkers intervened directly with frail elderly clients but did not make systematic, major attempts to develop the institutional and community supports often needed by the frail elderly.[6] These three studies illustrate the futility of trying to manipulate and secure for clients nonexistent community resources. They also point up the consequences of failing to consider the ecological context, a subject that will be discussed more fully later. Several studies are now available that suggest the importance of having community resources and multilevel intervention available in working with disadvantaged populations. For example, the Goldberg study conducted in England; a development project conducted in Vancouver, British Columbia; and Geismar and Krisberg's New Haven study are typical.[7]

Social workers have also learned something about the effectiveness of individualized interpersonal assistance offered by practitioners. But before discussing what has been learned, one should note that social work intervention in this area of practice overlaps considerably with interventions provided by other professional groups. Findings from evaluations of counseling, psychotherapy, behavior therapy, and applied behavior analysis as well as from micro-level social work intervention are relevant and useful in examining the effectiveness of micro-level practice.

If social workers were to rely on their profession's evaluative research on micro-level intervention conducted during the 1970s, they would have a thin data base indeed. Researchers in the allied disciplines generated a much larger volume of evaluative research during the past decade than did social work researchers. The findings of Smith and Glass regarding the difference in outcomes associated with type of problem, however, suggest limits to the ability to generalize findings from psychotherapy and behavioral therapy to social work practice. Although findings from allied helping professions are useful, they should be used with caution when generalized to social work practice.

An examination of research findings regarding interpersonal intervention leads to a number of conclusions. Evidence continues to mount suggesting that the various forms of planned interpersonal intervention are, on the average, more effective than nonspecific intervention. Evidence also suggests that various forms of interpersonal intervention are equally effective. These observations, which have been expressed by Luborsky and others, suggest that the common qualities of interpersonal intervention have effects and are currently among the most important components of intervention.[8] However, although there is extensive speculation about what these common components are, little definitive research exists concerning them. Nevertheless, there are some interesting hypotheses available based, to some extent, on research findings.[9] At present, variables of relationship and structuring seem to hold the greatest promise as components of effective intervention. A corollary to these findings is equally significant: in spite of the proliferation of technologies and techniques of interpersonal intervention, no meaningful research exists suggesting the superiority of one technology over another.[10]

At a more specific level, what contribution have components of micro-level social work intervention made to effectiveness? What does the research indicate about the effects on clients of the components of systems of interpersonal assistance such as organizational or agency variables, intervenor qualities, intervenor-client interaction or relationship qualities, and the various technologies and techniques of intervention? The following discussions consider the research findings in each component area, addressing the volume of available research, the quality of evidence, and the nature of the substantive findings.

Effects on Clients of Inter- and Intraorganizational Qualities

Most often, social work interventions are agency based and occur within a complex of human service organizations. How do the various arrangements within and between organizations affect clients in programs of interpersonal assistance? How do such arrangements affect workers and technologies of intervention that in turn affect clients?

Unfortunately, the amount of quality research available in this most important area is insufficient to permit reliable inferences, although Rothman and his colleagues have studied much of it and have applied the findings to organizational and community intervention.[11] The available research addresses questions of interorganizational relationships as well as relationships between organizational variables and those of worker process, but little attention has been given to the ultimate effects on individual clients. The work of Olmstead and Christensen is an instructive exception.[12] Also, the Midway experiment in Chicago was an attempt to examine organizational variables.[13] However, the important question of the contribution of agency or organizational variables to effective personal assistance has been largely unstudied.

Effects on Clients of Characteristics of the Worker

Considerable research exists in the area concerning the effects on the clients of the worker's characteristics, and much of it meets at least minimal scientific standards.[14] Among the qualities of the intervenor that have been found *not* to be associated with effectiveness are professional or disciplinary affiliation, demographic characteristics, having undergone personal counseling, and theoretical orientation.[15] Another set of intervenor qualities that holds promise but for which the evidence is inconsistent includes warmth, empathy, genuineness, and the quality and amount of experience.[16] Perhaps the only group of qualities studied that has produced generally consistent results has to do with the mental health of the intervenor.[17]

Effects on Clients of Worker-Client Interactions

Much research has addressed qualities of the client-worker interaction (that is, the quality of the interpersonal relationship), and it is in this area that the core of effectiveness seems to lie. Among these qualities are reciprocal empathy, warmth, and genuineness; worker-client complementarity; and communicated and perceived expectations.[18] The nonspecific or placebo qualities seem to lie in this area and to account for much of the effectiveness of current approaches to interpersonal assistance.[19]

Qualities of Clients Associated with Outcomes

Though considerable research exists concerning the qualities of clients associated with outcomes, the research fails to identify specific qualities.[20] Rather, this research says something about the limitations of particular agencies, intervenors, or technologies and suggests that regardless of the particular skill of the intervenor or the particular potency of the technology used, healthier clients tend to improve more and less healthy clients tend to improve less.[21] The findings indicate that it is not fruitful to look for absolute qualities in clients when studying the effectiveness of interventions; instead, researchers should consider the effects of the interaction of worker and client and client and technology.

Effects on Clients of Interpersonal Technologies and Techniques

Extensive research is available concerning the effects of various technologies and techniques, much of it of excellent quality.[22] A general conclusion from the findings in this area is that, on the average, technologies of interpersonal assistance are modestly effective, but none is more effective than any other or demonstrably more effective than a credible placebo technology.[23] However, if the criterion of effectiveness is not outcome but rather engagement and continuance, a somewhat different general conclusion emerges: more structured interventions and those that skillfully manipulate expectations and demands are more likely to succeed in engaging and keeping clients.[24]

Fischer has identified four areas that, in his estimation, currently provide validated techniques for social work practitioners to use.[25] The areas are the following:

1. *Structuring techniques.* These include techniques to prepare clients and workers for treatment, manipulation of expectancy and demand, techniques for enhancing the attractiveness of intervention, time limits, and contracting. Fischer asserts there is evidence supporting the general effectiveness of structuring approaches. This author, although agreeing with Fischer that this research is promising, is less convinced that it demonstrates the superiority of structuring over less structured methods of intervention. The argument lies more in the realm of efficiency than in effectiveness. For example, one type of structuring involves setting time limits, as contrasted with providing open-ended or continued service. Research comparing the effectiveness of these two forms of intervention (as illustrated by Reid and Shyne's study and by the more recent Butcher and Koss review) clearly suggests that planned short-term service is *as* effective as more prolonged forms of treatment but clearly not *more* effective than open-ended interventions.[26] Rather, the argument in favor of time-limited and similar techniques is one of efficiency. Briefer forms of intervention do seem to achieve generally equivalent effects at less cost. For example, in the Reid and Shyne study, the two forms of service achieved equivalent results, but the brief service pattern used 422 interviews and the continued service pattern 1562 to achieve the

same results. Moreover, the structuring techniques do increase the probability of continuance in service and thereby may enhance efficiency.

2. *Behavioral techniques.* Although behavioral techniques are often found to be quite effective for specified problems, this author does not agree with Fischer that very much is currently known about the elements active in producing these effects. Manipulation of expectancy and demand remains as an alternative explanation. Taking Fischer's example of systematic desensitization as a case in point, one need only study reviews by Marks or Kazdin and Wilcoxon: Although it is clear that systematic desensitization is effective for mild and moderate fears or phobias, it is not at all clear what it is about systematic desensitization that produces the results.[27] In fact, either the components of relaxation or exposure to the feared stimulus may be as effective as the total technology. The expectation-demand hypothesis remains plausible.

3. *Cognitive interventions.* Although the cognitive approaches are attractive, this author does not find evidence to back the claim that cognitive techniques are demonstrably effective. Relatively little controlled research concerning the effectiveness of the cognitive techniques is available.

4. *Relationship variables.* Such relationship variables as nonpossessive warmth, accurate empathy, and facilitative genuineness have been extensively researched. Reviews by Gurman; Mitchell, Bogarth, and Krauft; and Parloff, Waskow, and Wolfe suggest that these qualities are of increasingly questionable relevance.[28] To argue for their inclusion in practice models on the basis of proven effectiveness is therefore untenable at this point.

Implications for Practice and Research

A major agenda for the future must be clarification of the goals and objectives of social work practice. Serious attention must be paid to methods for implementing goal statements that will permit evaluation of effectiveness and efficiency. The development of the profession's ability to specify its goals should have the highest priority.

A second agenda has to do with evaluation research itself. It is alarming to find how little attention the profession is giving to evaluation research and evaluation of the effectiveness of its programs. There is extensive rhetoric in this area but very little activity. The evaluation activity of the 1960s has all but ceased; the profession has apparently pulled back from controlled evaluation of practice effectiveness. Instead, the emphasis is on practitioners' self-evaluation and on operational evaluations. Although this is laudable and should contribute to ultimate effectiveness, given the meager knowledge base supporting social work practice, it is essential that the profession invest extensive resources in evaluation research.

Building on the research findings concerning the qualities of apparently successful social work practice with disadvantaged populations, a third agenda should be to conceptualize multilevel practice interventions and evaluate their effectiveness. Such interventions should stress the interdependence of individual functioning with community and institutional supports.

A fourth agenda pertains to micro-level intervention stressing interpersonal assistance. In this area, two dimensions require future attention: (1) the study of the common components of effective intervention and how they are played out in various practice models, and (2) the evaluation of specific technologies (other than common components) hypothesized as having specific effects on practice. There has already been considerable activity in this area by allied disciplines, and similar work should be encouraged within social work.

Finally, if social work practice is to become more effective, a means must be found to integrate a scientific perspective into the system of social work education. The traditional dichotomy between practice and research must end, and a way must be found to place effectiveness at the center of social work education. If this were accomplished, effectiveness in practice would probably follow.

Problematic Practice Models

Lessons can be learned from studying some past and present practice models that have had undesirable characteristics. Four such characteristics are particularly problematic:

• Social work's practice models have tended to derive from highly specialized, theoretical frameworks that are usually restricted to a particular aspect of the person or the person's environment. Practice models based on such highly specialized frameworks have proved to be of limited use and, when applied to a wider range of clients seen by social workers, have resulted in serious distortions of clients' needs.

• Practice models have often failed to distinguish between descriptive-developmental-causal knowledge and prescriptive knowledge. As a consequence, models have been rich in content and often quite powerful, in that they provide a worker with a sense of understanding, but thin and wanting as prescriptive guidelines for intervening effectively. In this sense, social work's practice models have not been intervention models; they have too often elevated the goal of explanation over that of prediction. In other words, the profession has sought powerful models that would satisfy its need to understand clients, at the expense of building more precise models that would have a relatively high probability of achieving predictable results with clients. Social workers have assumed that predictable results would flow from powerful understandings. As Dubin has pointed out, this is a fallacious assumption.[29]

• Practice models have often been fixed and closed. The profession has evolved a limited number of practice models that have tended to be handed down from one generation of students to the next and taught through an apprentice mode with reliance on authoritative grounding.

• Practice models have emphasized criteria of process and effort. They have not been developed with an eye toward effectiveness (the extent to which goals and objectives are attained), adequacy of performance (the effectiveness of a model in relation to overall need), or efficiency (the effectiveness of a model in relation to alternative models as well as the differences in human and financial costs among models).

Drawing on these lessons of the past, this author would suggest several guidelines for building future models:

1. Social work intervention should be reconceptualized within an ecological-system framework. Intervention models must be conceptualized as systems composed of interacting environmental, organizational, technological, and personal events. Professionals must view themselves not as isolated technicians but as individuals functioning within larger interventional systems, usually social agencies that have complex, interorganizational relationships.

2. As it designs intervention models, social work will need to tap more diversified sources of knowledge. Single-theory models of intervention are too risky and incomplete. Knowledge from the behavioral and social sciences will need to be applied.

3. The profession should invest its limited resources in developing intervention models that provide guidelines for application. Such models can give direction to intervention rather than simply provide an understanding of the client in his or her situation.

4. The profession must develop open, evolving intervention models— ones seen as temporary, incomplete, and subject to constant review and revision. The emphasis would be on an eclectic use of information from diverse sources, and research findings and scientific validation would be central to such models. Students and practitioners will have to be adequately trained for the hard task of building these models.

5. Intervention models of the future should give primacy to adequacy of performance and efficiency. Simple effectiveness can no longer be the final question; effort and process surely should not be.

6. As intervenors who seek to help people individually or in groups, social workers must develop intervention models with predictable results. Dubin has suggested that the twin goals of science—explanation and prediction—do not necessarily go hand in hand.[30] Perhaps for the immediate future, social workers must be humble in their efforts to build models. They must strive for intervention models that will be somewhat precise and have a probability of guiding them toward predictable results with their clients, even though such models might not satisfy practitioners' cravings to understand causation or the complexities of the interactions with which they work.

7. Without an external guiding purpose, attention to efficient, personalized practice models grounded in scientific evidence could easily lead the profession to irrelevance. It is important, therefore, that an open, continuous consideration of the purposes and values of social welfare and social work should be central to the process of model development. Such an approach can in time lead to intervention models that not only would be more adequate and efficient but also would be more relevant.

Directions for the 1980s

Because a major source of difficulty for the profession has been in clarifying goals, intervention programs have been poorly focused and less than effective and efficient. As has been the case with intervention, the design of evaluation research has lacked clear purpose. Although the profession has sought to articulate goals within the framework of person and environment, conceptualizations that would give focus to this arena have been lacking. Recently, however, the notion of an ecological perspective has taken hold—an exciting development.[31] This perspective promises to sharpen the articulation of social work goals and to enhance the relevance of its interventions. Moreover, as illustrated in the work of Bronfenbrenner, ecological ideas could change evaluation research strategies.[32] The ecological perspective is consonant with those findings of evaluation research that repeatedly demonstrate the futility of intervening with people without considering their environment. The perspective also allows for the notion of the power of meso- and macro-level interventions. As Bronfenbrenner has so clearly described, human development and interventions aimed at facilitating it take on new meaning when considered within the ecological framework. Evaluation notions such as ecological validity and transforming experiments are powerful ideas with practical implications for the conduct of research. The ecological framework can help to focus intervention.

A second challenge for the eighties lies in the area of innovation. Social work practitioners must become innovators at the micro, meso, and macro levels because the profession's transactional focus—fixed on the interface between people and their environments—requires a continual redefinition of objectives in the context of rapidly changing circumstances. To be innovative, practitioners must hone (1) the ability to define and redefine goals, (2) a capacity for continual problem solving (requiring skills in utilizing information, assessing, setting objectives, planning and executing interventions, and monitoring for evaluation), and (3) the ability to tolerate uncertainty and to function independently and creatively.

Given the dynamic nature of the human condition, interventions that are effective today may become irrelevant and ineffective tomorrow. Relevance and effectiveness must be viewed as conditional and transitory, never to be taken for granted in a changing, turbulent world. The realities of practice in the 1980s will require sound problem-solving skills, creatively applied within an ecological framework, of practitioner and researcher alike.

Portions of this article are adapted from the author's presentations at the Council on Social Work Education 1978 Annual Program Meeting and the Jane Addams College of Social Work Research Symposium of January 26, 1979. The literature review supporting parts of this article was funded by the Ittleson Foundation, Inc., New York, New York. The contributions of the author's students at the University of Chicago to the ideas in this article are gratefully acknowledged.

Notes and References

1. Edward J. Mullen, James R. Dumpson, and associates, *Evaluation of Social Intervention* (San Francisco: Jossey-Bass, 1972).

2. Elizabeth Herzog, *Some Guidelines for Evaluative Research* (Washington, D.C.: U.S. Department of Health, Education & Welfare, 1959); and Joseph S. Wholey, "Evaluability Assessment," in Leonard S. Rutman, ed., *Evaluation Research Methods: A Basic Guide* (Beverly Hills, Calif.: Sage Publications, 1977), pp. 39–56.

3. William C. Berleman, James R. Seaberg, and Thomas W. Steinburn, "The Delinquency Prevention Experiment of the Seattle Atlantic Street Center: A Final Evaluation," *Social Service Review*, 46 (September 1972), pp. 323–346.

4. Mary Lee Smith and Gene V. Glass, "Meta-Analysis of Psychotherapy Outcome Studies," *American Psychologist*, 32 (September 1977), pp. 752–760; and Glass, Barry McGaw, and Smith, *Meta-Analysis in Social Research* (Beverly Hills, Calif.: Sage Publications, 1981). For a reanalysis of the Smith and Glass data, see Janet Trecy Landman and Robyn M. Dawes, "Psychotherapy Outcome," *American Psychologist*, 37 (May 1982), pp. 504–516.

5. Gordon E. Brown, ed., *The Multi-Problem Dilemma: A Social Research Demonstration with Multi-Problem Families* (Metuchen, N.J.: Scarecrow Press, 1968); and Edward J. Mullen, Robert M. Chazin, and David M. Feldstein, *Preventing Chronic Dependency: An Evaluation of Public-Private Collaborative*

Intervention with First-Time Public Assistance Families (New York: Community Service Society of New York, 1970).

6. Margaret Blenkner et al., *Protective Services for Older People* (Cleveland, Ohio: The Benjamin Rose Institute, 1974).

7. E. Matilda Goldberg, *Helping the Aged* (London, England: George Allen & Unwin, 1970); *The Area Development Project*, Research Monographs I (1968), II (1969), and III (1969), and *The Red Door: A Report on Neighborhood Services* (1968) (Vancouver, B.C., Canada: United Community Services of the Greater Vancouver Area); and Ludwig Geismar and Jane Krisberg, *The Forgotten Neighborhood: Site of an Early Skirmish in the War on Poverty* (Metuchen, N.J.: Scarecrow Press, 1967).

8. Lester Luborsky et al., "Comparative Studies of Psychotherapies," *Archives of General Psychiatry*, 32 (August 1975), pp. 995–1008; Smith and Glass, op. cit.; and Allen E. Bergin and Michael Lambert, "The Evaluation of Therapeutic Outcomes," pp. 139–190, and Hans H. Strupp, "Psychotherapy Research and Practice: An Overview," pp. 3–22, in Sol L. Garfield and Bergin, eds., *Handbook of Psychotherapy and Behavior Change* (2d ed.; New York: John Wiley & Sons, 1978).

9. Jerome D. Frank, *Persuasion and Healing: A Comparative Study of Psychotherapy* (New York: Schocken Books, 1974); Alan E. Kazdin and Linda A. Wilcoxon, "Systematic Desensitization and Nonspecific Treatment Effects: A Methodological Evaluation," *Psychological Bulletin*, 83 (September 1976), pp. 729–758; and Arthur K. Shapiro and Louis A. Morris, "The Placebo Effect in Medical and Psychological Therapies," in Sol L. Garfield and Allen E. Bergin, eds., *Handbook of Psychotherapy and Behavior Change* (2d ed.; New York: John Wiley & Sons, 1978), pp. 369–410.

10. Alan S. Gurman and Andrew M. Razin, eds., *Effective Psychotherapy: A Handbook of Research* (Elmsford, N.Y.: Pergamon Press, 1977); Bergin and Lambert, op. cit.; and Strupp, op. cit.

11. Jack Rothman, John Erlich, and Joseph Teresa, *Promoting Innovation and Change in Organizations and Communities* (New York: John Wiley & Sons, 1976).

12. Joseph A. Olmstead and Harold Christensen, *Effects of Agency Work Contexts: An Intensive Field Study*, Research Report No. 2, Vols. 1 and 2 (Washington, D.C.: U.S. Department of Health, Education & Welfare, Social Rehabilitation Service, 1973).

13. Edward E. Schwartz and William C. Sample, "First Findings from Midway," *Social Service Review*, 41 (June 1967), pp. 113–151.

14. Gurman and Razin, op. cit.

15. Sol L. Garfield, "Research on the Training of Professional Psychotherapists," pp. 63–83, and Donald M. Sundland, "Theoretical Orientations of Psychotherapists," pp. 189–221, in Gurman and Razin, eds., *Effective Psychotherapy: A Handbook of Research;* and Morris B. Parloff, Irene E. Waskow, and Barry E. Wolfe, "Research on Therapist Variables in Relation to Process and Outcome," in Garfield and Allen E. Bergin, eds., *Handbook of Psychotherapy and Behavior Change* (2d ed.; New York: John Wiley & Sons, 1978), p. 233.

16. Kevin M. Mitchell, Jerold D. Bozarth, and Conrad C. Krauft, "A Reappraisal of the Therapeutic Effectiveness of Accurate Empathy, Nonpossessive Warmth and Genuineness," pp. 482–502, and Arthur H. Auerbach and Marilyn Johnson, "Research on the Therapist's Level of Experience," pp. 84–102, in Gurman and Razin, eds., *Effective Psychotherapy: A Handbook of Research.*

17. Parloff, Waskow, and Wolfe, op. cit.

18. Ibid.; and Juris I. Berzins, "Therapist-Patient Matching," pp. 222–251, Mitchell, Bozarth, and Krauft, op. cit., Alan S. Gurman, "The Patient's Perception of the Therapeutic Relationship," pp. 503–543, G. Terence Wilson and Jan M. Evans, "Therapist-Client Relationship in Behavior Therapy," pp. 544–565, and David W. Johnson and Ronald P. Matross, "Interpersonal Influence in Psychotherapy: A Social Psychological View," pp. 395–432, in Gurman and Razin, eds., *Effective Psychotherapy: A Handbook of Research.*

19. Shapiro and Morris, op. cit.

20. Sol L. Garfield, "Research on Client Variables in Psychotherapy," in Garfield and Allen E. Bergin, eds., *Handbook of Psychotherapy and Behavior Change* (2d ed.; New York: John Wiley & Sons, 1978), pp. 191–232.

21. See, for example, R. Bruce Sloane et al., *Psychotherapy Versus Behavior Therapy* (Cambridge, Mass.: Harvard University Press, 1975).

22. See, for example, James N. Butcher and Mary P. Koss, "Research on Brief and Crisis-Oriented Psychotherapies," pp. 725–768, Alan S. Gurman and David Kniskern, "Research on Marital and Family Therapy," pp. 817–902, Lester Luborsky and Donald Spence, "Quantitative Research on Psychoanalytic Therapy," pp. 331–368, Richard L. Bednar and Theodore J. Kaul, "Experimental Group Research: Current Perspectives," pp. 769–816, Alan E. Kazdin, "The Application of Operant Techniques in Treatment, Rehabilitation and Education," pp. 549–590, and Ted L. Rosenthal and Albert Bandura, "Psychological Modeling: Theory and Practice," pp. 621–658, in Sol L. Garfield and Alan E. Bergin, eds., *Handbook of Psychotherapy and Behavior Change* (2d ed.; New York: John Wiley & Sons, 1978); William J. Reid, "A Test of a Task-Centered Approach," *Social Work,* 20 (January 1975), pp. 3–9; Kazdin and Wilcoxon, op. cit.; and Reid and Patricia Hanrahan, "Recent Evaluations of Social Work: Grounds for Optimism," *Social Work,* 27 (July 1982), pp. 328–340.

23. Gurman and Razin, eds., op. cit.; Bergin and Lambert, op. cit.; and Strupp, op. cit.

24. Arnold P. Goldstein and Norman R. Simonson, "Social Psychological Approaches to Psychotherapy Research," in Allen E. Bergin and Sol L. Garfield, eds., *Handbook of Psychotherapy and Behavior Change* (1st ed.; New York: John Wiley & Sons, 1971), pp. 154–195.

25. Joel Fischer, *Effective Casework Practice: An Eclectic Approach* (New York: McGraw-Hill Book Co., 1977); and Fischer, "The Social Work Revolution," *Social Work,* 26 (May 1981), pp. 199–207.

26. William J. Reid and Ann Shyne, *Brief and Extended Casework* (New York: Columbia University Press, 1969); and Butcher and Koss, op. cit.

27. Isaac Marks, "Behavioral Psychotherapy of Adult Neurosis," in Sol L. Garfield and Alan E. Bergin, eds., *Handbook of Psychotherapy and Behavior Change* (2d ed.; New York: John Wiley & Sons, 1978), pp. 493–548; and Kazdin and Wilcoxon, op. cit.

28. Gurman, op. cit.; Mitchell, Bozarth, and Krauft, op. cit., and Parloff, Waskow, and Wolfe, op. cit.

29. Robert Dubin, *Theory Building* (New York: Free Press, 1969), pp. 5–25.

30. Ibid.

31. Carel B. Germain and Alex Gitterman, *The Life of Social Work Practice* (New York: Columbia University Press, 1980).

32. Urie Bronfenbrenner, *The Ecology of Human Development: Experiments by Nature and Design* (Cambridge, Mass.: Harvard University Press, 1979).

Organizational Learning and Problem Finding

Charles A. Rapp
John Poertner

For social services, the coming years promise to bring increased competition for smaller amounts of money, increased demands for accounting for these funds, and tighter controls on eligibility. Social work administrators will be pushed to devote a larger part of their jobs to these functions than to programmatic issues and quality of service. A result is likely to be a reduction in the performance and effectiveness of the services for which agencies are funded. In the long term, the neglect of programmatic issues may be more threatening to administrators' place in society than are the current exigencies.

The challenges for social work administrators and managers are to develop tools that enable the efficient monitoring of an agency's services and techniques for using these tools to improve the effectiveness of services. In general, social service program managers are adept at managing budgets, "getting out the checks," and marshaling information for funding requests. These "housekeeping" functions have been well served by management information systems and other business applications.[1] In contrast, ten years of talk about accountability, the evaluation of one's own social work practice, and computerized tracking systems have not produced managers who use the information to improve program performance.[2]

Even casual observation in most social service agencies shows that managers rarely use systematically collected performance information to direct their operations and inform their decision making. The research suggests that managers do not know what information they need or how to use information purposively.[3] Part of the problem is the lack of attention given to determining the information managers *need*, designing reports that inform without overloading managers with information, and educating managers in the design and use of reports. Consider these quotes:

> Any manager who wants can have a desk or a closet full of computer printouts. However, these printouts never seem to contain the information that managers need to make important day-to-day decisions.[4]

> Most [management information systems] have not matched expectations or have been outright failures.[5]

> Every month I receive three boxes of computer reports which I place unopened in the storeroom closet.[6]

> Most reports help obscure rather than illuminate.[7]

This article describes a typology of performance information by which the social service program manager can monitor an agency's operations and locate problem areas. The typology is presented within the context of developing "learning organizations" that make a continuous effort to improve the effectiveness of services, social service productivity, staff morale, and acquisition of resources. Methods for measuring each performance area will be proposed and the strengths and weaknesses of each method discussed.

The Learning Organization

In general, social programs confront complex problems with untested interventions and pursue ambitious goals with limited resources.[8] If the program is in a highly political environment, it seeks to satisfy the agendas of multiple constituencies.[9] In such a situation, a management stance that expects continuous improvement in the delivery of services is indicated. Ineffective interventions, procedures, and agency policies must be discarded and replaced by new and promising ones that are based on the best available knowledge.

If funds are the lifeblood of an organization, then information is its intelligence. A provocative yet little realized promise of computerized information systems is that they become a tool for the learning organization to improve its performance.[10] A learning organization is one that takes periodic readings on its performance and makes adjustments so that performance is improved. This, then, requires three elements: (1) the ability of multiple levels of personnel to collect, store, and retrieve performance information in an accurate and timely manner, (2) the ability of these personnel to gain access to information that would guide the selec-

tion of management action, and (3) the ability and motivation of the
personnel to change and alter behavior based on the information.

The first element can be termed "problem-finding information." Although the management literature and curricula are replete with content
on problem solving, relatively little attention has been devoted to problem finding. Yet a number of people have argued that problem-finding
skills are a more potent predictor of successful managers than are problem-solving skills.[11] Problem-finding information is necessary to prevent
organizational crises, to evaluate staff, and to "keep the program ship on
course."

The second element involves access to problem-solving information.
Problem-finding information tells the manager little about what to do.
Problem-solving information is that which is needed to decide on a course
of action or a solution. It could include, for example, information on
successful social service programs, effective management practices, staff
training packages, or administrative regulations. Sources of problem-solving information range from colleagues and subordinates to journal articles, government publications, and research reports. The information
explosion is largely restricted to problem-solving information and brings
its own dilemmas of difficult access, unsolicited mailings, and information
overload.

The third element focuses attention on the role of the manager. The
learning organization requires not only adequate information but also
managers who are skilled and willing to translate the information into
action. In many cases, it is not a matter of the information being there or
mechanically getting the information to the manager, but a matter of the
manager's ability to exploit it. A study of federal executives, for example,
found that 44 percent of the respondents purposely discarded information
relevant to their decision making.[12] Factors that could influence managers' use of information include workplace contingencies, cognitive and
management style, format and timeliness of the information, and skill and
knowledge of the manager.

This article will focus only on the first element needed to develop the
learning organization—problem-finding information. Problem finding in
the learning organization requires reliable and valid measures of workers'
performance. However, four characteristics of social services make it
difficult to monitor the performance of social service workers. First, decisions related to the provision of services have been viewed as idiosyncratic to each case. The services provided are highly individualized and
not precisely described, and intervention is less a social technology than
a collection of vague methods. Because the delivery of services is done in

the privacy of an office or home, rarely can a manager or supervisor monitor a worker's performance by watching. In public agencies with huge caseloads monitoring would not be feasible even if delivery of services were not done in private. This situation differs from that in other organizations such as those engaged in automobile manufacture in which the supervisor can personally view the performance of subordinates.

Second, defining performance measures is difficult because of the social service organization's multiple constituencies. Constituencies include legislators, citizens, clients, staff members, courts, boards, the media, other agencies, and other professionals. Each group has interests, agendas, and claims on the organization that are not only different but often incompatible.[13] For example, using the reduction in the number of older people entering nursing homes as a measure of performance would be resisted by the nursing home lobby and a portion of the medical community but would likely be supported by legislators, policymakers, and advocacy groups.

Third, performance measures are often derived from the goals of an organization. But the goals of social service organizations are often vague or overly ambitious. The prevention of delinquency and the prevention of child abuse are examples of such goals. Social service agencies, including large public bureaucracies, have neither the resources nor the technologies to accomplish these goals. They can increase the number of employed teenagers and can protect children under their care from harm, but they cannot prevent delinquency or child abuse in an entire state or community. The height of this folly occurred in the early 1960s when social workers argued that casework services could eliminate poverty and thus were a force behind the social security amendments of 1962.

Fourth, measuring performance in a state agency is difficult because of the complexity of the delivery system. Purchase of services from private or community agencies is now the dominant mode of public social service delivery nationally.[14] Other agencies are often used that do not have formal agreements with the public agency. The service system itself is less a system than an amalgam of loosely knit agencies in which performance is partly determined by others not under the direct control of the managers in public agencies.

Although the four characteristics of social service agencies discussed in this section make it difficult to monitor the performance of workers, they do not *prevent* the development and use of performance measurement. The next section describes a typology of information by which an agency's manager can efficiently monitor the agency's programs and locate problem areas.

Typology of Performance Information

In social services, performance can mean different things. To some, performance relates to the number of clients served. Others would point to the satisfaction of clients. Still others would argue that a change in the client's condition is the only suitable indicator. Performance can also mean adherence to agency policies, time spent with clients, or the number of clients contacted or interviewed. Managers are often evaluated based on the amount of funds acquired, the amount of influence held in the community, or the job satisfaction of subordinates. Although several performance measures may be used, each reflects something different about the program and performance. Similarly, each has particular strengths and weaknesses; no single measure can capture all critical dimensions. Therefore, managers are forced to select which ones to use.

Managers cannot develop performance measures for every behavior or function in an organization. What is needed is a model that abstracts components of the organization and categorizes them so that they are measurable, subject to managerial intervention, and relevant to the learning organization. The categories must be critical to both the survival of the organization and its mission in relationship to the social services. The authors pose the following performance areas: (1) productivity, (2) effectiveness, (3) staff morale, and (4) acquisition of resources. For the learning organization, efficient problem finding means that the program's personnel must be able to take periodic readings on these performance areas and compare them to the agency's standards. The following sections will provide definitions of terms and describe alternative methods of measuring each performance area.

Productivity

Productivity is based on the amount of service provided and is measured through units of service.[15] Units of service reflect "program effort" (that is, all the activities performed by workers to meet their objectives) but imply nothing about the quality of service. There are four methods for measuring social service productivity. First, productivity can be measured by counting the number of people who are participating in a program. *Client count* is the most prevalent measure of productivity because it is easily understood and conveys something of meaning to laymen, workers, administrators, and funders. It can be used as an indication of the coverage of the target population and as a means of assigning caseloads. But client count is rarely sufficient as a measure of productivity. It assumes that all clients are receiving the same amount of service, that they are homogeneous, and that their problems are of equal intensity or severity. Client counts can also be inflated by program repeaters. For example, in manpower programs, the same client may receive placement services two, three, or four times.

Second, productivity can be measured by counting *service episodes*. A service episode reflects a complete period of service provision. One service episode could include recognition of the problem by the client, an effort to find help, a period of working with one or more professional helpers, and termination. A service episode encompasses more than one particular service. This method avoids the problem of repeaters included in client counts because each separate placement, as in the foregoing example, would be a service episode. The method of measuring productivity is particularly well suited for short-term or emergency services such as crisis hot lines or emergency room service. These services are quick and uniform, and the possibility of contact with clients more than once is high. The chief disadvantage of the measurement is that service episodes are not applicable to services that are long term or can vary considerably from client to client.

Third, productivity can be measured by counting *service events*. An event is a specific action on the part of the worker, client, or both. It is defined by discrete elements of the client-worker interactive process. It could be an interview, a telephone call, a case conference, a group counseling session, a home-delivered hot meal, a class session, a physical examination, a pregnancy test, or a child's placement in foster care. Ideally, one or only a few carefully chosen events are used to reflect the service activity that generates the program's service benefit. The primary strength of this unit of measurement is its validity. If carefully selected, it can be highly representative of the client-worker interactive process. In a program whose aim is to find alternative community living arrangements for elderly people in danger of being institutionalized, the number of interviews held with a client; the number of contacts made with key actors, for example, family members and potential landlords; and the number of visits made with the client to apartments or other facilities in which the client might reside may accurately reflect the major service activity of the program.

There is a major disadvantage with using events as the unit of measurement to report on program activities. Intuitively, it is probably obvious that normally some events in the interactive process between the client and worker are more crucial to the successful progression of that process than are other events. Moreover, these critical events usually require more effort or active involvement on the part of the participants. It follows then that a measure that counts all these events equally is not reliably measuring what occurs within the events themselves and is misleading. In this case, the weighting of events should be considered.

Fourth, productivity can be measured by counting *elapsed time*. Elapsed time might be oriented to the client, that is, a day of nursing home care received by the client or an hour spent by the client at a group therapy meeting. Elapsed time might also be oriented to the worker, for example, the number of hours he or she spent completing a foster home placement or the number of hours the worker spent in home services for the elderly.

The great advantage of elapsed time as a measure is its precision with respect to the use of resources. It is possible to show the hours of a worker's time and therefore resources allocated to different types of cases and to one particular client or to the caseload as a whole. The measure also is especially useful when making budget presentations because there is a direct correspondence between elapsed time of worker and cost factors in the program.

The great disadvantage of elapsed time is that it focuses on the expenditure of time by the worker without giving any attention to the number of clients served, their characteristics, the amount of help received, or even the service activity performed in the program. However, if any of the agency's constituencies has a primary interest in the use of resources and if the activity of the worker over time is in some sense constant, then this unit might be useful.

Effectiveness

Measures of effectiveness are outcome oriented, that is, they are based on changes in the client's condition. They reflect the quality of services. Productivity captures program activities, and effectiveness informs on the results of that effort.

Measures of effectiveness can be of three forms. First, effectiveness can be based on *behavioral change in clients*. For example, a couple engages a mental health center to help them reduce the number of verbal brawls they have. They report that arguments occur daily, and with the social worker's assistance, they set a goal of arguing a maximum of once a week. Performance could be measured by comparing the frequency of arguments before and after intervention or could be based on the degree of goal attainment.

Second, effectiveness can be based on *clients' satisfaction*. In the preceding example, the couple could be asked to complete a short questionnaire about their opinions of the service provided. If rating scales were used, the scores could be added and a cumulative satisfaction score compiled. The satisfaction of clients, as a measure of effectiveness, could increase responsiveness to clients and would be particularly valuable when clients are voluntary and pay for the services rendered. With these clients, the most critical dimension may be whether they thought favorably of the service rather than whether any change in their situation actually occurred. The weaknesses of the measure include biased responses owing to social desirability and its disregard for any substantial changes in clients. Publicly supported, social-control services such as protective services and programs for chronic mental patients demand more stringent measures of effectiveness than those that determine whether the client found a service helpful or enjoyable. These types of services do not attenuate the desirability or need for responsiveness to clients but call for other measures that are also needed. Unless an interview method is used, measures of clients' satisfaction cannot be used with illiterate clients. However, an interview method increases the likelihood of responses related to social desirability and increases personnel costs.

Third, effectiveness can be based on the *status changes* of clients. When this measure is used, delivery systems are viewed as a set of statuses through which clients move.[16] For example, manpower programs include such statuses as evaluation and testing, classroom training, on-the-job training, and both subsidized and unsubsidized employment. Mental health services for chronic clients include statuses such as institutional care, a halfway house, and independent living. These examples highlight an important feature of status changes: The statuses vary as to their "desirability" for clients and compose a hierarchy. For instance, unsubsidized employment for the mentally retarded is viewed as the most desirable status by professional, legislative, and public standards. Similarly, independent living for chronic mental patients is seen as the optimum status.

The use of status change as a measure of effectiveness has a number of appealing qualities. First, it has the ability to unify the agendas and performance expectations of the agency's multiple constituencies. For example, professionals (such as, social workers, psychologists, teachers, and doctors), law enforcement personnel, legislators, and the general citizenry see maintaining a child with the natural family as preferable to placement in foster care or institutional care. Public support is more likely to occur for programs designed to influence such statuses than for programs that focus on the satisfaction of clients as an outcome measure.

Second, status changes in any social service program are finite. In contrast, models of behavioral change and goal attainment are formulated through the interaction between the client and the worker and can be highly idiosyncratic. The finite property of status change can enhance organizational control and the process of supervision and allow for an increased focus by multiple organizational levels.

The one major drawback of status changes is that they are subject to administrative manipulation rather than based on the client's progress or needs. Deinstitutionalization of mental health services has been criticized for not leading to better care for clients, and in many cases it has led to worse care because discharges were often based on administrative criteria (for example, the budget and the need to attain yearly goals) rather than on the needs of clients.[17] There is another side to this weakness, however. Because status change seems amenable to administrative initiatives, such change can be perceived as a more reasonable basis for evaluating social service programs. If administrative actions do not contribute to outcomes of behavioral change, then such measures are not realistic. Measures chosen must be able to capture change based on organizational and programmatic effort.

Staff Morale

This performance area captures the job satisfaction of employees. The rationale for including this as a separate dimension is that work is an important life domain for most adults in America. In its attempts to help clients, the social service organization should concurrently contribute to the personal satisfaction and fulfillment of its employees. The recent attention to burnout among human service personnel testifies to the concern in this area. There is also some evidence, although somewhat equivocal, that links job satisfaction to levels of productivity.[18] However, the position here is that even if there is no link between these, staff morale is deserving of managerial attention on its own merits.

The measurement of staff morale in social service organizations is not as clear as that of productivity and effectiveness. However, several approaches can be identified. The most common approach involves the "informal sensing" of a morale problem by managers. This method probably does the job adequately with a relatively small program operation. If the operation is large, however, top-level managers tend to have less contact with each staff member, subordinate managers avoid passing on "bad news" to their superiors, and levels of morale vary considerably between units and people.[19] It is more difficult to know at any point in time the degree of satisfaction being experienced by organizational personnel except in the most general sense.

The limits on the informal sensing of staff morale have made it necessary to develop other approaches. One approach involves the systematic use of questionnaires. Questionnaires could be designed to measure level of dissatisfaction, as are many of the recent burnout instruments, or to measure level of satisfaction. In either case, the instrument would need to pass standard tests of reliability and validity, and the individual items must have the ability to be summarized into a single measure because a busy manager does not have the time to review extensive lists of items from a multitude of employees. In addition, an anonymous questionnaire should be used because it would increase the likelihood of accurate responses. Such instruments could be administered annually or semiannually. The strength of the questionnaire approach is its directness and its ability to take readings across the entire organization. Its major weakness involves the difficulty in developing an instrument that is reliable and valid.

Another approach to assessing morale uses unobtrusive, approximate measures such as absenteeism, turnover rate, or number of grievances filed. The principle strengths of this approach involve the ease of data collection and the direct link to agency performance in the case of absenteeism and turnover. Its major weakness concerns the accuracy with which these measures capture staff morale. Absenteeism and turnover rates are a function of many variables, morale being only one. The manager would have to devote time to interpreting these figures and inferring the degree to which staff morale was a causative agent.

Acquisition of Resources

Every social program needs to acquire resources from its environment to operate. Minimally, it needs to acquire funds, personnel, clients, and goodwill. Top-level managers devote the vast majority of their time to activities focused on acquiring these resources. In the current political climate, these activities assume increasing importance. Most organizations use well-developed accounting principles that provide a continuous measure of where dollars come from and how they are spent. Therefore, this area needs no discussion here.

Measuring the acquisition of personnel involves both the number of individuals and their qualifications. For example, an organization may want to increase the number of master's-level social workers in front-line positions or increase the amount of experience that new employees bring to the organization. The prospects of fewer jobs in the coming years could make these realistic goals. Personnel would also include the use of volunteers. Measures could include the number of volunteers, the number of hours of volunteer service, or the average number of volunteer service hours per volunteer.

Clients, as a resource to be acquired, assume a slightly different perspective than that discussed in the productivity section. For productivity, the concern is with individuals who have already achieved client status and as such are receiving services. In this section, the concern is with individuals before they attain such status. In other words, the section focuses on how many people apply or are referred for service. The social program needs a continuous flow of potential clients coming to the intake gates. Depending on the agency, measuring the acquisition of clients could be accomplished by counting the number of applicants or referrals received. For many programs, diversified sources of referrals can help promote stable operations. The manager may want to monitor the number of referrals from each source. This could include other agencies, former clients, and self-referrals. Perhaps all that is needed is an unduplicated count of any source making a referral during a given period.

Most social programs need a degree of public support or goodwill to survive. It is this public support that often translates into influence with which the program can alter its environment. Most managers seem only concerned with this critical resource during times when the program is being attacked or criticized. Measuring an amorphous area such as goodwill is difficult at best, with few well-tested methods. Telephone polls of the general population in an agency's catchment area could be used. This method, a major undertaking from design through analysis, would find that many, if not most people, never heard of the agency. Purposive sampling techniques may reduce the cost and enhance the relevance of the findings. Using this method, the agency decides the groups of individuals whose opinions it desires. For example, a youth diversion program would want to query juvenile judges, police officers, school administrators, teachers, and funders. Another method would be maintaining a scrapbook of newspaper articles that pertain to the agency. The number of positive and negative articles can be periodically tallied. Newspaper articles can also be used to help gauge the degree to which the public supports the underlying theory or ideology of the program. In the youth diversion program, the agency would want to monitor the frequency of proposals or pronouncements that call for such actions as "get tough on juveniles." This monitoring may indicate areas in which public education efforts need to be devoted.

Other Considerations

This article has proposed a typology of performance information and alternative methods of measurement. The careful selection of performance measures is a prerequisite for developing a learning organization. Several other components are needed to make such measures useful to social service managers.

First, the measures need to be organized into easy-to-read reports to facilitate use by busy managers. Managers should not have to sort through a stack of computer reports to find the few pieces of performance information they need. A key performance indicator system would be one solution.[20] The performance measures would be reduced to a two- or three-page report that provides an overall picture of agency operations.

Second, graphs portraying measured performance are often easier to read than data presented in tabular form. In addition, because graphic displays are more visual than data in tabular form, conclusions are more likely to "leap off the page." Moreover, graphs can easily capture trends in performance that are often useful to managers.

Third, each performance report should include both the current performance level and a standard by which to compare current achievement. A manager should not have to rifle through desk drawers and files to find the expected level of performance. For example, if adequate productivity performance has been set at forty clients a month, then this figure should be reported next to the number of clients actually served.

The learning organization, as a normative model of social service program management, may be useful in sustaining social service programs through these turbulent times. Although the demands on social service administrators in competing for funds will be greater than before, administrators should still devote a large part of their time to internal program performance. The typology of performance measures and guidelines for efficient performance reporting are a beginning attempt to specify the requisite tools for developing learning organizations.

Notes and References

1. Merlin Taber, "Information Systems for State Child Welfare Agencies: Their Promise and Their Problems," in Taber, Steven Anderson, and Charles A. Rapp, eds., *Child Welfare Information System* (Urbana: University of Illinois, 1975), pp. 1–12.

2. John Poertner and Charles A. Rapp, "Information System Design in Foster Care," *Social Work*, 25 (March 1980), pp. 114–119; and Taber, Anderson, and Rapp, eds.,*Child Welfare Information System* .

3. Russell Ackoff, "Management Misinformation Systems," *Management Science*, 14 (December 1967), pp. 147–156.

4. Poertner and Rapp, op. cit., p. 114.

5. Ackoff, op. cit., p. 147.

6. Conversation with Barbara Ryan, Regional Director, Illinois Department of Children and Family Services, Springfield, Illinois, 1977.

7. Robert L. Janson, "Graphic Indicators of Operations," *Harvard Business Review*, 58 (November–December 1980), pp. 164–170.

8. Merlin Taber and Daniel Finnegan, "Realistic Program Goals and Objectives: Outcome of an Analytic Process" (Urbana: University of Illinois, 1979), pp. 1–29. (Mimeographed.)

9. Patricia Yancey Martin, "Multiple Constituencies, Dominant Societal Values, and the Human Service Administration," *Administration in Social Work*, 4 (Summer 1980), pp. 15–27.

10. Taber, Anderson, and Rapp, *Child Welfare Information System*

11. Norman H. Mackworth, "Originality," in Dael Wolfle, ed., *The Discovery of Talent* (Cambridge, Mass.: Harvard University Press, 1969); and J. Sterling

Livingston, "Myth of the Well-Educated Manager," *Harvard Business Review*, 49 (January–February 1971), pp. 96–108.

12. Nathan Caplan, "The Use of Social Science Information by Federal Executives," in Gene M. Lyons, ed., *Social Research and Public Policies* (Hanover, N.H.: The Dartmouth/OECD Conference, 1975), pp. 43–59.

13. Martin, op. cit., pp. 15–27.

14. Bill Benton, Tracey Feild, and Rhona Millar, *Social Services: Federal Legislation Vs. State Implementation* (Washington, D.C.: Urban Institute, 1978).

15. Merlin Taber and Daniel Finnegan, "Social Service Productivity" (Urbana: University of Illinois School of Social Work, 1979). (Mimeographed.) The authors wish to thank Taber and Finnegan for the use of the material in this section.

16. Merlin Taber and John Poertner, "Modeling Service Delivery as a System of Transition: The Case of Foster Care," *Evaluation Review*, 5 (August 1981), pp. 549–566.

17. Ellen L. Bassuk and Samuel Gerson, "Deinstitutionalization and Mental Health Services," *Scientific American*, 238 (February 1978), pp. 46–53.

18. E. A. Locke, "Nature and Causes of Job Satisfaction," in M.D. Dunnette, ed., *Handbook of Industrial and Organizational Psychology* (Chicago: Rand McNally & Co., 1975).

19. Herbert Kaufman, *Administrative Feedback* (Washington, D.C.: Brookings Institution, 1973).

20. Janson, op. cit.

Information System Development for Cost-Effectiveness Analysis

Sheldon L. Rahn

Like the weather, cost-effectiveness analysis is something a lot of people talk about but not so many do anything about. The Critical Components Index presented in this article was developed to provide an operational tool for managers of human service organizations to use in developing an internal management information system that permits cost-effectiveness work to be done with discrete programs, either singly or on a comparative basis and with either randomized or matched client groups.[1]

The index was developed after examining currently operational agency information systems in four relatively large social and health service organizations in the province of Ontario, Canada. These four field studies were used to describe and classify the information categories currently in use and then to address the question of what additional information would be needed to undertake cost-effectiveness analysis in these four settings. The Critical Components Index, then, is the product of an interaction between field observation of a descriptive nature and the exercise of theoretical and conceptual considerations as to the kinds of data that are required for the analysis of cost outcome and cost-effectiveness.

A prototype format for cost-effectiveness analysis was prepared as a working tool reflecting the present state of the art at an operational level. (See Table 1.) This format has additional utility in demonstrating the dynamic characteristics among the variables employed. Program 3 is the "cheapest" on a simple unit cost basis (Column 1). But Program 3 turns out to be the most expensive with respect to average cost per closed case (Column 3), whereas Program 1, which seems the most expensive when

Table 1. Cost-Effectiveness Analysis Format for Selected During-Treatment Time Episodes or for Closed Cases[a]

	(1)	(2)	(3)	(4)	(5)	(6)		(7)		(8)
						Effectively Spent		Wasted		
Programs	Unit Cost per Interview Hour[b]	Average No. of Interview Hours per Episode or Closed Case	Average Direct Cost per Episode or Closed Case	Success Rate on Outcome Effectiveness (%)	Total Case-Related Expenditures	Amount	%	Amount	%	Average Cost per Successful Episode or Closed Case
Program 1 (present program)	$40	5	$200	30	$20,000	$6,000	30	$14,000	70	$666.67
Program 2 (planned alternative)	30	10	300	80	30,000	24,000	80	6,000	20	375.00
Program 3 (planned alternative)	20	20	400	60	40,000	24,000	60	16,000	40	666.67

[a]Each program consists of one hundred fabricated cases.

[b]The manual *Functional Budgeting for Canadian Voluntary Organizations* (Ottawa, Ont., Canada: United Way of Canada, 1972, p. 5) provides a format and procedures for deriving an average service unit cost. However, the United Way monthly time sheet captures worker time and salary cost only on a global "service," or "program" basis. For cost-effectiveness work, one needs worker time by program and case number for each client or client group to examine cost and outcome for selected cases for a certain time period or as closed cases. It is also important to be able to distinguish between case-related time, non-case-related agency activity, and community involvement time. For cost-effectiveness work, case-related worker time is primary. In United Way formats this is sometimes referred to as direct cost per unit. When non-case-related worker time and a program's fair share of overall administrative costs are added, a total cost per unit can be derived.

judged in terms of unit cost, is the cheapest on the basis of average cost per closed case. However, when a success rate is added, Program 2 turns out to be the winner, with the highest percentage of effectively spent money (Column 6) and the lowest average cost per *successful* closed case (Column 8).

Sorenson and Grove have articulated an important possible refinement under which cost per successful closed case can be supplemented by a matrix analysis of average cost per case for several levels of outcome ranging from no success to high success—and not just for closed cases but for cases at one or more points during treatment.[2] The average cost per successful closed case is derived by dividing the number of successful closed cases into total expenditures for both the successful and unsuccessful cases. Unfortunately, this single value *cannot* be used to decide which of two or three programs is really the most cost-effective. The reason is that a low success rate coupled with low total expenditures can make Program 1, for example, look just as cost-effective as Program 3 (Column 8).

What is missing in Column 8 is a dynamic tie-in to the further variable of problem reduction. Program 1 may have the same average cost per successful closed case as Program 3 ($666.67), but Program 1, with a 30 percent success rate, still has seventy unhelped cases (out of one hundred), whereas Program 3, with a 60 percent success rate, has only forty unhelped cases remaining.

Even though a 100 percent success rate is not really to be expected, from a societal and problem-reduction point of view, Program 1 (at a 30 percent success rate) would take twice as long as Program 3 (at a 60 percent success rate) to help 60 percent of the one hundred cases. Program 1 from this perspective would waste $28,000—as compared to $16,000 wasted in Program 3—to achieve a 60 percent reduction of problems. Viewed as a static model (as in Column 7), Program 1 wasted only $14,000 as compared to $16,000 wasted by Program 3. But as a dynamic model, the true superiority of Program 3 over Program 1 is revealed, even though Program 2 is the clear winner with the highest success rate and the lowest loss in wasted expenditures.

Needed Element

What is still needed is a final cost-effectiveness score that reflects, in a single value, the dynamic nature of these variables in their interrelationship. Pending such a development, the decision as to which of two programs is the most cost-effective can be made by examining for the highest success rate *and* the lowest percentage of wasted expenditures.

For the prototype format described here, unit cost could be derived by reference to the United Way manuals in use for some years now in the United States and Canada.[3] The United Way organizations have pioneered the technology for deriving service unit cost in social services, and their growing experience in the selection and use of a standardized set of service unit categories by agencies providing similar services to similar clienteles is making an important contribution to the program evaluation capacity of operating agencies. The chief limitation of the United Way technology to date is that the suggested form for compiling the time utilization of workers captures time data (and hence salary cost) by program only instead of by program *and* case number for each client or group of clients.[4] Information on both is necessary for cost-outcome or cost-effectiveness analysis in which unit cost data for cases active for a particular period of time or for closed cases only are required.

The peril of stopping with unit cost is illustrated in Table 1. If funding bodies were to make the mistake of basing allocation decisions on unit cost data alone, the impact upon the human service delivery system would be devastating. This is because it is so easy to reduce unit cost simply by disregarding standards and allowing the service to deteriorate. It is this reality that lends urgency to developing a full capacity for cost-effectiveness analysis in operating agencies.

Cost-effectiveness analysis is a summative research product. It is crucial to program evaluation but must be complemented by formative research work around the structural and process variables that may explain why a program is yielding a particular cost-effectiveness result.[5] The nature and severity of the problems addressed are, of course, just as relevant as an accurate definition and standardization of the specific intervention used.

The utility of cost-effectiveness data, when linked conceptually and operationally to the initial characteristics of clients and to the treatment activity, is in avoiding the unit cost pitfall and in facilitating a deliberate redesign and testing of programs to achieve greater cost-effectiveness. The degree of cost-effectiveness achieved depends, of course, on the state of knowledge about the human problems addressed as well as on the technology available for the application of that knowledge.

The information requirements for exercising the cost-effectiveness analysis format shown in Table 1 provided the conceptual framework for evaluating the adequacies and inadequacies of the four information systems examined in Ontario for this study. Nine critical information components were identified: client characteristics, case identification, worker identification, case data assembly, worker time utilization, intervention, quality assurance, unit cost, and outcome measurement. For each of the nine critical information areas a scale was developed designating nominal and operational categories in a continuum from least to most adequate. A numerical scaling procedure was used to attach numerical values to each option as separate points on an implicit ordinal scale. (Table 2, pp. 94–95.)

Because the unit of analysis in this system is the organization (and not an individual client, family, or worker), organizational documents are the source of the data—a class of information for which face validity can often be claimed or checked with relative ease.[7] Among the nine information components, outcome measurement in particular would need to have the validity of its criteria examined periodically by employing one or more separate measures of client functioning. Also involved in validity is the question of whether or not organizational procedures are in fact carried out in line with what is prescribed in organizational forms and documents. However, with the emergence of peer review audits on recording accuracy and performance quality, this is less of an issue than in earlier years.

The Critical Components Index, then, offers a cost-effectiveness capacity score ranging from 0 to 25. It can be used as a self-study instrument by management or as a tool in external consultation. When applied to the four Ontario service organizations, the scores were as shown in Table 3 (p. 96). It may be of interest to put these critical component scores in the context of organizational size, as in Table 4 (p. 98).

Systems Literature

Weiss was among the first to sketch the possibilities for gathering data continuously under an adequate internal information system for operating social and health service corporations. She stated: "Because the information is regularly and systematically collected on a longitudinal basis, it is possible to see the effects of program variations—both concurrent variations and variations over time."[8]

Rutman has given particular attention to the role of special evaluative research designs that may have to go beyond the established information system data base to examine the "linking rationale" between the human problem addressed, the program, and measured outcomes.[9] This is an important consideration because cost-effectiveness data alone do not reveal anything about the problem addressed, and with respect to program (intervention), they deal only with the dollar cost of the staff time and resources expended. However, average cost per successful closed case does provide an essential datum for inclusion in a full evaluative research design; cost-effectiveness data provide the crucial feedback that can motivate program evaluation work and planned innovation.

In recent years, a perceptive discussion of evaluative research problems and possibilities has been put forward in the literature.[10] What was

Table 2. Index of Nine Critical Components for Information System Development (Critical Components Index)[a]

Case Management (Range: 0–9)	Worker Activity (Range: 0–6)	Unit Cost (Range: 0–3)	Outcome Effectiveness (Range: 0–7)
<u>Client characteristics (history)</u>	<u>Worker time utilization</u>	<u>Unit cost</u>	<u>Outcome measurement</u>
No data 0	No data 0	No data 0	None 0
Unstructured 1	Treatment only 1	Per diem 1	Narrative recording 1
Structured 2	All time 2	Per hour 2	Global assessment scale 2
		Per closed case 3	Problem-oriented scale 3
			Subjective Goal Attainment Scaling 4
			Developmental inventory 5
			Objective Goal Attainment Scaling 6
			Single-subject design charting 7

<u>Case identification</u>	<u>Intervention</u>
None 0	No data 0
Alphabetical 1	Type only 1
Numbered 2	Type and modality 2

Table 2 (Continued)

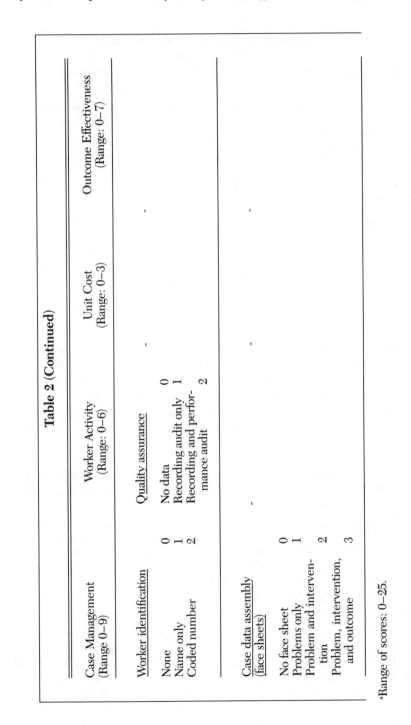

Case Management (Range 0–9)	Worker Activity (Range: 0–6)	Unit Cost (Range: 0–3)	Outcome Effectiveness (Range: 0–7)
	Quality assurance		
Worker identification	No data 0		
None 0	Recording audit only 1		
Name only 1	Recording and perfor- 2		
Coded number 2	mance audit		
Case data assembly (face sheets)			
No face sheet 0			
Problems only 1			
Problem and interven- 2			
tion			
Problem, intervention, 3			
and outcome			

aRange of scores: 0–25.

Table 3. Ratings on Nine Critical Components for
Four Service Corporations[a]

Component	Service Corporation			
	A	B	C	D
Client characteristics	1	1	1	2
Case identification	2	2	2	2
Worker identification	1	1	2	1
Case data assembly	1	1	1	1
Worker time utilization	0	2	0	0
Intervention	1	1	1	1
Quality assurance	1	0	2	1
Unit cost	1	0	0	0
Outcome measurement	5	4	1	1
Numerical score	13	12	10	9
Ideal capacity percentage	52	48	40	36

[a]Range of scores: 0–25.

not earlier so fully anticipated by clinicians or managers is the primacy of the clinician (or other front-line worker) both as data gatherer and a user. Earlier nomenclature seeking to distinguish the clinical information system from the management information system may now give way to a recognition that the major components do not split that way and that the information system is a unity that can serve several purposes or publics including clinician, management, policy board, funding body, and researcher.

In defining the term "accountability system" as an evaluation-oriented information system that includes data on outcomes, Weiss has further observed as follows:

> What makes it an accountability system? . . . one meaning is a system in which data are so special that individual staff members or staff units can be held accountable for their performance. Data are gathered that show the success record of individuals or units, the amount of work they did per success, their cost per success, and so on.[11]

Since 1974, accountability has been confirmed to be a shared responsibility. The focus for clinicians, supervisors, and managers is now on a collaborative approach to the design, development, and testing of alternative programs for any program that shows what appears to be a low cost-effectiveness result. It should also be noted that neither benefit-cost analysis nor output-value analysis is possible until cost-effectiveness data are at hand. In benefit-cost analysis, a ratio is struck between the cost of

successful treatment and the estimated dollar value of the lifetime benefits to society in terms of the future treatment costs avoided and the
future value of taxes paid by the person who has been helped. The cost
side of that ratio requires cost-outcome or cost-effectiveness data. Cost-
effectiveness analysis, on the other hand, looks at cost only in relation to
changes in client functioning (treatment outcome) while the client is in
treatment and perhaps in relation to functioning six months or a year after
treatment as well. As Sorenson and Grove have stated:

> Cost-effectiveness should be viewed as a subset of cost-benefit analysis.
> If the measured effects required for cost-effectiveness can be translated
> into monetary values, a cost-benefit analysis can be developed.[12]

In the decades ahead, funding decisions will be increasingly influenced by benefit-cost data. Both cost-effectiveness analysis and benefit-
cost analysis encourage a shift in communitywide planning and funding
procedures from a preoccupation with service programs to a focus on
identifying and reducing problems for the general population. Planning
and allocating bodies are rapidly modifying their program and budget
review work to require a focus on the problems of families and children
in the community, the nature and extent of those problems, and some
evidence of how much success and at what cost the operating agency can
be expected to perform in the new program and budget year.

Benefit-cost data will, of course, permit policymakers and funding
bodies to set priorities and make decisions on the basis of how much a
dollar spent now will save in comparison to the long-term costs to society
if nothing effective is done now. This kind of information can be expected
to accelerate spending for secondary prevention programs in which universal screening services—particularly for mothers, newborns, and preschool children—are tied to effective early intervention services and to
adequate income security programs and health care insurance.

However, the cost side of the benefit-cost ratio must reflect the current cost of successful intervention. Only cost-effectiveness analysis,
bridging from simple unit cost to benefit-cost technology, can provide an
average cost per successful closed case coupled with a unitary cost-effectiveness score.

Definition of Success

The definition of outcome success is, of course, a sensitive and central
issue. Although the definition could be based on social indicator data
(such as the population rate for developmentally delayed preschool children in a given municipal area), the validity for such data is very low;
more likely, the definition will be based on a point in the outcome measurement scale selected. Seven scaling options are identified in the index

Table 4. Critical Components Scores and Other Selected Variables for Four Service Corporations

Service Corporation	1978–79 Expenditures Budget	Percentage of Budget Spent on Information System Positions	Outcome Measure—(Level of Precision)	Critical Components Score	Percentage of Ideal Capacity Achieved
A	$ 4,834,000	2.3	5 (Developmental inventory)	13	52
B	2,510,915	2.3	4 (Subjective GAS)	12	48
C	29,630,169	1.6	1 (Narrative recording)	10	40
D	1,509,800	2.5	1 (Narrative recording)	9	36

of critical components shown in Table 2. The development of a definition of success is essentially a policy issue for service corporation boards and elected officials when public funds are involved. The options regarding the definition of success, or levels of success, will be conceptualized and articulated by clinicians, supervisors, researchers, and managers. The options will vary among programs addressing different human problems. The choice of options should be the responsibility of the policy board in consultation with the appropriate planning and allocating body.

Ultimately, the definition that is chosen will be reported and explained as part of the documentation prepared by each operating agency or governmentally administered service for discussion with a program and budget review panel each year—whether of a United Way or a governmental planning and allocating authority.

Conclusion

The terms "cost-outcome" and "cost-effectiveness" tend to be used interchangeably. For greater precision, cost-outcome analysis can refer to analysis of a single program and cost-effectiveness analysis to an examination of two programs on a comparative basis.

The author has noted the peril of relying on unit cost data alone and has provided an index of critical components for information system development. The index identifies certain information categories essential to cost-effectiveness analysis, and the rating scale provided can facilitate agency self-study in this regard.

Notes and References

1. This researcher is indebted to Robert C. Shaw, Executive Director; Mary M. Chase, Director of Research; and Mark Frankel, Coordinator of Clinical Services, at the Dellcrest Children's Centre in Downsview, Ontario, for initially stimulating him to conceptualize further around the possible utility of a classification tool. The Dellcrest group in early 1979 prepared a teaching and consultation document, which includes a provocative Data Capacity Matrix. The Dellcrest matrix incorporates thirty information system components and goes beyond cost-effectiveness analysis capacity to include cost-benefit analysis capacity as well. However, no rating scale is established.

2. James E. Sorensen and Hugh D. Grove, "Using Cost-Outcome and Cost-Effectiveness Analyses for Improved Program Management and Accountability," in Clifford C. Attkisson, William Hargreaves, and Mardi J. Horowitz, eds., *Evaluation of Human Service Programs* (New York: Academic Press, 1978), pp. 371–410.

3. See, for example, *Functional Budgeting for Canadian Voluntary Organizations* (Ottawa, Ont., Canada: United Way of Canada, 1978).

4. Ibid.

5. See Gary H. Miller and Barry Willer, *Information Systems for Evaluation and Feedback in Mental Health Organizations* (Ottawa, Ont., Canada: Evaluation

Research Training Institute, Centre for Social Welfare Studies, School of Social Work, Carleton University, 1975).

6. For a discussion of the use of a numerical scale in index construction, see Delbert C. Miller, *Handbook of Research Design* (New York: David McKay Co., 1970), pp. 89–90.

7. See Kenneth D. Bailey, *Methods of Social Research* (New York: Free Press, 1978). With respect to validity and reliability, Bailey notes (p. 288) that "Documents lend themselves to more rigorous checks on face validity than do other data gathering methods in social research."

8. Carol H. Weiss, "Alternative Models of Program Evaluation," *Social Work*, 19 (November 1974), p. 680.

9. Leonard Rutman, *Planning an Evaluation Study* (Ottawa, Ont., Canada: Evaluation Research Training Institute, Centre for Social Welfare Studies, School of Social Work, Carleton University, 1976), pp. 9–10.

10. See, for example, Peter W. Chommie and Joe Hudson, "Evaluation of Outcome and Process," *Social Work*, 19 (November 1974), pp. 682–687; Gary Miller and Barry Willer, "On the Validity of Goal Attainment Scaling as an Outcome Measurement in Mental Health," *American Journal of Public Health*, 66 (December 1976), pp. 1197–1198; Claudia J. Coulton and Phyliss L. Solomon, "Measuring Outcomes of Intervention," *Social Work Research and Abstracts*, 13 (Winter 1977), pp. 3–9; John Nackel, J. Goldman, and W.L. Fairman, "A Group Decision Process for Resource Allocation in the Health Setting," *Management Science*, 24 (August 1978), pp. 1259–1267; Scott Cummings and Mark S. Rosentraub, "Evaluation Research: How to Negotiate Scientific Rigor," *Social Work Research and Abstracts*, 14 (Fall 1978), pp. 16–24; Charles Cowger, "Organizational Considerations in the Application of Budgeting and Cost-Effectiveness Systems to Social Welfare Organizations," *Journal of Sociology and Social Welfare*, 6 (March 1979), pp. 211–220; John F. Rockart, "Chief Executives Define Their Own Data Needs," *Harvard Business Review*, 57 (March-April 1979), pp. 81–92; and Martin G. Kushler and William S. Davidson II, "Using Experimental Designs to Evaluate Social Programs," *Social Work Research and Abstracts*, 15 (Spring 1979), pp. 27–32.

11. Weiss, op. cit., p. 679.

12. Sorensen and Grove, op. cit. The authors discuss the difficulties to be encountered in long-term cost-benefit analysis work and review a short-term approach termed "output value analysis." They note that the original concept is set forth by J. Halpern and P.R. Binner in an article entitled "A Model for an Output Value Analysis of Mental Health Programs," *Administration in Mental Health*, 1 (1972), pp. 40–51.

Using Public Funds to Buy Private Services

Margaret Gibelman

A new era for the private social welfare system has begun. The Reagan Administration and Congress have, with considerable public support, initiated sweeping changes in the financing and methods of delivering social services. The attack on the capabilities of the public system to deliver services has intensified based on the assumption that government is the root cause of social and economic problems rather than the cure for them.[1] Accordingly, expanding the role of the private sector is seen as an appropriate strategy to circumvent the deficiencies of government as a provider of services. The devolution of government's role in the provision of services, however, raises serious questions about the capacity of private agencies to meet their increased responsibilities.

This article addresses emerging issues about the services clients receive when public responsibility for the provision of services is delegated to the private sector. Data for this discussion are drawn from the literature on public-private relationships and from an empirical study, conducted by the author, that assessed the impact of the use of government funds, through purchase-of-service arrangements, on patterns of social service delivery in the field of child protective services. A major question concerns potential differences in the types of services that public and private agencies provide. Are private agencies, as many have alleged, really the "stronger" providers of service? How are clients affected by the shift in responsibility to the nonpublic sector? This article provides new evidence that suggests optimism about the use of the private marketplace to provide services heretofore the responsibility of public agencies.

The argument has been advanced that a private social welfare sector no longer exists because a large majority of nonpublic agencies receive, through contracts, grants, or tax-exempt status, the benefits of government subsidies.[2] There are, however, important distinctions between public and private agencies. For purposes of this discussion, private agency refers to those organizations that provide social services as a primary function under the direction of a board of directors and that are financed through endowments, clients' fees, direct or United Way contributions, and, to varying degrees, government contracts. Contracts to support specific activities, however, represent only one source of income, and the agency is perceived by its clients and the professionals working within it to be nonpublic in nature. Private agencies are generally of two types, profit or nonprofit. This discussion is limited to nonprofit agencies, which are often known as voluntary agencies.

A public agency is defined as a governmental tax-supported organization whose powers and duties are prescribed by statute and administrative regulations. The scope of services provided by the public agency may vary from state to state and within localities of a state. Final authority for planning and administering public social services resides in a person or group elected by the voters or appointed by public officials. Publicly funded social services may be provided directly by the public agency or purchased from other public, voluntary, or proprietary agencies. When services are bought, this arrangement is usually actuated through a contract between the governmental agency (the contracting agency) and another organization (the provider). The purpose of this agreement is to purchase care or services provided to individuals or groups for whom there is a predetermined public responsibility.

Public-Private Relationships

Relationships between public and private systems of service have always been fluid, with pendulumlike changes occurring within the larger philosophical and political shifts affecting the whole of American social welfare. Relationships between the two sectors have, historically, ranged from highly independent to predominantly interdependent, with a growing emphasis on the latter. Until recently, public responsibility for the provision of services has usually meant direct public provision. Beginning with the War on Poverty legislation and the 1962 and 1967 amendments to the Social Security Act, national policies have encouraged a "mixed" public and private service delivery strategy in which private agencies are contracted to provide services to eligible individuals and groups who were heretofore the exclusive clients of public agencies.[3]

Traditionally, the private service system has been the provider of choice largely because of the residual nature of government services and the laissez-faire philosophy that has dominated government's approach to social welfare policies and practice. Long-standing perceptions that the public agency is a weak provider of service have encouraged the formation of a "partnership" with the stronger private sector. The emergence of purchase of service as an option for the delivery of public services has created the potential for new relationships between public and private service systems.

The desire to tap the private sector's capabilities also relates to the pragmatic need to expand the service delivery system to meet the needs of an enlarged population of clients. The gradual increase in the number of clients eligible for public services has occurred because certain services under the Title XX amendments to the Social Security Act can be offered, at a state's discretion, without regard to income. This is seen by some as a first step toward developing a personal social service system. In this schema, services ideally are available to all on the basis of need, with government responsible for paying the bill.[4] Purchase of service could thus potentially facilitate the provision of a range of services, through public-private collaboration, to a larger number of people. Will the use of private agencies, however, affect the types and quantity of services clients will receive?

Service Capability

The distribution of clients, services, social service personnel, and methods of financing services characteristic of public and private agencies suggests a differential standard. This set of polarities has represented in the conventional wisdom of the social work profession a two-tier service system in which the more valued psychotherapeutic, problem-solving services are provided by highly qualified personnel to the more advantaged clients through private agencies. In turn, public agencies tend to provide the more technical, concrete services using less-qualified staff to serve the more disadvantaged clients. Methods of financing services also vary by sector. Private agencies rely on clients' fees, endowments, United Way, and other contributions as well as government contracts, and public agencies are totally subsidized by government funds.

One possible outcome of using public funds to purchase services from private agencies is that a blurring of the distinctions between the two sectors could occur. Disillusionment with the performance of the public sector, accompanied by the stigma of government's association with an unpopular clientele, has perpetuated and accentuated the preference for the private sector as the "better" service delivery system. Contracting with private agencies, the traditional providers of choice, might eventually assist in obfuscating the association of public services as poor services for the poor.[5]

The merits and pitfalls of buying services from the private market instead of directly providing services is not a new debate. The social welfare field has long been concerned about which sector, public or private, is better able to deliver services, in what amounts, to which populations, and what the appropriate financial relationships should be. Despite the growing use of purchase of service, this arrangement has also been controversial partly because it reflects varying conceptions about public-private capability. Arguments related to contracting with private providers are frequently couched in terms of contrasting beliefs about the strengths of each sector and the appropriate role of government in delivering services. For example, speaking to the virtues of competition among providers of service, Buttrick notes that

> the idea of a welfare state does not imply that the state itself should dispense all welfare. . . . The provision of personal services gives no indication of possessing the kind of features that make monopoly the most efficient form of organization. . . . There may be considerable viability in competitive, free-choice methods of organization and delivery of services.[6]

The ascribed strengths of the private sector, based more on perception than hard data, are often emphasized by advocates of purchase of service. For example, private agencies are seen as promoting innovation in policy and administration, flexible programming, better service coordination, and responsiveness to immediate needs.[7] Likewise, a private-market strategy is preferred under the assumption that competition in this market results in a qualitative improvement in services, lower costs, a higher degree of choice of clients, and easier access to services.[8] The use of private agencies is also valued highly in light of the wish to avoid expanding the work force and associated costs of direct public service provision stemming from the rigidity of civil service regulations and union agreements; cost considerations are an issue here. The public agency, in contrast, has been viewed as the protector of the poor and the only sector that is capable of providing for and advancing the social well-being of all citizens.

To ensure that public mandates are met, government contracts with private providers can specify requirements about the types of clients to be served, including their presenting problems, socioeconomic status, or other characteristics relevant to the provision of services. When private agencies are given little discretion to choose their clients for the contracted program, a noticeable shift may occur in the distribution of clients from the public to the private sector. It is assumed that such a redistribution would be beneficial to the more disadvantaged clients who would benefit from receiving the "superior" private services. However, when private agencies are given some flexibility in selecting their clients, they might maintain their role as "gatekeepers" in deciding who is to be served and with what types of services. In part, the ability of private agencies to exercise such selectivity depends on the extent to which they have a monopoly on the services government wants to buy.[9]

Traditional distinctions between public and private agencies, then, lead to questions about the extent to which private agencies are equipped to offer a wide spectrum of services to clients usually served by public agencies. Do the services offered by these two types of agencies reflect a dual system of care, or have private agencies expanded the scope of their services to respond to the needs of all socioeconomic groups? In light of the current mandates to strengthen the private sector, the study reported here addressed several issues that face the social work profession:

• Does purchase of service result in an equitable distribution of services, particularly to the poor?

• Are there discernible differences in the types and quantity of services provided by public and private agencies?

• Is there evidence to suggest that the use of the private market will strengthen the provision of services heretofore provided by public agencies?

Study Design

The study reported in this article was undertaken to determine whether differences in service delivery patterns exist between a subdivision of a public agency and two private agencies under purchase-of-service contracts. All three agencies were located in a large northeastern state, whose purchase-of-service arrangements constitute a microcosm of the cross-sector contracting phenomenon. The sample consisted of sixty-three cases drawn from a sectarian family service agency and a nonsectarian children's agency, both of high repute, and fifty-seven cases drawn from the state's youth and family service agency. Thirty-nine direct service workers in these agencies were asked a series of questions by means of a closed-ended data-collection form administered by the investigator. The data were then subjected to statistical analyses; chi-square measures were used to determine the differences between public and private agencies in their service delivery patterns. The level of significance was defined at the .05 level.[10]

Child protective services was selected as the category for study because it is a service provided to, and potentially needed by, all socioeconomic groups served by either public or private agencies. Current research suggests that clients in need of protective services generally require a range of services, including both concrete (for example, homemaking and health care) as well as therapeutically oriented services (for instance, family or individual therapy), to ameliorate or prevent child abuse and neglect.[11] Child protective services represent a "clustering" of services in that several discrete (separate or individual) services such as marital counseling and advocacy may fall within this category. It was expected that within this service category, agencies would have relatively wide latitude in deciding on the types of services to be provided to clients and that differences, if any, in the nature and scope of services provided by the public and private agencies would be discernible.

All families in the sampled cases were referred for child protective services to the public agency that was mandated to investigate allegations of child abuse and neglect. Upon acceptance of a case, the public agency reached a determination either to provide services directly or refer the family to a contracted agency for service. The private agencies studied had the right to refuse a referral.

Results

Who Receives Services?

Traditional stereotypes hold that public and private agencies serve clients of different socioeconomic status. Because the private agencies under study could reject referrals from the public agency, some degree of selectivity about the characteristics of clients to be served could be exercised. The findings, however, negated the presence of a "creaming" phenomenon on the part of the private agencies.[12] The clients served by the two types of agencies were found to be remarkably similar on most variables related to family and normative social characteristics.

The population constituting the study's sample consisted largely of female-headed households, with an average of one to two children in the home and, frequently, members of the extended family, especially grandparents. A majority of the families were black and lived in a rented apartment or house in an urban area, with "fair" to "poor" neighborhood and structural housing conditions. The largest proportion of clients had Aid to Families with Dependent Children (AFDC) as their primary source of income. The adult females were most often unemployed, and for those cases in which an adult male was present in the home, an almost even division in the number employed and unemployed emerged. For both employed males and females, the majority held occupations in the skilled, semiskilled, and unskilled categories. Across the two types of agencies, the clients were relatively homogeneous.

Provision of Services

A number of dimensions related to the provision of services were studied, including the types of services clients received—individually and in categories of service—and the intensity with which services were provided (that is, how frequently clients were in touch with their workers either in person or by telephone). Together, these variables were expected to yield data supporting differences between the public agency and the private agencies under purchase-of-service contracts. Among the concerns raised about private agencies was their alleged tendency to focus on the provision of verbal, psychotherapeutic services to the sacrifice of the more concrete needs of clients. It was therefore expected that clients served by the private agencies would receive more psychotherapeutic, or "soft," services than concrete, or "hard," services.

Significant differences were, indeed, found in the types of services provided by the public and private agencies in eight of twenty-two areas of service. As depicted in Table 1, the more psychologically oriented services, as expected, were provided to a larger proportion of clients served by the private agencies. This situation was reversed in relation to the more concrete services such as day care and information and referral; these services were offered with greater frequency to the clients served by the public agency.

To test further the differences in the types of services offered by these agencies, a panel of experts was convened to determine the extent of

Table 1. Services Provided by Public and Private Agencies
by Rank Order[a]

Service	Public Agency Cases ($n=57$)	Percentage	Private Agencies Cases[b] ($n=63$)	Percentage
Information and referral	48	84	42	67
Individual therapy and counseling	34	60	52	83
Transportation services	23	40	40	64
Diagnosis and assessment	12	21	48	76
Family therapy	6	11	32	52
Day care	19	33	9	14
Financial management counseling	2	4	16	22
Marital counseling	3	5	13	21

[a]Services included in this table are those significant at or better than the .05 level. A range of other services was provided, such as parent educaton, medical and health services, crisis intervention, employment and vocational services, and group therapy. However, no significant differences were found between public and private agencies in their provision of these services.

[b]In general, more than one service was provided to each case.

agreement on which of the twenty-two discrete services fell into four predetermined categories: concrete services, counseling and therapeutic services, educational services, and monitoring and case management. Each of the discrete services was assigned to one of the four categories on the basis of the panel's classification. In the largest category, concrete services, fourteen discrete services were combined for analysis. As indicated in Table 2, however, no significant differences were found between the two types of agencies in the provision of concrete services. It had been expected that the public agency would provide its clients more concrete services than the private agencies would because this category includes the range of hard services such as emergency shelter, day care, homemaking, and placement services. The similarity between the two types of agencies in this category of service argues against the allegation that private agencies are unable or unwilling to address the concrete needs of their clients. This finding further suggests that private agencies may be demonstrating greater flexibility and utility in the types of services they provide than had previously been thought possible.

In regard to the provision of counseling and psychotherapeutic services, significant differences were found between public and private agencies. As indicated in Table 3, private agencies offered their clients more counseling and psychotherapeutic services than did the public agency. Such differences in the types of services offered between public and private agencies were also found in relation to educational services, which include employment and vocational counseling, financial management counseling, and parent education. Within this category of service, private

Table 2. Public and Private Provision of Concrete Services[a]

Number of Concrete Services Provided Per Case	Public Agency		Private Agencies	
	Cases $(n=57)$	Percentage	Cases $(n=63)$	Percentage
1	12	21	20	32
2–3	20	35	15	24
4–5	17	30	14	22
6–9	8	14	14	22

[a]The category of concrete services includes the following: homemaking, information and referral, employment and vocational services, emergency shelter, medical and health services, transportation, day care, housing services, intervention to mobilize extended family and friends, placement in foster care, placement in residential care, and advocacy. Figures are related to the following tests of significance: $\chi^2 = 4.35$, $df = 3$, and $p = .23$.

Table 3. Public and Private Provision of Counseling and
Psychotherapeutic Services[a]

Number of Counseling and Psychotherapeutic Services Provided Per Case	Public Agency		Private Agencies	
	Cases ($n = 57$)	Percentage	Cases ($n = 63$)	Percentage
0	18	32	2	3
1	19	33	24	38
2	15	26	18	29
3–5	5	9	19	30

[a]Counseling and psychotherapeutic services include the following: individual therapy and counseling, family therapy, marital counseling, group therapy, and crisis intervention services. Figures are related to the following tests of significance: $\chi^2 = 21.57$, $df = 3$, and $p = .0001$.

agencies offered a significantly higher porportion of such services to their clients than did the public agency. The same findings held true for the fourth category of service, monitoring and case management, which includes case management and diagnosis and assessment services. Thus, clients served by the private agencies had a significantly greater opportunity to receive all types of services than was true for clients served by the public agency.

Intensity of Services

It is generally assumed that the amount of interaction workers have with their clients will have a great deal to do with the ultimate outcome and success of service. The rationale behind this assumption is that frequent interaction enhances the opportunity for the rendering of effective services. The findings of the study reported here suggested that workers in the private agencies had much more frequent in-person interaction with their clients than did workers in the public agency. (See Table 4.) These differences also held true in relation to the frequency of telephone conversations, with workers in private agencies having significantly more frequent conversations with their clients.

Because all cases accepted for the sample were open for a minimum of three months and a maximum of nine months, variations in the workers' frequency of in-person interaction and telephone conversation cannot be explained on the basis of the period of time a client had been served in either type of agency. However, it was found that workers in the private

Table 4. Workers' In-Person Contacts with Families
Since Case Opening[a]

Number of In-Person Contacts	Public Agency		Private Agencies	
	Cases ($n = 57$)	Percentage	Cases ($n = 63$)	Percentage
1	32	56	13	21
2–3	19	33	26	41
4–5	5	9	17	27
6–9	1	2	7	11

[a]All sampled cases were open and in active service for a minimum of three months and a maximum of nine months. Figures are related to the following tests of significance: $\chi^2 = 19.91$, $df = 3$, and $p = .0002$.

agencies carried substantially smaller caseloads than their counterparts in the public agency, a finding that may account for the differences in the frequency of workers' interaction with clients. Thus, auspices appeared to have a dramatic impact not only on the type but also on the intensity of services provided to clients.

Conclusion

Delegating responsibility for the provision of services to private agencies, in the form of purchase-of-service contracts, may have a much more positive impact on services than traditional views of the private sector's capability suggest. The results of the study reported in this article pointed to an equitable distribution in the client populations served by public and private agencies.

Despite the right of these agencies, within limits, to screen the clients they accept for service, the socioeconomic characteristics of the families served were almost identical across the two types of agencies. The socioeconomic status of these families suggests that the private agencies are now serving those in greater need. The specificity of some purchase-of-service contracts about the clients to be served may encourage private agencies to reach out to populations different from those they traditionally serve.[13]

Given this similarity in the characteristics of clients served by the two types of agencies, the issue then becomes whether one sector evidences a greater service delivery capacity than the other. Although private agencies have been associated with the provision of psychotherapeutic services, the findings suggested that nonprofit agencies now use a range of treatment interventions to meet the needs of clients. Although the private agencies provided a higher proportion of counseling and psychotherapeutic services than did the public agency, this was only one of several categories of service made available. In contrast, the public agency focused more on concrete services but did not provide them in any greater proportion than did the private agencies. Thus, in relation to a number of variables related to the provision of services, the private agencies under purchase-of-service contracts proved to be the more versatile providers, as compared with the public agency. However, the limitations inherent in a case-study approach suggest the need for replication studies in other areas of the country. To the extent that the findings of the current study are borne out in future research involving different types of presenting problems and different types of private agencies (for example, mental health clinics), the benefits attributed to contracting will be further validated.

One implication of the differences in the types of services provided by public and private agencies is that, for a sizable number of clients served exclusively by the public agency, psychotherapeutic services may be limited or unavailable. In other words, such services may be offered only to those clients who are referred to private agencies for services. This situation may result in a dual system of care to clients of similar status wherein the full range of interventions is provided to clients in private agencies, but only the hard services are provided for those clients retained by the public agency. Although the provision of these concrete services may satisfy accountability needs in that they are easily definable and countable, the limited types of services offered by the public agency may not meet the needs of clients. In a political climate favoring the use of the private sector, the differential distribution in the types of services offered may create inequities for clients remaining within the public system for service.

The integral role of social workers in the private service sector is well established. The renewed emphasis on private agencies to deliver services heretofore within the domain of public agencies, however, is having an impact on the nature of practice within this setting. Increasingly, social workers in private agencies are relating to clients who represent a broader population than traditionally served by this sector and who need and demand a wider array of services. Changes are also occurring in the nature of work for practitioners employed by public agencies. The tendency of public agencies to concentrate on the provision of concrete services suggests that staff members need to be well versed in case management and information and referral, with less emphasis on direct intervention skills. Within the context of a shift in responsibility for the provision of services, modifications in the definition of the worker's functions are beginning to occur in both sectors. Although additional adaptations in roles and responsibility will occur, the use of public funds to purchase private services is proving to be a viable option to a purely public system of service.

Notes and References

1. Murray Comarow, "The War on Civil Servants," *Washington Post*, August 25, 1981, p. A19.

2. See Eleanor L. Brilliant, "Private or Public: A Model of Ambiguities," *Social Service Review*, 47 (September 1973), pp. 384–396; Amatai Etzioni, "The Untapped Potential of the 'Third Sector,' " *Business and Society Review*, 1 (Spring 1972), pp. 39–44; and Bruce L. R. Smith and D. C. Hague, eds., *The Dilemma of Accountability in Modern Government: Independence versus Control* (New York: St. Martin's Press, 1971).

3. The 1962 amendments to the Social Security Act authorized, for the first time, the federal reimbursement to states for purchasing their services from other public agencies. Provisions were extended in 1967 to include the purchase of service from voluntary and proprietary agencies. For a description of the use of contracting as a strategy to enhance popular participation in government decision making in War on Poverty programs, see Bruce L. R. Smith, "Accountability and Independence in the Contract State," in Smith and Hague, op. cit., pp. 31–69.

4. See Sheila B. Kamerman and Alfred J. Kahn, *Social Services in the United States: Policies and Programs* (Philadelphia: Temple University Press, 1976).

5. Shirley M. Buttrick, "On Choices and Services," *Social Service Review*, 44 (Spring 1970), pp. 427–433.

6. Ibid., pp. 429–430.

7. See Kenneth R. Wedel, "Government Contracting for Purchase of Services," *Social Work*, 21 (March 1976), pp. 101–105; Smith, op. cit.; Gordon Manser, "Further Thoughts on Purchase of Service," *Social Casework*, 55 (July 1974), pp. 421–427; Ralph M. Kramer, *An Analysis of Policy Issues in Relationships Between Governmental and Voluntary Agencies*, unpublished DSW dissertation, University of California School of Social Welfare at Berkeley, 1964; and John M. Wedemeyer, "Government Agencies and Purchase of Social Services," in Iris R. Winogrand, ed., *Proceedings of the First Milwaukee Institute on a Social Welfare Issue of the Day: Purchase of Care and Services in the Health and Welfare Fields* (Milwaukee: University of Wisconsin, 1970), pp. 3–20.

8. Arnold Gurin, *The Efficacy of Contracting for Services: A Mechanism to Improve Program Effectiveness and Efficiency for Administration in Human Services*, Summary Report, Grant No. 18-P-00170/1-01 (Waltham, Mass.: Florence Heller Graduate School for Advanced Studies in Social Welfare, Brandeis University, March 1980). This report was prepared for the U.S. Department of Health, Education, and Welfare.

9. Ralph M. Kramer, "Voluntary Agencies and the Use of Public Funds: Some Policy Considerations," *Social Work*, 15 (September 1966), pp. 53–61.

10. For a full discussion of the research, see Margaret Gibelman, *Public Purchase of Voluntary Agency Services: Assessing the Impact on Social Service*

Delivery, unpublished DSW dissertation, Adelphi University School of Social Work, 1981.

11. Henry C. Kempe and Ray E. Helfer, *Helping the Battered Child and His Family* (Philadelphia: J. B. Lippincott Co., 1972).

12. For a more extensive discussion of this topic, see Margaret Gibelman, "Are Clients Served Better When Services are Purchased?" *Public Welfare,* 39 (Fall 1981), pp. 26–34.

13. The increased outreach of private agencies to clients of low socioeconomic status are documented in Dorothy Fahs Beck and Mary Ann Jones, *Progress on Family Problems* (New York: Family Service Association of America, 1973).

Bringing Together Minority Professionals for Community Empowerment

Rufus Sylvester Lynch
Edward A. Brawley

In April 1979, the Center for Studying Social Welfare and Community Development, an organization for research, training, education, and community service, was incorporated in Pennsylvania by two black social workers. The primary purpose of the center is to bring together the talents, resources, and interests of a diverse group of minority social researchers, health and social service practitioners, and community leaders to address common issues and develop appropriate responses to problems, using the best knowledge and expertise available.[1] To carry out this purpose, the center attempts to bridge the gaps between the production of new knowledge and its application in practice settings, between academics and practitioners, between universities and communities, and between service providers and consumers.

The authors of this article view the center as an emerging institution and concur with the observation that there are "three elements which interact to define the shape of the changing or emerging institution. These are (1) *institutional variables*, (2) *linkages*, and (3) *transactions*."[2] After reviewing the factors that led to the establishment of the center, the authors examine it as an emerging institution by looking at such variables as its purposes, organization, structure, and activities and by describing some of its linkages and transactions with other groups and organizations. In addition, they present evaluative information on the center's first year of operation and discuss the potential of such organizations for increasing the power of minority professionals to draw on their own and society's resources in addressing the problems (in such areas as

114

community health care, housing, and education) and enhancing the quality of community life.

Purpose of the Center

Solomon has observed that "the theme of powerlessness among minority groups in the United States is a constant ringing in the ear of the nation."[3] Many members of minorities are familiar with the pain and hardships that result from a lack of power to change life situations. This powerlessness is also experienced by helping professionals, whose power to alleviate the hardships imposed on minority populations by unequal access to society's opportunities and resources "appears unalterably weak and ineffectual."[4] The personal experience of such powerlessness and its resultant frustration motivated the center's founders to look for an alternative to existing social institutions that would enable them and other minority professionals to have a greater impact on social policies, programs, and services. In essence, professional dissatisfaction coupled with a deeply felt need to make a substantive contribution to public service led to the creation of the center.

Holden asserts that the next several years will be critical for minority groups and particularly for blacks as they attempt to penetrate the existing power structure and to establish the mechanisms that will enable them to participate more effectively in the social, political, and economic structures of the United States.[5] Among the initiatives that he suggests will be required to achieve this participation is the establishment of minority-run "think tanks" that could develop future scenarios and strategies for black and other minority communities to follow. Although the center incorporates some of the characteristics of a "think tank," it tends to be less academic than that term suggests, in that the center stresses action as well as research. It is a laboratory for applied research or "action research" in the areas of social welfare and community development.[6]

The ultimate goal of the center is to empower the powerless to make positive changes in communities, social programs and services, and social policies, but the center's conception of empowerment differs somewhat from the conventional one. Usually, community empowerment is thought of as the mobilization of the most disadvantaged segments of a given community, often the welfare poor. This kind of empowerment generally involves securing the formal or informal participation of community members in the making of institutional decisions in which they have a vital interest. The center's purposes do not preclude such efforts to mobilize; indeed, the community forums it has presented on health care and the elderly have contained elements of this type of community empowerment. However, the center's membership is aware that the prospects for effective community participation in decision making regarding the human services, particularly on the part of low-income or minority groups, are not promising, and that strategies for community control in general can have quite conservative consequences.[7] (For example, a conservative consequence of community control of schools might be that busing aimed at racial integration would be blocked.) Thus, the center's conception of empowerment encompasses the additional ideas that (1) freeing competent and basically middle-class minority professionals to use their talents and energies more effectively on behalf of vulnerable or deprived groups, neighborhoods, and communities is potentially liberating to all concerned, and that (2) "voluntary associations are at the moment the best available device for forcing feedback into established policy-setting agencies as a means of altering social policy."[8] As such a voluntary association of primarily minority practitioners of social work and related human services, the center is dedicated to the empowerment of professional individuals, groups, neighborhoods, and communities.

Certain opinions about the empowerment of professionals were important in formulating the center's purposes: (1) the experiences in the workplace of both minority and majority members of the helping professions tend to be unsatisfying, (2) professional schools are not fulfilling the need of their graduates for relevant continuing education, (3) traditional professional organizations are not meeting the needs of all their members—especially their minority members, and (4) minority professionals do not have a strong network to provide opportunities for professional enrichment and advancement, primarily because they tend to be marginally and precariously involved with major social institutions.

The center's primary mission, as defined by its Board of Directors, is to educate people in this country and abroad about local, national, and international public welfare issues and concerns. Among its general goals, the center seeks to (1) lessen the burdens of local, state, and national governments by assisting in the drafting, analyzing, implementing, and disseminating of information regarding social and public welfare policy, issues, and regulations, (2) assist in studying and lessening community tensions, prejudice, and discrimination throughout the world, (3) assist in studying and alleviating manifestations of human suffering and distress and in educating the community to quality-of-life issues, (4) promote the exchange of ideas not only among members of the center but among all people, (5) study the socioeconomic and political conditions of neighborhoods and communities in the United States and abroad, and (6) study community problems of citizens of this country and of other nations by conducting seminars, international conferences, and research into educational techniques, in cooperation with other sociopolitical institutions created for purposes other than propaganda or the support or defeat of a candidate for public office.

Organization and Structure

Incorporated as a private nonprofit organization under Pennsylvania law, the center has the state and federal status of a tax-exempt and charitable organization. A Board of Directors, the Board of Fellows (made up of the total membership of the center), and an administrative staff share in the operation of the center. (The word "fellow" in "Board of Fellows," although considered to have a sexist connotation, was retained by majority vote of the center's membership in the absence of an acceptable alternative.) The composition of both boards and the administrative staff is predominantly female and minority. The center is funded by private donations, project grants, and contracts.

The seven-member Board of Directors is legally and fiscally responsible for the center, setting policy and providing overall direction and control. The Board of Fellows oversees the center's programmatic development. The thirty-three fellows include human service practitioners and scholars, the majority of whom have direct practice experience in human service delivery. In addition to functioning as a board, the fellows are organized in special-interest clusters, called colloquium groups, for the study of special topics or the development of individual or collaborative projects. The seven current groups are focusing on international studies, education and training, special projects, organizational development, research and model development, health and social services, and community and economic development. From time to time, individuals with special expertise may be appointed as consulting fellows to help work on specific projects or tasks.

The day-to-day operation of the center is the responsibility of the administrative staff, which currently includes an executive director, an associate director, and a secretary. In addition to handling routine management tasks such as the maintenance of records and accounts, the administrative staff investigates possible sources of funds and project opportunities and establishes and maintains working relationships with local and national groups and organizations. Staff members also develop promotional materials, present public testimony for the center concerning social welfare and related issues, advise the Board of Fellows of the center's activities and consult with them about project proposals and activities, and perform any other tasks deemed necessary for carrying out the goals and objectives of the center.

First Year and Future Activities

As might be expected, a great deal of energy during the center's first year of operation was devoted to organizational and logistical matters. The processes of securing legal incorporation and tax-exempt status; finding accommodations, necessary equipment, and supplies; and establishing a viable and visible organization were accomplished, as was the often difficult process of clarifying organizational purposes, goals, and the roles and responsibilities of directors, fellows, and staff.

Despite this heavy investment of time and energy in organizational activities, the membership initiated several specific projects designed to advance the center's programmatic purposes. Although some projects had to be deferred or abandoned, primarily because of insufficient funds, it is useful to look at the following list of projects planned, to get a sense of the range of concerns of the center:

1. The conducting of a case study of a neighborhood organization's efforts to combat crime, ease tensions, and restore safe living conditions for residents of an area in west Philadelphia
2. A conference designed to enable public school officials, public administrators, and educators to explore interdisciplinary research and promising approaches to common problems
3. A study of the aims, values, and methods of networking and its potential for promoting individual welfare and strengthening communities
4. The development of a model transitional boarding home in Philadelphia for persons awaiting placement in an adult foster home or hospital admission or for persons needing short-term respite care
5. The development of a training program and resource manual for the boards of directors of five voluntary organizations in southeastern Pennsylvania
6. The compilation and publication of the proceedings of the Tenth Annual Conference of the National Caucus on the Black Aged
7. A nationwide study of the feasibility of using subsidized taxicabs for the transportation of the frail and impaired elderly
8. The conducting of a series of five workshops in Pennsylvania on the changing roles of and relationships between black males and black females
9. A conference focusing on the problems of teenage pregnancy
10. A proposal to the National Endowment for the Humanities to compile an oral history of forty prominent black jurists whose contributions to civil and social justice have not been documented

Of the projects listed, those completed were the research project on a subsidized taxicab program as an alternative transportation system for the frail elderly and the publication of the Proceedings of the Tenth Annual Conference of the National Caucus on the Black Aged. Because of the success of the latter project, the center was asked to compile and edit the proceedings of three regional miniconferences (held in Detroit, Atlanta, and Los Angeles) on the black aged in preparation for the 1981 White House Conference on Aging.

In addition to the projects originally planned, the center collaborated with the Philadelphia Office of Adult and Aging Services to develop and test a model training program for the proprietors of boarding homes. It also conducted two community forums in Philadelphia on the need for more effective health care and human services at the neighborhood level; these forums served as vehicles for improving collaboration and coordination among relevant organizations and individuals. In addition, the center established a scholarship for one minority student in the schools of social work of Bryn Mawr College, Temple University, University of Pennsylvania, and University of Pittsburgh, as well as an annual award for persons who make outstanding contributions to the fields of education and training, public administration, research, and human service practice.

Under a grant from Pennsylvania-Delaware Community Action, Inc., the center recently completed a study and produced a position paper on the needs of the elderly in Pennsylvania, the way in which these needs are currently being addressed, and what needs are going unmet. This study produced data, which may have national significance, on the roles of area agencies on aging and community action programs in serving distinct segments of the aging population. Another project that may have national significance is a collaboration with the University of Pittsburgh's School of Social Work to develop technical assistance models for four different state departments or offices on aging to help them implement the Age Discrimination Act of 1975.

In addition, the center has made a substantial effort to build productive relationships with a variety of governmental, human service, academic, and community-based organizations. During its first year, the center reached out to more than fifty community groups, public and private organizations, and academic institutions. Although not all these efforts have borne fruit yet, some successes are reflected in the projects already described, many of which have required the development of collaborative relationships.

Finally, because it is an organization that advocates creative and socially responsible public policy, the center has tried to make its voice heard in a variety of arenas. For example, the executive director has testified on behalf of the center at federal and state public hearings and has maintained regular contact with a broad range of federal and state officials and legislators.

As an emerging institution, the center has been shaped by the interaction of its institutional variables or characteristics, its linkages, and its transactions. The linkages and transactions just described have been especially important to its development because they reflect the center's resolve to be connected to social institutions committed to goals that are consistent with those of the center.

Evaluation

Following the center's first full year of operation, the membership undertook a structured self-evaluation to assess how well the center was operating. The evaluation process included (1) an analysis of the center's operations, based on broadly accepted criteria for assessing private nonprofit organizations, (2) an evaluation of the center's records, to determine the extent to which the goals and objectives of the center were being accomplished, (3) a questionnaire survey of the Board of Fellows, and (4) interviews with the Board of Directors, to gain their views on the operation of the center.

The center appeared to conform to nationally accepted standards in terms of the composition and operations of its Board of Directors; its purpose, program, expenses, promotion, fundraising, and budgetary processes; and its accountability. However, the assessment procedure sensitized board members to some points they had overlooked. Because the center had no regular source of income and was supported primarily by cash and in-kind donations from the founders, relatively little attention had been given to establishing an adequate system of financial management and reporting. The evaluation revealed this weakness and, despite the fact that the center had little money of its own, some necessary fiscal controls such as an annual budget were implemented.

The evaluation revealed that some of the center's objectives were stated in terms too broad and diffuse to permit evaluation—for example, "to provide reality-based research and learning experiences in a wide range of social service and community settings in line with present developing social needs." It became clear that the center's objectives would have to be stated in more specific terms if they were to be useful guides to action and tools for evaluating performance.

The questionnaire administered to all members of the Board of Fellows was designed to elicit their views on the concept and operation of the center. Although the rate of response was small (thirteen respondents or 40 percent) and the representativeness of the responses is not known, the data provide an additional perspective on the functions and achievements of the center. Most of the fellows who responded said they understood the purpose of the center and agreed that among its many benefits, the center had given them opportunities for research activities, information sharing, new personal and professional associations, and professional growth and learning. Most respondents also stated that their contacts with the center were sufficient and satisfactory, that they approved of what the center had accomplished during the first year, and that they were pleased about their involvement with the center.

In interviews, all members of the Board of Directors assessed the strengths and weaknesses of the center during its first year of operation. Board members cited several factors as contributing to the progress made so far. They noted that the concept of the center appeared to have been validated in that several significant projects had been initiated and developed. The center's structure seemed to them sufficiently flexible to allow for many types of participation, interactions, and activities. They saw the executive director's role as crucial in developing the center's visibility and credibility in the community, in translating the initiatives of the fellows and others into specific projects, and in acquiring operating funds.

However, the board members pointed out some weaknesses in the concept and operation of the center, primarily related to the disparate commitments and contributions of the fellows and directors. They noted that most fellows have full-time occupations and a range of other commitments and that they are geographically dispersed. Some, they asserted, were insufficiently committed to the center's success. The board members also saw lack of money as a serious problem, faulting themselves for their failure to invest more time and energy in raising operating funds. Finally, they expressed concern that an undue share of the burden of ensuring the center's survival had fallen on the executive director and a few others, a situation viewed as nonviable in the long term.

In summary, the evaluation revealed many strengths and successes. This was especially true of the center's capability to initiate and successfully carry out a variety of projects that contribute to its mission of serving the community. However, some areas of organizational structure and procedure need to be given more attention if the center is to survive and prosper.

Conclusion

Like most community organizations, the center was created to exert influence.[9] Many of its goals parallel those found in the process of community organization: "the improvement of social provisions for some disadvantaged or disenfranchised population" and "the enhancement of social relationships to bring about a greater capacity on the part of some target population to deal with common problems."[10] The center is not a community organization in the conventional sense, however, because its purposes transcend any given community and it attempts to place its concerns and activities within a global perspective. Boehm described this viewpoint thus:

> There is a growing recognition that we don't live alone, that we are part of the main, so that when there is famine or war or violence somewhere in Africa or Asia, we are involved not only on moral grounds but also because our own well-being, social, economic and political is at stake. . . . how to deal with these problems is, at this point, not entirely clear but what seems to emerge is a sense of commitment to human well-being on a global scale.[11]

The establishment of the center exemplifies the revitalization of the voluntary social welfare sector in the United States.[12] Like other voluntary organizations concerned with social welfare, it "provides individuals with allies, options, outlets, and power" and "provides society with innovation, experimentation, criticism, and reform."[13] But again, it differs from most voluntary social welfare organizations in that it is committed to making "the linkage between where people live in the neighborhood or small community, the city, the state, the federal government, and the world."[14]

The processes of clarifying the concept and mission of the center and of implementing programs and linkages on a global scale are incomplete; it would be misleading to suggest otherwise. The process of role definition is evolutionary, and the authors believe that it must be allowed to take its course. Most members of the center are willing to tolerate the occasional confusion and risks inherent in the ambiguities surrounding the center's mission rather than preempt the natural developmental and definitional processes that are taking place. They recognize that seeking a precise definition of mission for the sake of certainty can result in a much narrower and more limited conception of the center than is desirable.

The center's developers hope to create a new type of organization that can be replicated by or can serve as an impetus for other human service practitioners, researchers, and community leaders who want to develop a mechanism for empowering minority professional individuals, groups, neighborhoods, and communities. They are aware that the center, although unique in many ways, is only one of many attempts to respond on a practical and theoretical level to similar problems.[15] They believe that, under the present circumstances in which "the traditional establishments have deeply vested interests in protecting themselves and their reality as the turbulence increases [and] the inclination is strong to enclose and retrench," it is vital that substantial effort be devoted to developing alternative mechanisms for addressing people's needs, particularly the needs of more vulnerable groups.[16] The center's members hope that more of their professional colleagues throughout the country and abroad will be encouraged to mount their own experiments in community empowerment. As Harris asserts,

> Permanent solutions to problems such as poverty, inadequate health care, domestic violence, and long-term needs of older Americans and the handicapped will come only when substantial numbers of people in communities all across the country are personally involved, committed to, and supportive of, the solutions to these problems.[17]

Notes and References

1. In the context of this article, the word "minority" applies to black, Hispanic, Asian, and Native Americans. With the exception of Native Americans, members of the aforementioned groups have participated fully in the center's activities, and efforts are being made to involve Native Americans.

2. Robert R. Mayer, *Social Sciences and Institutional Change* (Rockville, Md.: U.S. Department of Health, Education & Welfare, 1979), p. 3.

3. Barbara Bryant Solomon, *Black Empowerment: Social Work in Oppressed Communities* (New York: Columbia University Press, 1976), pp. 11–12.

4. Ibid., p. 383.

5. Matthew Holden, Jr., *The Politics of the Black "Nation"* (New York: Chandler Publishing Co., 1973), pp. 179–212.

6. Kurt Lewin, *Resolving Social Conflicts* (New York: Harper & Row, 1948).

7. Marilyn Gittell et al., *Limits to Citizen Participation: The Decline of Community Organizations* (Beverly Hills, Calif.: Sage Publications, 1980); and Norman I. Fainstein and Mark Martin, "Support for Community Control among Local Urban Elites," *Urban Affairs Quarterly*, 13 (June 1978), pp. 443–468.

8. Donald N. Michael, "Influencing Public Policy: The Changing Role of Voluntary Associations," in Ralph M. Kramer and Harry Specht, eds., *Readings in Community Organization Practice* (2d ed.; Englewood Cliffs, N.J.: Prentice-Hall, 1975), p. 86.

9. Edmund M. Burke, "Citizen Participation Strategies," in Kramer and Specht, eds., *Readings in Community Organization Practice*, p. 203.

10. Joan Levin Ecklein and Armand Lauffer, *Community Organizers and Social Planners: A Volume of Cases and Illustrative Materials* (New York: John Wiley & Sons, 1972), p. 11.

11. Werner W. Boehm, *Human Well-Being—Challenges for the Eighties—Social, Economic and Political Action* (New York: U.S. Committee of the International Council on Social Welfare, August 1978), p. 44.

12. Brian O'Connell, "The Independent Sector and Voluntary Action," in National Conference on Social Welfare, *Social Welfare Forum, 1980* (New York: Columbia University Press, 1981), pp. 39–52.

13. Ibid., p. 40.

14. Arthur J. Naparstek, "Community Empowerment: The Critical Role of Neighborhoods," in National Conference on Social Welfare, *Social Welfare Forum, 1980*, p. 57.

15. See, for example, Eustolio Benavides III, Mary Martin Lynch, and Joan Swanson Velasquez, "Toward a Culturally Relevant Fieldwork Model: The Community Learning Center Project," *Journal of Education for Social Work*, 16

124   *Lynch and Brawley*

(Spring 1980), pp. 55–62; David Biegel and Arthur Naparstek, "Organizing for Mental Health: An Empowerment Model," *C/O Journal of Alternative Human Services*, 5 (October 1979), pp. 8–14; Biegel and Wendy Sherman, "Neighborhood Capacity Building and the Ethnic Elderly," in Donald E. Gelfand and Alfred J. Kutzik, eds., *Ethnicity and Aging*, "Adulthood and Aging Series," Vol. 5 (New York: Springer Publishing Co., 1979), pp. 320–340; Pastora San Juan Cafferty and Richard M. Krieg, "Social Work Roles in Assessing Urban Development," *Social Work*, 24 (May 1979), pp. 225–231; Benjamin Cuellar, "The Chicano Agency: A Study of Social Service Agencies Serving the Spanish Speaking in Santa Clara County, California," unpublished Ph.D. dissertation, Columbia University School of Social Work, 1981; Melvin Delgado, "A Hispanic Foster Parents Program," *Child Welfare*, 57 (July/August 1978), pp. 427–431; E. Daniel Edwards et al., "Enhancing Self-Concept and Identification with 'Indianness' of American Indian Girls," *Social Work with Groups*, 1 (Fall 1978), pp. 309–318; Douglas Glasgow, "A New Community Building Focus," in National Association of Black Social Workers, *Survival and Beyond*, proceedings of the Sixth Annual Conference of the National Association of Black Social Workers (Detroit: Multi-Tech, 1974), pp. 167–177; Shirley Jenkins, *The Ethnic Dilemma in Social Services* (New York: Free Press, 1981); Jack A. Kirkland and Fred Smith, "Organizing and Working in Black Communities, Past, Present and Future: Highlighting the WEB Approach," in National Association of Black Social Workers, *Black America: Reawakening for the Future*, proceedings of the Eighth Annual Conference of the National Association of Black Social Workers (Chicago: CCT Press, 1976), pp. 98–125; Doman Lum, "Toward a Framework for Social Work Practice with Minorities," *Social Work*, 27 (May 1982), pp. 244–249; Claudette McShane and John Oliver, "Women's Groups As Alternative Human Service Agencies," *Journal of Sociology and Social Welfare*, 5 (September 1978), pp. 615–626; M. Morgenbesser et al., "The Evolution of Three Alternative Social Service Agencies," *Catalyst*, 3, No. 3 (1981), pp. 71–83; Clara Peoples, "Community Organization—You Can Do It Too," in National Association of Black Social Workers, *Survival and Beyond*, pp. 282–291; and Joseph H. Strauss et al., "An Experimental Outreach Legal Aid Program for an Urban Native American Population Utilizing Legal Paraprofessionals," *Human Organization*, 38 (Winter 1979), pp. 386–394.

16. Michael, op. cit., p. 82.

17. Patricia Roberts Harris, "Caring Communities for the Eighties," in National Conference on Social Welfare, *Social Welfare Forum, 1980*, p. 2.

Part Three
Responding Creatively to a Turbulent World

Editor's Comments

Part Three examines the growing edge of social work practice as it relates to the encounter between the social worker and the consumer of social work services. Each article in this section addresses a new arena for social work practice, a new population at risk whose needs pose special practice questions, or new knowledge and approaches for working with a population long familiar to social workers. The articles represent a continuing professional concern, namely, that of discovering, testing, and disseminating improvements and innovations in practice.

The first article, by Akabas, deals with a new arena for the practice of social work, namely, the industrial setting. Akabas reaffirms the necessity for the social worker to attend not only to the person in this new area but also to the work situation. No doubt Helen Harris Perlman would thoroughly approve. The fourth article, by Graham, Hawkins, and Blau also deals with social work in a host setting, but the setting considered is historically the first into which social work moved. These authors discuss an innovative way in which to conceptualize and deliver social work services in the medical arena. The traditional social work role is reformulated and is described as the management of the stress that results from an illness, its treatment, the necessity of dealing with a health care organization, and subsequent life adjustments that may be necessary. The formulation suggests that the management of stress requires appropriate treatment, just as the management of an illness does. The consequences of this reformulation for the status of social work and the frequency of its use should prove most interesting.

The third article, by Tonti and Kosberg, like the fifth article, by Ballew and Ditzhazy, deals with social work practice with a population long familiar to social work. The former focuses on the "old-old," the latter on families in which child abuse occurs. In both cases the authors apply theories and techniques used in other aspects of social work to work with these two populations, both of which are increasing in size and growing as a cause for concern. The article by Ballew and Ditzhazy also deals with a recurrent tension in social work by focusing on the balance between prevention and treatment. It describes secondary rather than primary prevention, for it discusses families that are neither the labeled and involuntary clients already in the long-term protective service caseload nor those who once were or may again be so labeled but are not now served. These families are judged at risk, and for them service provision may make the crucial difference between an episode of abuse occurring or not. A model that should prove transferable is given. Furthermore, the authors offer an evaluation tool and a diagnostic tool that should prove helpful to others in the field.

The last article in Part Three, by Black, discusses some of the consequences for social work practice of the recent explosion of knowledge in genetics, a seemingly distant field. It focuses mainly on the subject of adoption and also deals with issues surrounding children born of incestuous and consanguineous unions. The implications of the discussion should alert readers in many other areas of social work practice to questions that are raised for families facing decisions prompted by the diagnosis of genetic handicaps, for couples who are considering having a baby, and for a society in which radioactive exposure is a hazard. Also social workers should become aware that they practice in a world in which job applicants undergo genetic screening in certain industries and in which "genius" sperm banks, artificial insemination, and test-tube babies are no longer just the elements of science fiction.

The second article in this section, by Harrison, Kilpatrick, and Vance, requires a longer introduction than the others. It is an excellent discussion touching on a small and specialized segment of social work's clientele— dual career families. The dual-career family is, statistically, a small part of a large phenomenon—a steady and increasing growth, in the last thirty-five years, in the number of women who work outside the home. Poor women and minority women have long been part of the labor force, but their counterparts who are richer and who are majority group members have begun to join them in record numbers. The social work and social welfare issues posed by these trends have only begun to surface. Because this is the only article in the volume to deal with working women, it is perhaps appropriate to provide a context within which it may be considered.

Nearly two-thirds of all women of prime working age—18 to 65 years old—now work for all or part of the year. In the last twenty-five years, the participation in the labor force of women with husbands and with children under 18 rose 2½ times, whereas the rate for women with husbands and with children under 6 rose by more than a factor of 3.[1] Almost half of all women workers have no husband, although many have children to support. These are the divorced, separated, and widowed as well as the never married. In addition, more than one-quarter of all women workers are married to men earning less than ten thousand dollars a year.[2] Both groups of women work out of dire economic necessity.

---

[1] Howard Hayghe, "The Effect of Unemployment on Family Incomes in 1977," *Monthly Labor Review*, 102 (February 1978).

[2] Esther Wattenberg and Hazel Reinhardt," Female-Headed Families: Trends and Implications," *Social Work*, 24 (November 1979), pp. 460–467.

Contributing to the economic pressures on women to enter the labor force is the failure of the support payment system to assist divorced or separated women heading a family. In a recent study, only 3 percent of all eligible female-headed families received enough support or alimony to move the family above the poverty line.[3] Another study of applicants for Aid to Families with Dependent Children (AFDC) showed that half of the women who were eligible to receive child support or alimony did not, while those who did averaged thirteen hundred dollars per year.[4] Additional pressures probably result from an ever-rising level of economic expectation on the part of American families, as well as from the women's movement, which preaches self-fulfillment in work, among other tenets.

Degler reminds us that the stresses women face today have existed for thousands of years, as has the "female-headed household" in surprisingly large numbers.[5] However, the largest bulk of women workers in the past and in the present can in no way be described as having careers. They work in low-status, low-skilled, low-paying jobs that are most often in those occupations traditionally relegated to "women's work." About half of all women workers are in segregated occupations in which 75 percent or more of the workers are female. These include secretaries, waitresses, bookkeepers, nurses, school teachers, and, yes, social workers. Female-intensive occupations fall at the lowest end of the income scale for all occupations, and women in general are clustered in the lowest ranks of the job and pay hierarchy.[6] Last, we are all aware that in spite of a number of pieces of legislation forbidding discrimination in hiring, pay, or conditions of work based on sex, women still earn fifty-nine cents for every dollar earned for comparable work by a man. And that gap has remained unchanged for at least two decades.

Thus large numbers of women work out of economic necessity to support or help support themselves and their children. Given the data just described, we see the feminization of poverty as the number of female-headed households rises. In addition, the jobs women hold usually offer little in the way of satisfaction or personal growth. Most women also have two other full-time jobs: child care and housekeeping. Two-parent

---

[3]Martha Griffiths "Can We Still Afford Occupational Segregation?" in Martha Blaxall and Barbara Reagan, eds, *Women and the Workplace* (Chicago: University of Chicago Press, 1976).

[4] Subcommittee on Economic Growth and Stabilization, U.S. Congress Joint Economic Committee, Ninety-fifth Congress, First Session, *American Women Workers in a Full Employment Economy: Compendium of Papers* (Washington, D.C.: U.S. Government Printing Office, 1977), p. 3.

[5] Carl Degler, *At Odds: Women and the Family in America from the Revolution to the Present* (New York: Oxford University Press, 1980).

[6] Griffiths, op. cit.; and Subcommittee on Economic Growth and Stabilization, op. cit.

households may or may not share the tasks related to these jobs in a way the members deem equitable, but one-parent families have no such option concerning a division of labor. One can begin to see the array of social work and social welfare efforts that may be prompted by this picture. These range from helping family members work out a division of family maintenance tasks and leisure time, to fighting for increased funds for developing a greater number of child care resources at affordable prices, to fighting for equity in pay and working conditions, to seeking more adequate AFDC programs in which clients received services in a less demeaning way.

Poor women seeking jobs, more well-to-do women seeking careers, and any woman moving into a field traditionally dominated by men face common problems of discrimination in getting a job, a promotion, and adequate pay; sexual harassment; strains concerning sex roles and sexual stereotypes; difficulties with colleagues at work; and friction among family members as all try to cope with new roles and added tasks. These are all areas in which social workers can be helpful if they are sensitive to the issues raised by the extent to which woman are working—and must work—outside the home. It is not surprising that women facing all these stresses are predominately the users of social services. The reader is asked to consider the article by Harrison, Kilpatrick, and Vance within this context.

Industrial Social Work: Influencing the System at the Workplace

Sheila H. Akabas

Social work faces a turbulent world, indeed, a world in which resources decline while demand for services rises, a world that heaps scorn on our profession for whatever is troubling society, with no credit for the services that have remedied the worst problems facing the aged, the abused, the disadvantaged, and the ill. Is it any wonder that the profession is in turmoil and filled with self-doubt? In industrial social work, this self-doubt is expressed in a debate as to whether or not social work belongs in the world of work, and if so, what its role should be. The author's views, based on many years of experience in the field, are that not only does social work belong in the world of work, but also that it is no more dangerous a turf than many other settings in which we practice. Rather, it is an ideal place to carry out our dual goals of direct service and system change. In fact, it may serve as the profession's vehicle for capturing the resources and attention its mission warrants.

This article will review some of the historical and contextual issues in industrial social work, define the conflict that seems to exist around practice in this arena, note the developments in mental health promotion that help social work achieve acceptance in the world of work, and, finally, suggest a model for social change based on that acceptance—acceptance of social workers as experts with skills of use to work organizations.

The concept that the practice of industrial social work might have a social change component is apparently a new idea. In the context of the 1960s, when this field of practice began to grow, many held that the professional role in the world of work should be restricted to individual direct service.[1] This was based on a realization that organizational change efforts, gone awry, had played a key role in aborting the development of

industrial social work in earlier decades. But it can be argued that the
1980s provide a new context that warrants expansion of industrial social
work's practice goals—expansion to social change. Indeed, our professional code of ethics, with its mandate that we be agents of both care and
change, allows us to do no less.

What follows uses a definition of industrial social work as practice at
the workplace or in direct contractual arrangement with workplace organizations. Work organizations, either employers or trade unions, represent the usual sponsoring auspices for industrial social work programs.
The service delivery programs themselves are targeted primarily at the
100 million members of the labor force in their status as workers. Many
industrial social work efforts also provide services to family members in
their status as dependents of covered employees. Attention may also be
directed at helping populations outside the world of work (such as the
disabled and unemployed) in their effort to gain entry into that world.
Services may vary from those intended to remedy specific problems such
as substance abuse, inadequate educational preparation, or physical or
emotional handicaps, to those that encompass care for the full range of
human problems.

Likewise, the intervention goal may range from job maintenance to
general well-being; from tertiary rehabilitation to education and prevention. Modalities, too, encompass the spectrum of options available to the
profession. The definition covers, as well, the situations in which the
interaction between social policy and the organizational actors—trade
unions and employers—are at issue.[2] Included are such functions as community economic development, legislative analysis, occupational social
welfare benefit planning, and corporate philanthropy. In short, the turf
for industrial social work comprises those policy, planning, and service
delivery activities at the intersection of social work and the world of work.
This developing and expanding field of practice has achieved the critical
mass necessary to assure its survival. The question to be explored here is
the nature of that survival—or, practice for what?

Historical and Contextual Issues

The world of work has experienced marked changes in recent decades,
the culmination of forces that have been in motion for some time. The
majority of workers in the United States now produce services rather
than goods, perhaps requiring different effort and attitude from workers
than what was necessary when they were machine-paced. Furthermore,
the number of women who work has changed drastically. Married women
and mothers are most likely to be in the labor force, sharpening within
the workplace our realization that the idea of separate worlds—of work

and family—is only a myth.[3] The work organization has changed as well. Family businesses or single-unit employers (and even more so, family farms) have given way to large bureaucratic organizations that are certainly multisite, and often multinational, in character. The workplace is bureaucratized, and its responsiveness to individual need has declined accordingly. Finally, fewer worksites have a mediating force between worker and management because the proportion of workplaces that have unions representing the labor force has fallen.

Some might suggest that these changes combine to cause present problems of low and shoddy productivity from American workers, that shoddiness is the product of uncaring and alienated workers who are too far separated from the consumers of their production. It is important for the worker to understand the consumer's needs. (For example: a hunter is unlikely to make a poor arrow if he knows he may have to use it against an oncoming, angry wild beast.) We can call both labor and management to task—labor because they bargained away management's right to fire for botched work; management because they did not care how long any particular product lasted—in fact, planned obsolescence is the order of the day.

Thus, although some twenty years ago it seemed logical that social workers should help individuals and not meddle in organizational issues to change systems, today such a position is insupportable. The world, today, is in worse shape than twenty years ago, and it is in worse shape, at least in part, because it is handling badly the very issues and problems at which social workers are expert. The potential exists for change based on the profession's mutual interests with the world of work.[4]

Nor is it so new for social workers to be entering the world of work. A look at the profession's historical experience confirms that we have always recognized work as important in people's lives.[5] It comes as no surprise that the Vaillants in their research should have found that the capacity and willingness to work in adolescence is the most predictive of a host of variables correlated with adult well-being.[6] Besides having the word "work" in their professional title, social workers have a history of concern about people in their roles as workers. Principles established by Freud (the ability to love and to work as the two hallmarks of adult functioning), Erikson (the significance of mastery in the development of self-image), and Robert W. White (the sense of "effectance" and competence resulting from organized activity) all tell us of the significance of work in human well-being.

Social work's support of full employment, vocational rehabilitation, and manpower training attests to the profession's political identification with job outcomes. In fact, the connection between social work and the world of work has been constant, sometimes as trusted ally (as during the Great Depression, when social workers realized that, alone, they could not solve the extensive nature of client problems and developed liaisons with trade unions); sometimes as rejected intruder (as when the early "ladies of charity" judgmentally refused to feed the families of strikers and earned the lasting wrath of the incipient trade union movement); and sometimes as neutral outsider (as when the profession turned itself inward with a psychoanalytic approach not compatible with the needs of work institutions or their potential client populations).[7]

Area of Conflict

Through this lengthy history of contact between social work and the world of work, one theme has been consistent: the ongoing epidemic of breast-beating as some of the profession's conscience-stricken spokespersons struggle with their unaccustomed alliance with power. There *are* problems inherent in this, as in any practice arena. It is possible that high wages and sumptuous corporate dining rooms or the ideological rhetoric of unions can co-opt social workers from their commitment to objective professional practice. But this author believes that the "conscience-stricken . viewers with alarm" show too little confidence in our professional behavior and, therefore, overstate the case and cause for alarm.

Consider an article by Bakalinsky in a prominent journal. Even the title is pejorative: "People vs. Profits: Social Work in Industry."[8] By posing an either/or situation, she eliminates the possibility that both can exist simultaneously. She has not learned what the Japanese have discovered: that people are responsible for profits. The secret behind profits may not be for the world of work to become a social welfare organization, but it is surely for the world of work to value highly and care effectively for its human beings. The Japanese have achieved high productivity not by capital investment in plant and equipment (their per capita investment is less than ours) but by capital investment in developing the skill, knowledge, and commitment of its work force.

Illiteracy is less than 1 percent in Japan. Proportionally, they train ten engineers to every one we train. Their workers have interchangeable skills rather than sharing a division of labor with a machine. When an auto company was having trouble selling cars, it did not place workers on indefinite layoff, but sent the factory personnel out selling. Who can sell a car better than the person who makes it? In Lincoln, Nebraska, when a Japanese motorcycle company experienced a slowdown in demand, they loaned their paid workers to the city—no forced unemployment for people whom they wanted to count on for future skill and commitment. These companies are extremely profitable. The issue is *not* people versus profits.

We should not reject work organizations. It is too easy to hide behind an assessment of value incongruence. Certainly, in our work with unions and employing organizations, we cannot ally ourselves with the formal power of management when they would deny the interests of less powerful persons in the work system. Yet neither should our latent message be, "We dare you to show us that you care about people."

A good example of such a message appeared in the literature after Skidmore and others wrote their historic piece on the social work project at the Kennecott Copper Corporation.[9] A social work journal carried a comment by Jacobson questioning whether professionals ought to be working in a setting that (1) engages in strip mining, (2) has been ordered to reduce pollutant emissions at some of its sites, (3) dominates the copper industry in Chile, and (4) has limited ecological concern.[10] The article implied that by delivering social services to employees working for Kennecott, the social workers were actively promoting these socially unacceptable practices. And, of course, Jacobson's answer to his question of "ought?" was "no."

Although sharing a concern over these practices by Kennecott, the present author suggests that Jacobson posed the wrong issues. At no point was he willing to deal with whether the services provided Kennecott workers had been needed and helpful to these workers (an important question for a "helping" profession), or why it would have been *better* to offer those same services (because one can assume that the profit-seeking employer would not have provided unneeded services) to those workers in the community at public expense rather than at the worksite at corporate expense. Improvement in its workers' well-being (and, therefore, the quality of its labor force) would accrue to Kennecott as those workers' employer in either event, whether services were provided in-house or in the community.

Two issues are important here. First, social workers are not omnipotent. We cannot control all the acts of our employers. Following Jacobson's argument to its logical conclusion, we should not work for the federal government because it is building a military arsenal; we should not work for state prison authorities because their institutions are frequently discriminatory and punitive; we should not work for counties because they often pay insufficient allowances to welfare clients. The point is clear: we do not require that all the actions of public employers pass stringent tests of humanism, and we cannot do so with corporations or unions either. The best we can expect is to assure that our own behavior meets the ethical standards we are pledged to uphold by our professional code of ethics.

The second issue is that if we want to change these organizations, we are more likely to do so from within than by our "oughts" registered from outside. Staying on the outside makes us feel good, but it does not allow us to accomplish our professional objectives; nor does it permit us to influence one of the most significant sectors of the American community today.

We need to act in work organizations as we do elsewhere, ethically and wisely. Clearly, we do not want management to become more profitable at the expense of workers. Clearly, we have a responsibility to speak out if an action is perceived as wrong, destructive, or unacceptable. But in the world of work, as in any setting, if we follow good professional practice, that is, if we assess organizational readiness for change and then develop recommendations based on an adequate understanding of the organization and, its needs, we may be able to influence the system toward the very goals that tend to elude us elsewhere.

In the world of work organizations, as everywhere, change requires patience. But time is on our side. If we partialize goals, we can develop an attainable agenda. Over time, sufficient trust will develop to advance that agenda and to expand the attainable as well.

Mental Health Promotion

Germain has suggested a social work mission appropriate to the world of work: to see individuals and their environments as inseparable, constituting a transacting system, with the goal of practice being not only "to be concerned about individuals and their capacity for human relatedness, autonomy, spontaneity, and active participation," but to structure "environments that will nourish these qualities."[11] Examples of working with the system to achieve these goals abound.

Consider a workplace where the company was concerned about alcoholism among its employees. The analysis of a team of consultants indicated that the setting had adopted a "culture of drinking."[12] Socialization of new workers into the setting involved drinking together at lunch, then camping in the nearby bar after work. "Just one more before you leave" was the nightly injunction. "Drying out" was perceived as antisocial. The company's alcoholism prevention program was a failure. A substitute culture had to be developed to replace the norm of alcoholism. The consultants recommended installing an electronic game area on the premises with the use of staggered lunch periods, so there would be room for everyone. A recreational program of intramural sports was also instituted. The junior high school near the plant opened its gym to workers after hours, and a local YM-YWHA in an area near many workers' homes made facilities available to the group on Saturday mornings. A countervailing culture seems to have been produced. The workers' view of management has changed from seeing them as monitors to enablers. Some employees have begun to play basketball instead of drinking, and although it is too early to conclude anything, the system may be on the road to change.

Other accomplishments in the workplace represent significant systemic change. For example, social workers in the personal services unit of a city civil service workers' union determined that many people were coming to them for help in qualifying for social security disability benefits when short-term disability benefits ran out and the people remained unable to return to work. The professionals recognized that earlier intervention might return more persons to work and at least would mitigate the crisis of having to prepare documents for long-term disability eligibility at the last moment. [13]

Research uncovered that a major proportion of those drawing short-term disability did so for less than one month. For those disabled longer than thirty days, serious psychological, social, and financial problems could be predicted. An intervention has been developed whereby the insurance carrier alerts the personal services unit of all claimants drawing benefits for more than thirty days. A social worker contacts such individuals and assures them that their benefits are secure. At the same time, the social worker offers the new claimants—who still think of themselves as workers—an opportunity to explore issues around both present care and future return to work.

The results of this early contact between social worker and claimants are remarkable. As they explore new options together, better decisions are made. The social worker may encourage the workplace to accommodate the disabled (both through structural and attitudinal changes) or may increase the workers' investment in returning to their prior work. Long-term disability applications, now reduced in number, are expedited. In short, the *system*, and the way it deals with the disabled, has changed because "private troubles" were made into "public issues" and were then redressed. [14] The gain to management is considerable in that few financial losses are greater in magnitude than are those resulting from the premature and unnecessary retirement on pension of a productive worker. Furthermore, in the grapevine around the city in which this program was instituted, other individuals and organizations have heard about the change. Diffusion of innovation has occurred as similar systems have adopted the early rehabilitation intervention model. [15]

Thus, the world of work can be seen as a functional community in which it is possible to deliver destigmatized, universal services to 100 million individuals and influence organizations in a way that will enhance systemic responsiveness to people and their lives. [16] The following discussion focuses on how this might be done.

Potential for Social Change

Social workers' entry into the world of work usually comes based on that world's need for—and the workers' ability to provide—direct service to constituent populations. We are not being hired to, and we do not begin by intending to, change systems. But by providing direct service—and doing it well—change occurs on many levels.

First, our very existence in-house causes change because introducing a new function serves to change any organization. Second, by doing our job well we create pressure for more service (another organizational change). It is noteworthy that more and more programs open and few if any close. Third, by adopting an ecosystems practice approach that involves engaging systems in benign, and possibly helpful, interventions with and for our clients, we begin to develop alliances in the workplace, engaging others in helping us do our job (with the implicit agreement that they can count on help from us in doing their jobs). Thus, without purposeful planning, we begin to remodel the work organization. The transition to the role of organizational change agent is almost inevitable.

But we have a tendency to become impatient. Unwisely, we expect organizational change to occur at a fast pace. As social workers, we may come into the workplace with a vision. But as with individual clients, we need to wait until the workplace is ready for our vision—or we may lose it. We need to bring along certain individuals, powerful and otherwise, before we can hope to change work organizations. Brager and Holloway's formulation that low-ranking people have power seems relevant to social work in the workplace.[17] They point out the conditions under which power can be exerted, including (1) selection of realizable goals, (2) analysis of the forces involved in the present equilibrium, (3) identification of forces that could be changed to shift the existing balance, and (4) the use of structural and technological interventions, as well as people-changing interventions, to achieve goals.

Given these conditions, Resnick has suggested a relevant model—changing organizations from within.[18] The three elements of a change effort include (1) a catalyst (the industrial social worker), (2) an action system (every union and employing organization has a mini system of human services that can be the foundation for such an action system), and (3) a clearly defined goal. Resnick, too, cautions of the need for time and patience. The change agent must understand the organization well, have identified an action system, and be aware of sources of resistance (including being ready to abandon a goal if too much resistance is identified).

In the workplace, possible goals can range from gaining insurance coverage for outpatient mental health care to initiating a flextime system; from developing a voucher system for day care to providing training to supervisors on performance reviews; from developing a new policy on corporate giving to instituting a requirement for advance notification on required overtime. Since change requires effective communication and extensive interactional work, social workers by training and inclination have a natural advantage in efforts to achieve change within a world of work organization. In fact, the industrial social worker can become the informal, in-house consultant for organizational change.

Research suggests that success in implementation of a consultant's innovation recommendations is directly correlated with the consultant's level of expert knowledge, understanding of the particular setting or organization to which the innovation is to be applied, and support of those who have to implement the innovation.[19] Consultation is the natural work of a social worker. The subject matter of human resource management and social responsibility is our turf. There are at least three important reasons why social workers can predict greater success today than at previous times in initiating changes as "in-house" consultants in the world of work: (1) the world of work's use of experts is high, (2) the interest of the world of work in the issues about which social workers are expert is strong, and (3) the growth in training industrial social workers means that there are social workers being educated about the specific nature of world of work organizations. In sum, it is reasonable to conclude that an organizational change designed to improve the world of work's responsiveness to human beings and their needs both within the workplace and in the community in general is not only feasible but is actually being accomplished by social workers in labor and industrial settings.

This recital—and expanded view of the possible—would be incomplete without a warning as well. A great deal is at stake in the world of work settings. For many clients, their future employment, ability to maintain their families financially, sense of self, and status and accomplishments are all on the line. The world of work lacks norms of professional behavior and confidentiality that we hold as our basic professional responsibility. We always walk a tightrope there, and must be mindful, in the extreme, of protecting individual confidentiality, recognizing that work institutions are not concerned primarily with human well-being.[20] We may be disappointed in our change effort. We may not help all the individuals who come to us.

Where we currently stand, on balance, however, is much more positive than negative. The world of work is becoming more complex. The necessity of complying with government regulations, learning to maintain a labor force, and dealing with problems related to technological change and economic losses has confirmed the need of work organizations for experts in human resource management. One can discern a pronounced trend among employing organizations and trade unions toward utilizing the specialization of social work to deal with human problems.[21] To professionals with a duality of objectives—direct service and social change— the world of work may not offer license to try to change the world, but it does offer the opportunity to use professional technology to analyze and understand the workplace and to set in motion a process that involves incremental progress toward making that world a different—and better— place for people. This, indeed, is the promise of industrial social work.

Notes and References

1. Hyman J. Weiner, Sheila H. Akabas, and John J. Sommer, *Mental Health Care in the World of Work* (New York: Association Press, 1973).

2. Paul A. Kurzman and Sheila H. Akabas, "Industrial Social Work as an Arena for Practice," *Social Work,* 26 (January 1981), pp. 52–60; and Akabas and Kurzman, "The Industrial Social Welfare Specialist: What's So Special?" in Akabas and Kurzman, *Work, Workers, and Work Organization: A View from Social Work* (Englewood Cliffs, N.J.: Prentice-Hall, 1982), chap. 9.

3. Rosabeth Moss Kanter, *Work and Family in the United States: A Critical Review and Agenda for Research and Policy* (New York: Russell Sage Foundation, 1977).

4. Daniel D. Cook, "Companies Put Social Workers on the Payroll," *Industry Week,* 210 (September 21, 1981), pp. 73–74, 79.

5. Helen Harris Perlman, *Persona—Social Role and Personality* (Chicago: University of Chicago Press, 1968), chap. 3, pp. 59–86.

6. G. Vaillant and C. Vaillant, "Natural History of Male Psychological Health: Work as Predictor of Positive Mental Health," *American Journal of Psychiatry,* 139 (1981), pp. 1433–1440.

7. Sheila H. Akabas, "Labor: Social Policy and Human Services," *Encyclopedia of Social Work,* Vol. 1 (17th issue; Washington, D.C.: National Association of Social Workers, 1977), pp. 737–744.

8. Rosalie Bakalinsky, "People vs. Profits: Social Work in Industry," *Social Work,* 25 (November 1980), pp. 471–475.

9. Rex A. Skidmore, Daniel Balsam, and Otto F. Jones, "Social Work Practice in Industry," *Social Work,* 19 (May 1974), pp. 280–286.

10. Robert Jacobson, "Industrial Social Work in Context," *Social Work,* 19 (November 1974), pp. 655–656.

11. Carel B. Germain, "An Ecological Perspective in Casework Practice," *Social Casework,* 54 (June 1973), pp. 323–330.

12. Michelle Fine, Sheila H. Akabas, and Susan Bellinger, "Cultures of Drinking: A Workplace Perspective," *Social Work,* 27 (September 1982), pp. 436–440.

13. Sheila H. Akabas, Michelle Fine, and Roslyn Yasser, "Putting Secondary Prevention to the Test: A Study of an Early Intervention Strategy with Disabled Workers," *Journal of Primary Prevention,* 2 (Spring 1982), pp. 165–187.

14. C. Wright Mills, *The Sociological Imagination* (New York: Columbia University Press, 1959), p. 8.

15. Ila Jarvikowski, *Early Rehabilitation at the Workplace* (New York: World Rehabilitation Fund, 1980).

16. Sheila H. Akabas, "The World of Work: A Site for Mental Health Promotion," in Felice Perlmutter, ed., *New Direction for Mental Health Services: Mental Health Promotion and Primary Prevention* (San Francisco: Jossey-Bass, 1982), pp. 33–44.

17. George Brager and Stephen Holloway, *Changing Human Service Organizations* (New York: Free Press, 1978).

18. Herman Resnick, "Tasks in Changing the Organization from Within," in Resnick and Rino J. Patti, eds., *Change from Within* (Philadelphia: Temple University Press, 1980), pp. 200–216.

19. "Studies of Program Consultation in Community Mental Health Centers," in *Consultation*, 1 (Fall 1981), pp. 57–58.

20. Sheila H. Akabas, Susan Bellinger, Michelle Fine, and Richard Woodrow, *Confidentiality Issues in Workplace Settings* (New York: Industrial Social Welfare Center, Columbia University School of Social Work, 1981).

21. Sheila H. Akabas and Seth A. Akabas, "Social Services at the Workplace: New Resource for Management," *Management Review*, 71 (May 1982), pp. 15–20.

Social Work Practice with Dual-Career Middle-Class Families

Dianne F. Harrison
Allie C. Kilpatrick
Patricia V. Vance

Amidst the turbulence in U.S. society, the family has not remained untouched. Social workers have increasingly witnessed profound changes in family structure ranging from single-parent to blended-family households, all of which require innovative practice efforts. Primarily during the past few decades, the dual-career family structure has emerged as another significant form of family life requiring the attention of the social work profession.

The term "dual-career family" was coined by Rapoport and Rapoport to define the type of family in which both heads of household pursue careers and at the same time maintain a family life together.[1] In this definition, "career" is used to indicate sequences of occupational jobs that are developmental in character and that require a continuous and high degree of commitment. "Family" is defined as involving at least a marital pair and one child living as a domestic unit.

The concept of the dual-career family has theoretical significance and empirical validity in three contexts: (1) the relationships between family and occupation, (2) variant patterns in the social change process, and (3) sex-role issues in contemporary society. Inherent in all three of these contexts are stresses and strains that can appear as families develop structures that meet their needs but that have few societal supports. Because dual-career families are by definition two-income families, a majority of these households are in the middle or upper economic class. This article focuses primarily on such families. The reader should be aware, however, that many working-class families manage dual careers.

142

All these contexts are indicative of changes in a turbulent society. The increasing incidence of dual-career families is likely to continue given the growth in rates of higher education and in employment opportunities for women, together with greater societal acceptability of this type of family structure. Social work must address itself to this phenomenon.

This article reviews the historical development of the concept of dual-career families with their inherent characteristics, stresses and strains, and gains and rewards. Social work practice issues are discussed with particular emphasis on assessment and treatment. Finally, implications for social work education and actual agency practice are presented.

Historical Review

Development of the concept of the dual-career family has been divided into phases that describe three generations of research. The Rapoports have labeled these as (1) the precursor, (2) the pivotal, and (3) the third generations.[2]

The Precursor Generation

The precursor generation lasted until the late 1960s and focused attention on changes in sex roles. Researchers in this period did not use the concept of the dual-career family and did not use family structure as a central organizing concept. The studies of Fogarty, Rapoport and Rapoport; Nye and Hoffman; and Gavron did, however, make it clear that a formulation of the concept of dual-career family was needed.[3]

The Pivotal Generation

During the pivotal generation, from 1969 through 1973, the concept of dual-career family emerged and issues associated with its functioning were outlined. Particular issues described included characteristics of dual-career families, stresses and strains, and gains and rewards.

Characteristics. Several early family experiences have been found that may predispose certain individuals to seek combinations of domestic and occupational involvements. These individuals include: only or first children; girls who were their "father's sons"; people whose mothers worked (particularly those whose mothers enjoyed working); boys who had a particularly warm relationship with their mothers, thus making them perhaps more empathic and responsive to the needs of women; and people who had some elements of tension in their family background that paralleled the high tension level found in dual-career families.[4]

Other reported characteristics of dual-career families are (1) the mesh of a husband's responsiveness to his wife's needs with the wife's reliance on her husband's support and approval and (2) the emphasis on occupations as a primary source of personal fulfillment. In general, dual-career families were found to be more egalitarian and modern in sex-role attitudes and to have a greater capacity for departing from traditional family roles than families without dual careers.[5]

Stresses and Strains.   All the studies during this period emphasized the stressful character of maintaining the dual-career family pattern under the circumstances prevailing in the 1960s. These stresses were conceptualized as (1) dilemmas evolving from: overload (both emotional and physical); normative values in violation of internalized norms from childhood socialization (such as the belief that mothers should stay at home with their children); role-cycling (demands of occupational roles of husband or wife versus their family roles); networking (many couples cannot sustain the kind of social relationships that their more conventional friends and relatives expect); and identity (centering around sex-role changes, variations, trade-offs, status, amount of money earned, amount of education, and what name the wife is to use), (2) conflicts between earlier and later norms, home and work expectations, and ideals and actual feelings, (3) barriers such as domestic isolation and sex-role prejudices and stereotypes, and (4) problems such as the inability of the wife to find an appropriate job with enough flexibility to accommodate domestic requirements, competing with members of the opposite sex, keeping personal aspirations within limits that the marriage can tolerate, and arranging domestic help and child-care services.[6]

Several studies suggested that the wives in dual-career families bear a disproportionate share of the burdens of stress management. Poloma, for example, identified four stress- and tension-management techniques used by dual-career wives in particular.[7] These techniques were making a favorable definition of the dual-career situation (emphasizing the advantages rather than the pitfalls); clarifying values (establishing that in conflict situations the family demands take precedence); compartmentalizing (keeping work anxieties and conflicts out of the home as much as possible); and compromising (resolving differences between their ideal career aspirations and reality).

A new concept identified was that of "tension lines" consisting of points beyond which individuals feel they cannot be pushed except at risk to themselves or the marital relationship. Tension lines were considered inevitable in that, along with tremendous stress, the dual-career pattern had no models or social supports. Families create their own coping patterns through sensitivity to family tension lines.[8]

Gains and Rewards.   Most of the studies emphasized the advantages of dual-career families. Financial gains were one advantage, although most families paid highly for support services such as child care. The gains felt by wives were more in terms of self-realization. Husbands valued wives who were seen as developing and fulfilling themselves and who were also manifesting an egalitarian pattern of which husbands approved.[9]

The Third Generation

In the third generation, extending from 1974 to the present, studies are more diverse than previously in methods and objectives. The research completed during this period reflects the specialized interests of academic, policymaking, feminist, and therapeutic orientations. Findings from a variety of studies that are of special interest to social workers include (1) the occupational system's characteristic rigidity, demands, and male biases have stressful impacts on dual-career families; (2) separations, commuting, and job-sharing can be handled without destroying the marital relationship; (3) geographical mobility on the part of husbands has a deleterious effect on career-oriented wives, but wives' wishes and interests are ineffectual in the situation; (4) societal norms are in a stage of "lip-service" democracy with respect to equity in sex roles; (5) dual-career wives who are married to fellow professionals are more work-productive than career wives who are not married to fellow professionals; (6) family values are significant as intervening variables in the acceptance of unconventional patterns by husband and wife; and (7) perhaps only a "superwoman" can successfully combine a professional career, marriage, and motherhood given current cultural norms.[10]

Several researchers have used the concept of life stages in their studies. In their reinvestigation of women originally interviewed in 1969, Poloma and associates explored patterns of career development for women and identified four major career types: regular career, interrupted career, second career, and modified second career, each related to the developmental stages of the children in the family.[11]

Treatment Issues: Assessment and Intervention

The preceding section has identified characteristics and sources of stress related to the dual-career lifestyle. The purpose of the following section is to provide social workers with brief guidelines for the assessment and treatment of dual-career couples and families who seek professional help.

Assessment

As suggested earlier, stressors that can plague the dual-career family may originate (1) outside the family system (on the job or with relatives); (2) within the family itself (in the marital relationship); or (3) with individual family members (growing out of each spouse's values and behaviors).

Each of the potential sources of stress may interact with and exacerbate the strains created by the other stress areas.

The present authors have previously described specific techniques for analyzing these sources of stress, recommending a multimethod approach to assessment—an approach that involves not only interviews with the family, but observations, self-report questionnaires, and at-home behavioral monitoring.[12] The present discussion, based on clinical experience and recent literature on problems of dual-career couples, will review typical areas of difficulty that the social worker should be aware of and attend to during assessment.[13]

Couples seeking treatment may initially complain of conflicts that include problems in one or more of the following areas: division of labor; lack of spouse support; lack of time for children, spouse, self, or career; an inadequate child care system; guilt or anxiety regarding perceived failures as parents; lack of sexual desire or interest; and feelings of alienation or actual withdrawal from the marital relationship. In addition to such presenting complaints, the social worker should review several other possible problem areas. For example, their further investigation may reveal the existence of some degree of unspoken competition between spouses or of conflict related to the distribution of power within the marital relationship.[14]

Basic differences in values, interests, or desires may be exacerbated by external pressures (such as those related to health or religion) and by dual-career pressures.[15] The social worker should assess the couple's communication and problem-solving skills, noting in particular their ability and willingness to be direct, open, and flexible in stating their own needs and meeting those of their partner. The couple's previous coping mechanisms and problem-resolution styles can be determined through such techniques as self-disclosure by the clients, role-playing, and observation.

As in any marital or family difficulty, the personality traits and psychological predispositions of the individuals involved will be important influences in the extent and duration of the conflict.[16] As Rice noted, dual-career couples are typically verbal, intelligent, achievement-oriented, perfectionistic, and likely to rely on cognitive analysis for problem solving.[17] As a result, in anxiety and conflict situations they are more prone to defend their positions through intellectualization, rationalization, and isolation of affect from thought processes.[18] Such individuals may also depend a great deal on external reinforcers (such as job advancement) for self-esteem. If such reinforcers are threatened by pressures within the home, a tremendous amount of conflict may result.

Another area that the social worker should assess with dual-career couples is the degree of Type A behavior manifested.[19] The Type A personality is characterized by a sense of urgency, competitiveness, and impatience, which may be intensified by the structure and nature of dual-career families and result in increased stress and incidence of both physical and emotional difficulties. People with Type B personalities are typically more relaxed than those with Type A qualities and tend to react to internal and external stressors with less anxiety and more sense of control and thus would presumably have fewer physical and emotional difficulties. It may be that the dual-career lifestyle fosters Type A behavior in individuals who, under different circumstances, exhibit Type B behavior. The Activity Survey of Jenkins and associates is a helpful tool for estimating the degree of Type A behavior.[20]

Intervention

Following initial assessment, the worker should direct the couple in defining and prioritizing problems and concerns. The present authors have previously advocated a systems perspective for both assessment and treatment.[21] Using this model, the point of intervention is determined by weighting the ideals with the practical solution, and early intervention is directed at the largest possible system level (such as job pressure or child care) to eliminate at least one source of stress, diffuse any crisis reaction, and "buy time" to devote to more involved individual or joint problems.

Rice suggests that an overall treatment principle with dual-career couples should be to establish (or reestablish) some sense of equity within the marital relationship.[22] Several treatment techniques can be used to help accomplish this major objective and other goals that the couple and social worker may seek. As a starting point for problem solving, the majority of couples can probably benefit from training in communication and listening skills. Learning to specify and assert one's needs and expectations and to understand the other's point of view can facilitate discussions about competition, power distribution, and division of labor. It is important during such training that the social worker encourage the expression of both affective and cognitive content.

The social worker should also attempt in the beginning of treatment, prior to problem solving if possible, to accelerate the exchange of positive reinforcers between spouses.[23] This can be done by arranging to have the couple spend time alone together, encouraging them to share pleasing behavior in nonconflict areas, and suggesting to the couple that they schedule "love and caring" days whenever possible.[24] These activities can create a more positive atmosphere for later problem solving.

Once communication skills have been taught or improved and a positive atmosphere has been established, various strategies for enhancing problem-solving abilities can be utilized. Several authors have described

general techniques for conflict resolution that involve (1) defining sources
of conflict, (2) determining what the couple will agree to in terms of
resolution, (3) specifying new behaviors required, (4) reviewing alternative strategies, (5) implementing a plan, and (6) evaluating the outcome.[25]
It may be that the couple's original marriage contract requires revision
with respect to each spouse's goals and expectations. This general problem-solving model can be used for such revisions.

More specific skills may be needed in the management of time and
stress to conquer the "overload" and Type A problems. In these areas,
the couple can be assigned to read several popular books to augment the
social worker's efforts.[26] Seidan, in describing time management techniques for dual-career couples, also suggests using Gordon's Parent Effectiveness Training model as a "no-lose" method for resolving conflicts
without initiating power struggles.[27]

As noted earlier, a common area of concern for dual-career parents is
the effect of their lifestyle on children. This may be manifested in guilt
or anxiety (usually on the part of the mother) or in both parents developing feelings of failure with respect to child rearing and family relationships. Research findings indicate that such parents can be reassured by
the social worker that children in dual-career families thrive best when
their parents are satisfied with their work lives and child care arrangements and when the caretaker is stable and responsive.[28]

It is also helpful, at times, to restructure the children's attitude toward
the stress of the dual-career family.[29] Understanding the contributions
parents make through their careers and the rewards that both parents
and children reap as a result can lessen resentful attitudes on the part of
children and foster more supportive reactions.

Finally, it is especially important that the social worker's own values
toward dual-career issues (such as whether mothers with young children
should work or whether fathers should help equitably in household tasks)
be carefully examined so that such values will not interfere with or dictate
the treatment process. Because many dual-career issues are gender oriented, both male and female social workers may be perpetrators of value-
laden and biased treatment. Rice suggests using cotherapists of each sex
as a way of avoiding these potential problems.[30]

The preceding suggestions have been offered as brief guidelines for
working with dual-career families and will necessarily be subject to change
depending on clients' unique situations and reactions, cultural influences,
the therapist's skills, and the time and resources available in a given
agency. The scant literature available on the treatment of dual-career
families is based primarily on clinical and personal experiences. More
research is needed that empirically evaluates the effectiveness of various

treatment strategies that have been proposed as well as the relationships between the characteristics of individuals and couples and the outcome of treatment. As the incidence of this type of family structure increases, the need for social work intervention will correspondingly increase. Social workers should be prepared for this population with empirically tested, empirically sound treatment regimes.

Implications for Education and Training

If the profession of social work is to be responsive to the needs of dual-career families, practitioners must be prepared to provide appropriate services to them. One step in this direction is through curriculum offerings in schools of social work and in programs of agency staff development and in-service training.

Curriculum Content

A number of factors are converging to heighten the sensitivity of social work educators and agency practitioners and trainers to issues such as sex-role stereotyping, the changing roles of women, and the unique stresses of dual-career marriages. Standards for the accreditation of social work programs now address sex discrimination, and schools are advised through guidelines of the Accreditation Commission of the Council on Social Work Education (CSWE) to be certain that the curriculum achieves the elimination of sex-role stereotyping.[31] National Association of Social Workers (NASW) Standards for Social Work Personnel Practices revised in 1975 now include standards on affirmative action and nondiscrimination.[32] Two of social work's major professional associations—the CSWE Commission on the Role and Status of Women and the NASW National Committee on Women's Issues—have developed vehicles to promote women's interests and increase awareness of inequities and problems. Only social workers who have been completely isolated over the last decade could remain unaffected by the women's movement and the profession's efforts to raise practitioners' consciousness. Such awareness is an early step in the process of improving social work curricula and agency training materials.

Once committed to the need to address the potential stresses inherent in emerging family structures, how does the social work educator proceed? The traditional alternatives in academe are to develop a new course or to insert content in relevant areas throughout the curriculum (or to do both). An example of the new course is "Socialization and Stress in the Female Life Cycle," which is taught at The Florida State University.[33] Particular attention is paid in this course to the role of women in dual-career marriages. As students learn to understand the dynamics of such relationships and the ways to handle probable stresses, they will be better prepared to work with clients in these situations and also to handle their own life situations should they become partners in dual-career marriages.

It is also appropriate for faculty members to introduce supplementary materials into existing courses that they teach. Each of the prescribed curriculum areas in social work programs (such as human behavior and the social environment, social work practice, social policy, research, and field instruction) is appropriate for the inclusion of materials regarding dual-career families. Some writers are now addressing this subject, but the authors of this article have found that only occasionally is the matter handled in depth in social work textbooks.

The area of human behavior may serve as an example of what can be done. A common approach to the teaching of behavior is the concept of the life cycle or life-span development, which lends itself well to the inclusion of material regarding dual-career marriages as a new family structure to be studied. For example, Bloom presents a "life span development table" depicting "normative stages."[34] This lists, in the affective development of young adults aged 22 to 30, not only the emergence of psychological and social maturity but also social stresses in occupational area, family, and social life. He suggests:

> As greater numbers of women attain higher levels of education, and as better jobs become more available to them, fewer are likely to settle for traditional marriage and parenthood roles. In fact, some of the traditional patterns of homemaking and child care are on the way to becoming obsolete. They are largely based on nonpaid, small-unit, only partially mechanized hand labor, while the larger economy features wages and fringe benefits, mass production, and mechanization. As a result, home and family life have counterbalancing allures, but also maladaptive features—especially for wives and mothers.[35]

In another text on human development, Craig discusses the powerful socialization influence of the father who cares for the young child and points out that fathers are as capable of nurturing children as are mothers. She speaks of the dual-career situation:

> Working mothers must combine their traditional role as nurturer with their occupational or professional goals. Maternal employment often shifts some child-care and household responsibilities from wife to husband. This may cause marital stress. If both parents are pursuing careers as well as raising children, they must both make some compromises. Since it has only recently become commonplace for women to combine career and family, today's working women and their families cannot look to previous generations for role models. They must devise solutions to the many new problems they meet as they go along.[36]

Neither Bloom nor Craig expands much on the comments quoted here. The question of what to do with this information about the potential stresses and strains of dual-career marriages is left, appropriately perhaps, to other areas of the curriculum.

Courses on social work practice provide an appropriate forum for instruction on strategies for working with dual-career couples. With increasing frequency, new books in this area address such issues as sexism in social work practice, emerging new family patterns, the influence of the women's movement on the development of new treatment approaches, self-actualization of women, resocialization, and assertion training. However, it still remains for the individual instructor to draw upon a number of such resources to develop a comprehensive, organized body of material for teaching students how to intervene with the problems of the dual-career marriage.

Books on basic research methodology could use as examples and for illustration the employment of married women, the rise in numbers of dual-career couples, and the characteristics of dual-career families. Creative instructors may do so on their own, but the market awaits a research methods book that makes extensive use of such data.

Perhaps the greatest and most obvious need for strengthened resources on the topic of dual-career families is in the area of social welfare policy and services. Again, the diligent educator may find materials scattered across the field but not in an organized or comprehensive form. Field instruction materials are as diverse as the agencies offering field placements to students. There is scant evidence, however, that agencies are any more effective than educational institutions in preparing students to counsel dual-career couples; major responsibility typically rests with the field instructors and with students themselves for locating relevant materials if the case of a dual-career couple is assigned.

Administrative Practice

As has been pointed out earlier in this article, reduction of job pressures (eliminating the external or largest possible source of stress) would be a first approach in working with dual-career couples experiencing difficulty. It is critically important for the social work profession to monitor its own personnel practices and policies and to serve as an appropriate model for other fields of employment. This implies that administrators of social agencies (and of social work education programs) should strive to reduce stress for any dual-career employees on their staff. The authors have discussed previously the particular responsibility of schools of social work in developing a model milieu for dual-career couples employed in academe. Similarly, persons being trained for administrative positions in social agencies need to be sensitized to their potential role responsibility in relation to stress reduction for dual-career employees.

The following guidelines for social work administrators are illustrative of points that need to be considered:

1. Recruitment efforts should make it clear that both women and men are being sought for positions at all levels. Assumptions should not be made regarding a person's availability for a position based on the spouse's employment situation. Such assumptions fail to recognize the couple's right to be recruited independently.[37]

2. Initial salaries offered employees should be equitable; that is, persons with equivalent credentials should receive similar salary offers.

3. Assignments should afford employees equal opportunities to assume responsibility and receive recognition and promotions.

4. Consideration should be given to developing part-time positions as career options rather than as temporary exceptions.

5. Parental leave, not necessarily maternity leave, policies should be developed.

6. Sick leave or personal leave (with pay) should be available for either parent who needs to care for a sick child (an option often available only to mothers).

7. "Interrupted" employment policies need to be developed to allow a parent to "stop out" by design, during school holidays and summer vacation months, without jeopardizing the position.

8. "Flextime" should be allowed so that parents can plan coverage at home more effectively.

9. Decisions regarding hiring a professional couple should be made on the basis of their qualifications, considering their relationship only if one would have decision-making or supervisory authority over the other or where one partner's decisions might affect the other.

Interventions such as these at the level of the employment system could reduce stress in the lives of dual-career families. Innovative changes in administrative practices might ultimately reduce the number of couples needing direct intervention because of overwhelming stress at the individual level.

Conclusions and Suggestions for Future Research

An important contribution of the concept of the dual-career family is that it has provided a framework for analysis that extends beyond the individual to include the marital partner, children, and influential external systems (such as the job, relatives, and societal agents). Social work's response to dual-career families must be directed toward these various system points, encompassing not only clinical efforts but administrative, policymaking, organizational, and educational efforts as well. The profession's responses should be based on empirically acquired knowledge rather than simply based on anecdotal evidence or personal experience.

Existing research studies of dual-career families are primarily descriptive in nature, outlining characteristics and particular stresses and strains. Several areas and issues of concern require further study. More definitive analyses of the dual-career family structure as compared to other types of structures are needed. Attention should also be paid to the consequences of the dual-career structure on the individuals (job performance, role strain, coping mechanisms), the marital dyad (relationship satisfaction, problem-solving abilities), the family unit (child rearing, family developmental tasks), and the children (school performance, peer relationships).

The possible existence of a Type A family pattern that potentially exacerbates overload problems should be investigated. As suggested earlier, studies should be designed that evaluate the effectiveness of various interventive strategies as well as the relationships between the characteristics of individuals and couples and treatment outcome. Ingredients of successful dual-career family management, including inherent rewards and benefits, should be examined to provide models for families who are experiencing difficulties and as a basis for building social supports. Finally, it is equally critical that the profession of social work monitor and evaluate its own personnel policies and practices in areas related to the employment of dual-career family members.

Notes and References

1. Rhona Rapoport and Robert Rapoport, *Dual-Career Families Re-examined* (New York: Harper & Row, 1976).

2. Robert N. Rapoport and Rhona Rapoport, "Dual-Career Families: Progress and Prospects," *Marriage and Family Review*, 1 (1978), pp. 1–12.

3. M. P. Fogarty, Rhona Rapoport, and Robert Rapoport, *Women and Top Jobs: An Interim Report* (London, England: Political and Economic Planning, 1968); M. P. Fogarty, Rhona Rapoport and Robert Rapoport, *Sex, Career, and Family* (Beverly Hills: Sage Publications, 1971); F. E. Nye and Lynda W. Hoffman, eds., *The Employed Mother In America* (Chicago: Rand McNally & Co., 1963); and H. Gavron, *The Captive Wife: Conflicts of Housebound Mothers* (London: Routledge & Kegan Paul, 1966).

4. See A. C. Bebbinton, "The Function of Stress in the Establishment of the Dual-Career Family," *Journal of Marriage and the Family*, 35 (August 1973), pp. 530–537; T. Neal Garland, "The Better Half? The Male in the Dual-Profession Family," in M. C. Safilios-Rothschild, ed., *Toward A Sociology of Women* (Lexington, Mass.: Xerox, 1972); Lynda Lytle Holmstrom, *The Two-Career Family* (Cambridge, Mass.: Schenkman Publishing Co., 1972); and Rhona Rapoport and Robert Rapoport, *Dual-Career Families* (Middlesex, England: Penguin Books, 1971).

5. Rapoport and Rapoport, *Dual-Career Families;* and for a more thorough

review of the literature on characteristics of dual-career families, see Allie C. Kilpatrick, "Dual-Career Families: An Assessment of Consequences and Issues." Unpublished manuscript, Florida State University, 1980.

6. Rapoport and Rapoport, "Dual-Career Families: Progress and Prospects."

7. Margaret M. Poloma, "Role Conflict and the Married Professional Woman," in Safilios-Rothschild, ed., *Toward a Sociology of Women*.

8. Rapoport and Rapoport, "Dual-Career Families: Progress and Prospects."

9. Ibid. For a review of gains and rewards found in later studies, see Allie C. Kilpatrick, Dianne F. Harrison, Patricia V. Vance, and Daniel S. Montgomery, "Stress and Strains of Dual-Career Families: Implications for Social Work." Paper presented at the Fifth Annual Conference on Professional Social Work Development, Florida Chapter of the National Association of Social Workers, September 27, 1980, Hollywood-By-The-Sea, Florida.

10. See B. Rosen, T. H. Jerdle, and T. L. Prestrich, "Dual-Career Marital Adjustment: Potential Effects of Discriminatory Managerial Attitudes," *Journal of Marriage and the Family*, 37 (August 1975), pp. 565–572; A. Farris, "Community," in Rhona Rapoport and Robert N. Rapoport, eds., *Working Couples* (New York: Harper & Row, 1978); R. P. Duncan and C. C. Perrucci, "Dual Occupation Families and Migration," *American Sociological Review*, 41 (April 1976), pp. 252–261; J. Frost and A. Nordlund, "Sex Roles and Lip Service: Some Swedish Data," paper presented at the Eighth World Congress of Sociology, Toronto, Ont., Canada, August 1974; R. Bryson et al., "The Professional Pair: Husband and Wife Psychologist," *American Psychologist*, 31 (January 1976), pp. 10–16; C. D. Epstein, "Law Partners and Marital Partners: Strains and Solutions in the Dual Career Family Enterprise," *Human Relations*, 24 (December 1971), pp. 549–563; Rapoport and Rapoport, *Dual-Career Families Re-examined*; and Margaret M. Poloma, Brian F. Pendleton, and T. Neal Garland, "Reconsidering the Dual-Career Marriage: A Longitudinal Approach," *Journal of Family Issues*, 2 (June 1981), pp. 205–224.

11. Poloma, Pendleton, and Garland, op. cit.

12. Kilpatrick, Harrison, and Vance, op. cit.

13. For recent literature, see David G. Rice, *Dual Career Marriage, Conflict and Treatment* (New York: Free Press, 1979); Colleen L. Johnson and Frank A. Johnson, "Parenthood, Marriage, and Careers: Situational Constraints and Role Strain," pp. 143–161, and Charles Lawe and Barbara Lawe, "The Balancing Act: Coping Strategies for Emerging Family Lifestyles," pp. 191–203, in Fran Pepitone-Rockwell, ed., *Dual-Career Couples* (Beverly Hills, Calif.: Sage Publications, 1980).

14. Rice, op. cit.; and Anne M. Seidan, "Time-Management and the Dual-Career Couple," in Pepitone-Rockwell, ed., *Dual-Career Couples*, pp. 163–189.

15. Lawe and Lawe, op. cit.

16. Ibid.

17. Rice, op. cit.

18. Ibid, p. 97.

19. Meyer Friedman and Ray Rosenman, *Type A Behavior and Your Heart* (New York: Fawcett Books, 1974).

20. See C. D. Jenkins, R. H. Rosenman, and M. Friedman, "Development of an Objective Psychological Test for the Determination of the Coronary-Prone Behavior Pattern in Employed Men," *Journal of Chronic Diseases*, 20 (1967), pp. 371–379.

21. Kilpatrick, Harrison, and Vance, op. cit.

22. Rice, op. cit.

23. Neil S. Jacobson and B. Martin, "Behavioral Marriage Therapy: Current Status," *Psychological Bulletin, 83* (1976), pp. 540–556.

24. Richard B. Stuart, *Helping Couples Change: A Social Learning Approach to Marital Therapy* (Champaign, Ill.: Research Press, 1980), pp. 1–81.

25. See, for example, Neil S. Jacobson and Gayla Margolin, *Marital Therapy: Strategies Based on Social Learning and Behavior Exchange Principles* (New York: Brunner/Mazel, 1979); and Lawe and Lawe, op. cit.

26. See, for example, Martha Davis, Elizabeth Robbins Eshelman, and Matthew McKay, *The Relaxation and Stress Reduction Workbook* (Richmond, Calif.: New Harbinger Publications, 1980); Harold Greenwald, *Direct Decision Therapy* (San Diego, Calif.: EDITS Publishers, 1973); and Alan Lakein, *How to Get Control of Your Time and Your Life* (New York: Signet Books, 1973).

27. Seidan, op. cit.; and Thomas Gordon, *P.E.T.: Parent Effectiveness Training in Action* (New York: Bantam Books, 1978).

28. M. C. Howell, "Employed Mothers and Their Families—I," *Pediatrics,* 52 (August 1973), pp. 252–263. See also Mary Rowe, "Choosing Child Care: Many Options" in Pepitone-Rockwell, ed., *Dual-Career Couples,* pp. 89–99.

29. Kilpatrick, Harrison, and Vance, op. cit.

30. Rice, op. cit.

31. *Guidelines for Implementation of Accreditation Standards on Non-discrimination (Women)* (rev. ed.; New York: Council on Social Work Education, 1976). (Mimeographed.)

32. *NASW Standards for Social Work Personnel Practices,* Policy Statement No. 2 (Washington, D.C.: National Association of Social Workers, 1975), pp. 12–13.

33. See Leila C. Deasy, *Socialization and Stress in the Female Life Cycle.* Unpublished bibliography, Florida State University, Tallahassee, 1981.

34. Martin Bloom, *Life Span Development* (New York: Macmillan Publishing Co., 1980), p. 6.

35. Ibid., p. 290.

36. Grace Craig, *Human Development* (Englewood Cliffs, N.J.: Prentice-Hall, 1980).

37. Barbara S. Wallston, Martha A. Foster, and Michal Berger, "I Will Follow Him: Myth, Reality, or Forced Choice—Job-seeking Experiences of Dual-Career Couples," *Psychology of Women Quarterly,* 3 (January 1978), pp. 9–21.

A Transactional Model for Work with the Frail Elderly

Mario Tonti
Jordan I. Kosberg

It is undeniable that professionals in the human services will be in contact with an increasingly older population, be it in work with clients in agencies, patients in hospitals and other facilities, or participants in programs. This will come about as a result of the increasing number and proportion of elderly persons in the population as well as the increase in the median age in the United States to 35.5 years.[1] It is estimated that the proportion of those in this country who are over 65 years of age has almost tripled since 1900 and could grow to almost 20 percent of the population by the next century.[2] Another projection has indicated that the number of individuals 60 years of age and older will increase 31 percent by the year 2000.[3]

The "graying of America," however, does not refer only to the continuing growth in the number of elderly people in the United States. It also refers to the fact that the oldest among the elderly constitute the fastest growing segment of the population at this time. Between 1960 and 1970, the number of people 75 years of age in America increased three times faster than the number of those 65 to 70 years of age, and between 1970 and 1976, the number of individuals 40 to 60 years of age increased by 1.9 percent while the number of those 85 years of age and older increased by 39.1 percent.[4] Currently, there are about 23 million people 65 years of age and older in this country, and by the year 2030 it is estimated that this number will be 55 million. Those who are 75 years of age and older will then number as many as those who are 65 years old today.[5]

Although there is hardly a perfect correlation, in general, the older the person, the greater the probability that he or she will suffer from

156

physical or mental impairment, loss of functioning, and poor health. Therefore, the oldest among the elderly, those 75 or older, who are sometimes referred to as the "old-old," will present the greatest challenge to professionals working with and for the aged. Social workers in particular will be called on to maintain the independence of the elderly, thus enabling them to live in the community and remain outside an institutional setting. Such efforts will necessitate the existence of community resources such as supporting services as well as appropriate knowledge and skills among those working with elderly clients and their families.

Work with the Elderly

The authors believe that work with and for the elderly is different from work with other client groups. These differences have implications concerning the understanding of the problems of the elderly and the solutions to these problems. For example, in addition to representing economic losses and subsequent financial adjustments, retirement has social and psychological ramifications for the individual. Furthermore, the aged as a group, and especially the oldest of the old, are likely to have health problems resulting in changes in lifestyles, mobility, and self-perceptions. Family relationships, too, can be affected by the passage of time, for with aging comes the loss of spouse, friends, and—more likely than ever before because of the increasing longevity of the aged—grown children. Such losses make the existence of informal support systems for maintaining the independence of an aged person a matter of great importance. Finally, the influence of psychological dynamics on the individual's proximity to death is an issue with which those who work with the elderly must contend.

The realization that working with elderly populations is different from working with those that are younger is reflected in the plethora of gerontological and geriatric specialties available in professional education in various fields. This is certainly true for social work education. Models of intervention of a more generic nature have not been found to be suited to work with older and frailer clients. Consequently, specific practice skills for work with older populations have been increasingly discussed. For example, Brody and then Spark and Brody explored working with the elderly client in the context of the family, and Boszormenyi and Spark focused on intergenerational family therapy.[6] More recently, a variety of special skills and techniques used in social work with the elderly and their families has received attention.[7] For these reasons a life model is proposed in this article for use in intervention with the frail elderly.

Life Model

The life model as developed by Germain and Gitterman and others postulates that social work intervention should be concerned with the transaction between the individual and the environment.[8] The model's strength lies in its emphasis on understanding the environment and in its lack of insistence that the individual change. These aspects of the model are especially appropriate for work with the frail aged, who have often had to cope with a series of losses in regard to health, resources, and significant others. In the life model, the goals of social work intervention with the frail aged become the enrichment and organization of the elderly person's environment to attain a better fit with his or her changing needs and abilities and the maintenance of a quality of life that is satisfactory to the client and to those who care about the client. In summary, the life model directs the social worker's attention to the elderly person's relationships with family, neighborhood, and environment. Intervention is then directed to the transactions between the aged and their environment in order to maintain a viable life balance between them.

One of the valid criticisms of the model is that it is not specific enough for implementation on the practice level. In the person-environment equation, what practice principles flow from the model that allow practitioners to operate skillfully at the various points of life transitions? The framework of the life model that will be considered in this article examines transactions in which there is too much environmental press or too little environmental stimulation. The objective of the intervention described on either end of the continuum is to adjust the transactions between the environment and the client so that there is a better fit vis-à-vis the coping ability of the elderly individual. Case examples from the authors' practice will be used to illustrate this principle.

Unresponsive Environments

The first environments to be considered are those that are unresponsive to the elderly person in a variety of ways and fail to provide sufficient support. These environments may consist primarily of the community, friends and neighbors, or family.

Insufficient Formal Supports

The community as environment mainly includes the formal systems that provide service and care to the frail elderly. Found within these formal systems are "golden age" centers, other social service programs, and medical services, such as those provided by doctors, hospitals, and clinics.

In this area a lack of sufficient services for the care of the frail elderly is common. Accessible medical care, day care facilities, home health aides, and chore services are among the supports often unavailable to elderly individuals.

A case in point would be that of Mr. and Mrs. B, a frail couple living in their own home, who have a pension as well as social security and who are therefore not eligible for Medicaid. As a result, Mr. B has not received the kind of medical care he needs for his multiple health problems. The appropriate intervention in this situation would be to establish Mr. and Mrs. B in a clinic or medical program that would work with them concerning their financial constraints.

Insufficient Informal Supports

Contact with and support from those who live nearby are crucial to the maintenance of the elderly person. Because of their proximity, neighbors can provide care on an ongoing basis and also be available when special situations or crises arise. However, the issue of proximity has a negative side to it for those who are isolated and without sufficient neighbors or friends. The object of intervention in such instances is to reinvolve the elderly individual's neighbors in a manner that is acceptable to him or her. Programs such as the Retired Senior Volunteer Program and other neighborhood volunteer groups are fine avenues for accomplishing this task. In addition, social groups for the frail elderly are virtually untried in the field, and participation in such a group would help increase outside contact and eliminate isolation for the elderly client.

An example of intervention in an environment failing to provide sufficient informal support can be seen in the case of Mrs. R, a 79-year-old woman living alone and isolated in a small, run-down house. Mrs. R was afraid to go out and did not have contact with anyone except her landlord, who occasionally complained about her poor upkeep of the house. When Mrs. R started drinking heavily and her health and living conditions deteriorated, her social worker involved her, the landlord, and several neighbors in a meeting to discuss the situation and possible options. Prior to this, the neighbors had no idea who lived in Mrs. R's small house, and they agreed to visit Mrs. R on a regular basis. The landlord, apprised of the situation and with the social worker's help, was able to improve the quality of Mrs. R's home. The social worker also planned to involve Mrs. R in a group being formed in the near future.

Insufficient Family Supports

It is the family that society and the individual consider first when there is a need for support and caretaking, and the family in most cases provides care when an elderly relative is in need. However, the capacities of families to provide support is based on their current structure, their history, and their problem-solving abilities. Social work intervention may therefore be required in a variety of circumstances in which the elderly client is receiving insufficient family support.

For example, there are many elderly people who have no family living near them or who have no family at all. The best alternative for these individuals is to utilize friends and neighbors as surrogate family. Those elderly people who have some family but whose relatives live a distance away can often gain a sense of belonging through phone calls or occasional visits. Family members who live closer can provide physical as well as moral support. However, there are many situations in which long-established patterns have separated family members who live close to each other but who are nevertheless unavailable to each other. In cases such as these, the reestablishment of family ties is often a delicate task that requires a great deal of skill on the part of the social worker. Furthermore, the presence of family members who are currently involved with the frail elderly client, such as children or spouse, does not eliminate the need to recontact peripheral family members. These relatives may be supportive of both the elderly person and those who may be providing care to him or her.

Literature concerning the caretakers of the elderly is now being developed. Studies often indicate that one person, usually the spouse or daughter, cares for the elderly individual, and this represents another instance of a lack of environmental support.[9] Respite care, support groups, and educational opportunities have proved effective in supporting those who are caretakers of the elderly, but members of the extended family may still be needed to help provide continuity of care to the elderly as well as emotional respite for the caretakers.[10]

The case of Mrs. C illustrates many of the issues commonly arising concerning the elderly and their families. Mrs. C, age 81, lived with her daughter, Mrs. J, who was 65. The interaction between mother and daughter was often conflictual and occasionally destructive to both of them. After several contacts, Mrs. C's social worker came to realize that much of the conflict between mother and daughter was fanned by the lack of involvement of Mrs. C's two sons. With Mrs. C's approval, the worker contacted the sons, one of whom lived in town and one of whom lived in another city, and worked with them to increase their contact with their mother and sister. Although there was considerable resistance on the part of the son who lived in town, he eventually became more involved with his mother and sister. The brother who lived out of town invited his mother for a visit, and she accepted. This provided an important respite for both Mrs. C and her daughter.

Interventions in Other Environments

Although some environments are unresponsive to the needs of the elderly, others are fragmented, inappropriate, or full of conflict. As in dealing with environments that fail to meet the needs of the elderly, the worker encountering environments like these may need to intervene with community, neighbors, or family.

Fragmented Formal Involvement

In instances of fragmented formal involvement, individuals are the victims of fragmented services. Often the aged are clients of several agencies and the recipients of a variety of medical services. Frequently the results are services that conflict with each other and individuals who are overmedicated and have no clear sense of which service relates to what problem. One of the best methods of correcting such a situation is to organize a meeting among representatives of all the agencies involved. Such meetings should include the client and clarify roles and responsibilities relating to the client's different needs. One individual acting as an ombudsperson is often helpful in negotiating complex service delivery systems for the client. In the medical arena, seeing a family-practice physician or other holistically oriented physician often provides an alternative to constantly making the rounds of medical clinics.

The experience of Mr. and Mrs. S illustrates these points. Aged 68 and 71, respectively, Mr. and Mrs. S were clients of several clinics at two different hospitals. Their medical bills for various prescriptions were well over eighty dollars per month, and their multiple medications were having some negative side effects. In addition, Mr. and Mrs. S were confused about whom to contact for which ailment, and they spent a great deal of time in clinic waiting rooms. Their social worker remedied this unfortunately common situation by bringing the couple to a family-practice clinic. Their circumstances were explained to the family physicians, who reviewed all the records and reduced their medicine intake, as well as their medical costs and time spent at the clinics. As a result, Mr. and Mrs. S received better medical care and felt more in control of their situation.

Inappropriate Informal Involvement

On occasion, one does find too much neighborhood involvement in the life of the frail elderly client. This overinvolvement can take the form of harassment of the elderly individual by adolescents or unscrupulous neighbors who seek to take advantage of someone who is vulnerable. When this is the case, the worker often must operate as an agent for the protection of the elderly client and intervene either directly with the community or indirectly through the police or other social action groups.

This kind of protective role was assumed by the social worker of Mr. J, a confused man of 68 whose parents died and left him a small inheritance. Mr. J was invited to live with neighbors who then began to use his money to purchase cars and expensive gifts without his understanding. The worker's team confronted the family with the aid of an attorney and brought legal action against them. Mr. J was removed and placed in sheltered housing.

Conflicting Family Involvement

In contrast to some of the situations described earlier, many of the frail elderly have families who are actively involved in caring for them. Sometimes, however, the quality of the family's involvement is chaotic. When the chaos results from a lack of clarity concerning roles and responsibilities, a task-centered family meeting is the most efficient way to help family members organize themselves to care for their elderly relative.

During such a meeting, members of the family (including the elderly individual) are requested to state their concerns, both about their own lives and about the life of the elderly person. The object is to have family members talk about their desires and capacities for involvement with the required tasks of caretaking. The worker then clarifies tasks and questions unreasonable levels of "sacrifice" made for the care of the elderly client. It is often wise to formalize the final agreement as a contract, with the worker helping the family understand the fluid nature of the client's and family's needs. However, it should be noted that there are families for whom the issue is more than just a lack of organization. Families with histories of abuse, alcoholism, mental illness, or other dysfunctional patterns may require in-depth family therapy as the major intervention.

An example of a family conference can be seen in the case of Mrs. O, whose social worker called a meeting to help sort out family difficulty concerning the planning of Mrs. O's care. Present were Mrs. O, age 93, her two sisters, her three daughters, and her three granddaughters. All of those involved were concerned about Mrs. O, but several had conflicting opinions about the best way to care for her. Mrs. O had demanded that she not be placed in a nursing home, and the family argued about alternatives. They blamed each other for a lack of commitment to Mrs. O and boasted about their individual sacrifices. After helping family members focus on the issue, the social worker was able to work out a compromise in which Mrs. O would live with a sister who could care for her.

Coping Capacities of the Elderly

The elderly, then, may encounter a wide variety of environments that are unresponsive, fragmented, inappropriate, and marked by conflict in varying degrees. White and others have discussed the necessity for individuals to maintain a sense of competence in dealing with their environment.[11] For the frail elderly, however, the struggle to maintain this sense is extremely difficult because their coping abilities have been reduced by deteriorating health, limited economic resources, and personal losses. The task of the social worker in the life model is to help the individual maintain a sense of competence in transactions with the environment. The focus in working with frail individuals is primarily on acknowledging their strengths, accepting their limitations, and developing new coping strategies that allow them to continue to have a fulfilling life. Individuals appear to have difficulty maintaining viable exchanges with their environment when they attempt to exercise either too little control or too much control over it.

Inadequate Environmental Control

Individuals who underutilize control of their environment are often described as dependent. The difficulty with this term is that it does not describe the systemic implications of someone's exercise of too little control over the environment. Systems theory indicates that those exerting too little control must be supported by overfunctioning elements in other areas to maintain a functional balance. Therefore, when their functioning has regressed, the frail elderly may provoke intense involvement of family, neighbors, or community agencies during medical and emotional crises. The danger of such involvement is that it tends to perpetuate itself, thus keeping the environment's input high and the client's control low. One of the best safeguards against this trap is the clear contract drawn up by a social worker with all involved parties. Such a contract should be written on the basis of a realistic appraisal of the current and future functioning of the elderly client.

There are, of course, individuals who have a lifelong history of undercontrolling their environments or using dependence as a control mechanism. Attempts to upset the balance within their support systems will be met with powerful resistance by those involved. Systems therapy with families and others needs to be considered in such cases if there appears to be a desire by the client or a threat from his or her support system to abandon long-held roles abruptly.

A pattern of dependency and undercontrol was evident in the case of Mrs. L, whose case was transferred from one social agency to another. The first agency believed that Mrs. L was a helpless individual who required social service intervention in all areas of her life. However, when a social worker from the second agency assessed the situation, she felt Mrs. L had many unrecognized strengths that needed to be developed. With much resistance from the referring agency and some from Mrs. L, the worker established a service plan that would enable Mrs. L to do more for herself. The worker encouraged all concerned parties to allow Mrs. L to try handling more of the choices in her life. To date she has succeeded in taking over many more of her own decisions and has firm control over her use of the services she does need.

Excessive Environmental Control

Physical frailty does not always necessitate a lessening of the control and power elderly people hold in the systems within which they operate. Many frail individuals attempt to maintain their prior levels of functioning and control over their environment. As their needs increase, they struggle against accepting help from others. Unfortunately, the strategies these people use to maintain their independence can often be dysfunctional or dangerous to themselves.

The task of social workers is to help the frail elderly assess the functionality of their current coping strategies and, often, discard those that are dysfunctional and develop new ones. The danger here lies in damaging the elderly person's sense of competence in the process and in challenging his or her life circumstances by eliminating coping mechanisms. A useful rule of thumb is that one should never suggest the abandonment of a coping strategy without being able to suggest a new one to replace it. New strategies are often based on helping clients accept their need for environmental control and redirecting this need into a more functional avenue or outlet.

Like those who are undercontrolling, the elderly person who is overcontrolling operates in an existing system. If this system is predicated on the elderly client's being constantly in charge, the system will resist changes in which responsibilities are distributed more evenly among system members.

These principles are illustrated by the reactions of Dr. A and his family to an anticipated change in their lives. Dr. A had been a strong father and a "take charge" individual all his life. At age 84 he could no longer practice medicine and wanted to move with his wife to a smaller apartment. His family waited for him to direct them as to where and how to help him. However, Dr. A was confused, and his confusion subsequently permeated the family. The situation deteriorated for everyone until his social worker met with family members to help them plan the move. The family slowly began to realize that Dr. A needed more direct assistance and could no longer "run the entire show."

Implications

The authors believe that the life model of social work intervention with the frail elderly has the flexibility necessary to help workers meet the diversity of their elderly clients' needs. Use of the model also enables the worker to focus on various levels—community, neighborhood, family, and individual—to derive support for clients. Adherence to the model involves several implications in the areas of practice, education, and policy, and these will be summarized.

Practice

Social workers dealing with the elderly should be skilled in work on a one-to-one basis as well as in work with families and groups and with planners and policymakers. All these skills may be required in working with an elderly client, depending on the client's problems and on the supports and resources that are available or need to be mobilized.

Given an environment of increasing economic constraints, social work agencies must consider cost efficiency in their operations. In the life model, the professional social worker with an MSW could perform the vital role of assessing individual elderly clients and could then supervise the interventions undertaken by BSW workers or paraprofessionals. Such a division of labor is possible with the life model and is cost efficient for the agency.

Education

Schools and departments of social work, especially those preparing students for careers in the field of aging, should begin to train professionals to practice within a life model framework. This training would focus on aging as a normative life stage and would emphasize an understanding of the fit between human systems and the environment. Those who are already working in the field of aging should be encouraged to pursue additional training in needed knowledge and skills so as to become familiar with the life model. If pervasive retraining were undertaken to acquaint practitioners with the life model, the ramifications for social work education, especially continuing education departments, would be prodigious.

Policy

Community care systems must be flexible enough to permit the individualized provision of care to each client. This runs counter to the common practice of having clients conform to organizational requirements concerning problem definition and mode of intervention. The life model emphasizes the need to modify the characteristics of an elderly client's environment, be it community, neighborhood, or family system, rather than to have the client adjust to the often adverse characteristics of the environment.

In addition, the life model stresses the need for social workers to help communities assess the availability of resources to be used in working with a frail elderly client. Social workers operating from a life model perspective must organize communities to establish programs that will fill gaps in services and support for the aged. Finally, workers need to educate service providers to shape their interventions in a way that maximizes the positive aspect of services while minimizing any disruptive effect that services may have.

Notes and References

1. H. B. Brotman, "The Aging Society: A Demographic View," *Aging* (January–February 1981), pp. 2–5.

2. F. R. Eisele, ed., "Political Consequences of Aging," *Annals of the American Academy of Political and Social Sciences*, 415 (September 1974), p. iv.

3. D. G. Fowles, "U. S. 60+ Population May Rise 31% to 41 Million by Year 2000," *Aging* (June–July 1975), pp. 14–16.

4. U. S. Bureau of the Census, *Current Population Reports*, No. 643 (Washington, D. C.: U. S. Government Printing Office, 1977), p. 25.

5. Robert L. Kane et al., *Geriatrics in the United States: Manpower Projections and Training Considerations* (Santa Monica, Calif.: Rand Corporation, 1980).

6. Elaine M. Brody, "The Aging Family," *Gerontologist*, 6 (1966), pp. 201–206; Geraldine M. Spark and Elaine M. Brody, "The Aged Are Family Members," *Family Process*, 9 (June 1970), pp. 195–210; and Nagy I. Boszormenyi and Geraldine Spark, *Invisible Loyalties: Reciprocity in Intergenerational Family Therapy* (New York: Harper & Row, 1973).

7. See Jordan I. Kosberg, ed., *Working with and for the Aged* (Washington, D.C.: National Association of Social Workers, 1979).

8. See Carel Germain and A. Gitterman, *The Life Model of Social Work Practice* (New York: Columbia University Press, 1980); and Carol H. Meyer, *Social Work Practice: The Changing Landscape* (New York: Free Press, 1976).

9. See Ethel Shanas, "The Family as a Support System in Old Age," *Gerontologist, 19* (April 1979), pp. 169–174.

10. George Getzel, "Social Supports and Self-Help Groups: State of the Art," *Journal of Gerontological Social Work*, 1 (Spring 1979), pp. 251–255.

11. See Robert W. White, "Strategies of Adaptation: An Attempt at Systematic Description," in George V. Coehlo et al., *Coping and Adaptation* (New York: Basic Books, 1974); and Carel B. Germain, ed., *Social Work Practice: People and Environments* (New York: Columbia University Press, 1979).

Innovative Social Work Practice in Health Care: Stress Management

Cathey A. Graham
Cynthia J. Hawkins
William H. Blau

Given the current economic and societal strain as well as the changing lifestyles in the United States, patients are subjected to an increasing barrage of stressors, which according to leading researchers in medicine elicit the early onset of distinct patterns of disease.[1] Conservative estimates indicate that between 50 and 70 percent of all medical complaints are stress-linked.[2] Moreover, the course of these illnesses and the prognoses for the patients suffering from them can be affected by the patients' abilities to minimize and cope with stress.

Health practitioners as well as their clients have become increasingly aware of the need for an effective approach to stress management as an important part of health care. Patients are seeking specific skills and knowledge to call upon in coping with daily stress. The underlying message that comes with patients' expression of this need may be a statement of their motivation to assume a more active role in their own health care as they are faced with the limited resources of the current health care system.

The Stress Management Program, an outgrowth of the Cardiac Rehabilitation Department at Huntington Memorial Hospital in Pasadena, California, is designed to address this need. Members of the target group for this social work program are patients who are referred by physicians and health care teams to undergo adjunctive therapy for stress-related symptoms.

167

Medical social workers have traditionally helped patients and their families to cope with stress resulting from the mental and physical discomfort of illness and treatment. Traditionally, these clinicians have also provided patients with help in minimizing stress associated with (1) posthospitalization adjustment to illness, and (2) changes in lifestyle resulting from illness. Social workers' role in humanizing medical treatment has been long established: among other services, social workers provide counseling, patient education, discharge planning, psychosocial evaluation, financial counseling, and crisis intervention in most major medical facilities. Given this background, social workers' active participation and leadership in current stress-management programs represent a natural evolution of their traditional role in hospitals as well as in other health care facilities.

A comprehensive stress-management program is, however, dramatically different both conceptually and practically from the traditional services provided by medical social workers. Conceptually, the new model emphasizes treatment rather than ancillary services. In the traditional medical setting, the stress reduction provided by social workers was useful in that it facilitated treatment but was not itself treatment. In the present model, stress management is typically a specific treatment for the symptoms bringing the patient to the hospital; at Huntington Memorial Hospital, a physician who refers a patient for stress management usually anticipates that the treatment will have a positive effect on one or more symptoms, rather than merely making the patient more amenable to medical treatment.

From a practical standpoint, organization and delivery of these innovative social work practices are modified from the traditional structure in which all social work services were included in the overall treatment package provided by the general medical hospital. Currently, at facilities such as Huntington Memorial Hospital, social workers provide specialized stress-management services such as biofeedback and relaxation training on a fee-for-service basis. Patients receive specific billings for these treatments, as they do for other professional rehabilitation services. The revenue produced by the social work staff in providing these treatments enables the program to be largely self-supporting.

Interdisciplinary Cooperation

Acceptance of a stress-management program in a hospital requires a high level of interdisciplinary communication and cooperation. The unique contribution of a social worker as a provider of treatment is given the most respect when the services provided are (1) recognized by physicians as valuable and necessary, and (2) distinct from medical diagnosis and the chemical and surgical treatment of disease—areas to which physicians devote their primary energies.

Current health care is overloaded with patients' demands for medical treatments for complaints that are maintained and exacerbated by the patients' chronic stress—stress that may have been a major factor in the etiology of the symptoms. Faced with the needs of a patient suffering from a stress-related disease, a physician is often unable to do more than provide a palliative drug prescription and advise the patient to reduce his or her stress level. When the patient asks, "But *how* do I reduce stress?" many effective physicians are delighted to refer the patient to a stress-management specialist rather than to ignore the problem or offer simplistic advice that the patient is unable to heed.

Given a positive and respectful relationship between physicians and social workers providing stress-management services, patients with psychosomatic symptoms and patients with organic but stress-related symptoms both receive high-quality care. This care is offered without the patients being blamed for the symptoms and without exhausting the health care system's ability to provide services or the patients' financial resources. It is a positive innovation that social workers can now provide direct treatment for such patients within an interdisciplinary facility rather than merely provide crisis counseling and discharge planning after the hard-pressed medical system has failed to meet the patients' needs.

Medical Treatment and Psychotherapy

In the authors' opinion, the failure of the traditional health care system to treat patients with chronic, stress-related symptoms adequately has been a result of a simplistic conceptualization of symptom formation, a conceptualization that until recently has dominated the delivery of most medical services. In this simplistic schema, symptoms are either real (organic manifestations of physical disease) or psychogenic (caused by the mind and essentially imaginary). This view of illness has led to patients being classified as having organic illnesses (that should be treated by medicines, surgeries, and so forth) or as having psychosomatic complaints (secondary to a mental or emotional disorder that should be treated by psychotherapy). As Bakal notes, however, in psychosomatic disorders ". . . organic changes do take place. The symptoms are real. . . . The problem discovered in trying to isolate illnesses that are psychosomatic from illnesses that are not is simply that few illnesses, *if any*, have either an 'emotional' or a 'physical' cause [italics added]."[3] Symptoms may range from those that are entirely physical to those that are primarily imaginary, with almost all complaints having both organic and psychogenic aspects. Nevertheless, many physicians have used the terms "psychosomatic" to refer to symptoms that they could not cure or fully understand and that they, therefore, believed were maintained by the patient for psychological reasons (secondary gain). The current approach to psychosomatic symptoms is to recognize that they are real but that disease can be exacerbated or minimized by the patient. This means that the patient is no longer to blame for the symptoms but is often able to be responsible for reducing the symptoms' severity, just as he or she may increase the severity to life-threatening proportions. Stress management makes the positive statement, "You can control your symptoms," rather than the negative statement, "You are to blame for your symptoms."

Of course, a secondary gain in maintaining the symptoms exists for some patients who do not want to give up their symptoms because they experience some reward from having them (for example, receiving attention or being able to avoid making a decision about a significant conflict). The authors believe, however, that secondary gain is rarely the sole or major basis for patients' common physical symptoms. A combination of physical and psychological factors is more typical to the etiology of the symptoms, and analysis of each patient's complaints and history can point the way not only to medical alleviation but also to techniques through which the patient can take control of his or her body to minimize or eliminate the symptoms.

When the symptoms are of essentially psychogenic origin, as when secondary gain is a major factor in their maintenance, psychotherapy is indicated. Psychotherapy may be conducted by psychiatrists, social workers, psychologists, or other practitioners and is, historically, the first treatment per se that social workers conducted in hospitals. Stress management may include psychotherapy, whose techniques are often helpful in teaching clients to take control of their own physical and emotional symptoms. Nevertheless, stress management does not necessarily include psychotherapy and instead may use essentially educational techniques. Moreover, when psychotherapy is included in the authors' program of stress management, there is no presumption that the patient's symptoms are neurotic rather than real or that resolving childhood conflicts will rid the patient of present symptoms. In contrast, psychotherapy, in the context of stress management, focuses on the patient's ability to control his or her responses to external stress and to develop a lifestyle conducive to physical health. This model does not negate the possibility of medical symptoms arising from deep inner conflicts that only extensive analysis can fully resolve. However, the authors' current work focuses on the symptoms as real experiences that the patient can modify using practical techniques, even if he or she has not resolved all the psychological conflicts that may contribute to the etiology of the symptoms.

Establishing the Treatment Contract

Medical social workers have traditionally helped patients to understand their rights and obligations in hospitals. Often used to help encourage patients' compliance to hospital regulations and procedures, social workers may also act as advocates for patients, informing hospital administration of problems patients have in fulfilling their part of the contract between the provider and the patient.

When social workers offer direct treatment as in the Huntington Memorial Hospital's stress-management program, the workers must take an active role. They must establish and maintain a therapeutic contract with their patients. The social workers' understanding of the nature of a health services contract is necessary for the competent and ethical implementation of this responsibility.

A valid contract is always essential to the legitimate provision of health services. In emergency situations, a patient's condition may limit his or her conscious participation in developing a contract, but a contract must exist, either as a written agreement or as implied by a specific situation. It is imperative for health services providers to recognize that, in ordinary circumstances, their opinions as to patients' need for treatment are insufficient to establish contracts. Practitioners' misunderstanding of this limitation on professional action has in the recent past led to excesses that are clearly in violation of good practice. One may be outraged by legal action against a physician for saving the life of an unconscious victim without obtaining a signed consent-for-treatment form; one may be similarly outraged when hospital regulations require a severely injured patient arriving at the emergency room to sign financial forms before being treated; likewise, one may be outraged when patients are treated with involuntary hospitalization or sterilization as the result of professionals' unilateral determination of their insanity or lack of fitness for parenthood.

At Huntington Memorial Hospital each course of direct treatment provided by a social worker is based on a carefully prepared contract with the patient that includes the participation (in person or by referral) of the patient's primary physician and, in many cases, of other members of the treatment team. The final contract is established only after (1) evaluation of the patient, (2) consultation with other professional staff, (3) discussion with the patient of how the treatment may alleviate his or her symptoms, (4) feedback from the patient indicating that he or she understands the requirements, costs, and potential benefits of the treatment, and (5) informed consent of the patient to participate in the treatment prescribed.

Following a patient's referral for stress management, the contract is established in the context of a screening evaluation. During the evaluation, the symptoms leading to the referral are discussed, as are the patient's current medical status and treatments (including medications), previous treatments, and the primary concerns of the referring physician. The social worker obtains the patient's personal and family health histories, which delineate physical and mental problems as well as provide a basis for evaluating the patient's risk factors, such as sedentary work and leisure, recent major life changes, and use of alcohol, nicotine, caffeine, and other legal or illicit drugs. The patient's past and current psychosocial history is assessed, including information about the patient's vocation, recreation, social life, and sex life. Particular attention is given to the patient's lifestyle and attitudes toward work, achievement, spiritual values, relationships, and play. Knowledge of these intimate aspects of a patient's life is privileged, and one aspect of the contract between the patient and the provider is agreement by the patient to discuss these areas in hope that the provider's knowledge and skill be of help.

During the screening interview, the social worker determines the type of stress-management intervention that appears most appropriate to the patient. For example, a high-powered executive whose lifestyle has contributed to a major stroke or heart attack and who has suddenly realized that he or she must change or die might benefit from crisis intervention followed by training sessions emphasizing biofeedback and relaxation techniques. In contrast, a patient suffering from chronic low-back pain that has not responded to medical treatments by numerous physicians might benefit from an initial course of biofeedback sessions targeted to the symptoms and linked to long-term group or individual psychotherapy aimed at reducing psychic conflict that might engender secondary gain for the symptoms. In any case, the treatment approach that seems most efficacious is discussed with the patient, whose agreement to proceed with the mutually determined course of treatment is recorded. Hence, a contract that is clear, procedurally correct, and relevant to the needs of the patient is established between the patient and the provider.

Motivation of the Patient

Everyone has heard of cases in which the operation was a success but the patient died. Stress-management professionals typically face a situation in which a potentially successful treatment program has been proposed and developed, but the patient drops out. The success of the treatment is clearly related to the degree of responsibility the patient is willing to take in the management of his or her symptoms. During the screening evaluation, the social work clinician assesses the patient's ability and willingness to take control of his or her bodily processes, physical habits, and states of mind associated with the symptoms.

The typical patient who attends the screening evaluation on referral by his or her physician is motivated to receive help from a "healing person." Unfortunately, in the authors' experience, only slightly more than half these patients are truly open to recognizing that they themselves—using techniques, procedures, and in some cases, equipment provided by their professional therapists—must be the primary healers in their treatments. Moreover, patients are expected to chronicle both their symptoms and their therapeutic activities on a regular basis and to report their progress or lack of progress to the clinicians.

A significant portion of the screening interview at Huntington Memorial Hospital is, therefore, designed to determine if the patient understands the nature of stress management and is willing to become involved in such a course of treatment. If by enrolling in the program the patient is merely complying with orders from his or her doctor, the participatory nature of stress management is explained. Once the patient understands the true nature of stress management, he or she can make an informed decision as to whether the program is likely to be of benefit.

Theoretical Background

The services provided in the authors' stress-management program are derived from theory and practical experience. The General Adaptation Syndrome, a concept developed by Selye, describes the physiological consequences of stress and the impact of these reactions on health.[4] As stress is intensified or prolonged, the body's ability to resist decreases, and stress-related disorders occur. Chronic stress can be deadly—complete exhaustion of adaptation energy leads to the death of the individual. Pelletier extends this concept to psychological stress, proposing that many psychophysiological disorders result from the body's tendency to react to psychological stress with the same mechanisms used to cope with physical stress.[5] The "fight-or-flight" response is the body's way to provide a short-term, intensive reaction to physical stress or threat; however, people become increasingly susceptible to illness when this emergency response becomes chronic in a society whose members live under nearly constant psychological stress.

Further evidence of the "stress connection" in human illness has been found by Holmes and Rahe who examined the relationship between specific life changes and the development of illness.[6] Their findings (which included extensive interviews with 394 individuals of different ages and various socioeconomic levels) indicated that life changes are factors in the rapid development of disease. Holmes and Rahe were able to assign relative "risk values" to the specific life changes most frequently associated with the patient's becoming ill in the subsequent year. Listed in order of decreasing impact, these life changes include death of a spouse, divorce, marital separation, jail term, death of a close family member, and retirement.

There is ever-increasing evidence that a person's likelihood of becoming ill is affected not only by stressful life events but also by the individual's personality, that is, how he or she reacts to the life events. Cardiologists Friedman and Rosenman found striking similarities in the personality types of their cardiac patients.[7] Based on the results of their study, they developed the concept that individuals with "Type A" personality styles are more vulnerable than others to the early onset of coronary artery disease. The Type A behavior pattern was described as

> an action-emotion complex that can be observed in any person who is aggressively involved in a chronic, incessant struggle to achieve more and more in less and less time, and if required to do so, against the opposing efforts of other things or other persons. It is not psychosis or a complex of other worries or phobias or obsessions, but a socially acceptable— indeed often praised—form of conflict.[8]

In contrast, persons possessing a "Type B" pattern have the ability to relax without feeling guilty, to work at a natural pace without agitation, to enjoy free time, to express creativity, and to have fun. These individuals are less vulnerable to the development of premature coronary artery disease.

Numerous other researchers including Benson, Folkow and Neil, and Sternbach have substantiated these somewhat gloomy conclusions: chronic stress (physical or psychological) is as hazardous to physical health as it is universal in this society, and essentially normal patterns of personality and lifestyle are associated with the onset of specific life-threatening illnesses.[9] Fortunately, other recent research has resulted in this happier finding: individuals are far more capable of taking conscious control of their physiological processes than had previously been thought possible. Using biofeedback and other techniques such as relaxation training and hypnosis, subjects can develop highly refined control over their muscular tension and even over the so-called "involuntary" aspects of the physiological arousal involved in reacting to stress. Applying these self-control techniques in conjunction with patient education and in an atmosphere of interdisciplinary cooperation, stress-management programs have been successful in treating patients with a variety of disorders, including migraine and tension headaches, ulcers, gastrointestinal dysfunction, hypertension, bruxism, torticollis, Raynaud's disease, tinnitis, neuromuscular dysfunction, asthma, and chronic pain. Stress-management techniques may also be of value in treating psychological problems such as anxiety, depression, and insomnia.[10]

Services Provided

1. Individual Biofeedback Training. As a clinical treatment modality for stress-related symptoms, biofeedback is used to assist the patient in learning to control his or her physiological state. Biofeedback instruments provide the patient with immediate, accurate information about muscle tension and physiological arousal. Electromyographic (EMG) feedback about muscle contraction can be applied directly in training patients to relax their muscles. The hands and feet of a person experiencing chronic stress are typically cold and sweaty as a result of the autonomic nervous system's fight-or-flight response. Biofeedback temperature training enables patients to warm their hands and feet and thereby quiet their bodies' excessive autonomic arousal. Similarly, electrodermal (galvanic skin response or GSR) changes indicate autonomic arousal, which may be brought under conscious control by GSR training. Training patients to increase the temperature of their hands and feet has been found to be useful in the control of migraine headaches and Raynaud's disease. EMG muscle relaxation has been useful in control of tension headaches and bruxism. A variety of other disorders have proven amenable to treatment by biofeedback as a single modality or, as in the treatment of hypertension, in combination with other modalities.[11]

2. Individual Relaxation Training. Relaxation training may consist of progressive relaxation as developed by Jacobson (in which an individual systematically tenses and relaxes each muscle group), autogenic training as developed by Schultz (in which an individual focuses attention on heaviness and warmth in the extremities), and the Quieting Response technique, developed by Stroebel (in which an individual learns to relax rapidly at the time of disturbance).[12]

3. Home Practice. Clinical sessions are augmented by extensive training for the patient in relaxation and biofeedback. Most patients are instructed to maintain journals describing their headaches and other symptoms, many patients are given cassettes of recorded relaxation instructions, and almost all patients are instructed in the regular practice of relaxation techniques at home.

4. Stress-Management Workshop. This is an eight-week course designed to teach relaxation skills and stress-management concepts. Lectures cover topics such as chronic versus acute stress, life changes, Type A behavior, good health, relaxation, and biofeedback. A portion of each class session is spent in relaxation training.

5. Individual and Group Psychotherapy. Psychotherapy may be used as an adjunct or an alternative to stress-management training. Psychotherapy may help the patient to make realistic attitude changes as well as to help the patient resolve personal conflicts and practical problems that may be troubling him or her.

Specialized Training

The graduate training for a master's degree in social work does not fully prepare workers to provide stress-management treatment for seriously ill patients; moreover, inexperienced graduates may be ill-prepared to offer effective supportive services to patients suffering from long-term physical illnesses. Although graduate training provides the clinician with the theoretical understanding necessary for successful interventions with varied client populations, few social workers leave graduate school fully prepared to cope not only with clients in crisis but with the following: (1) a bureaucracy that may resist recognition of the social worker as a competent provider of treatment, (2) patients who reject any help offered because of past experiences with clinicians who "burned out" rapidly when faced with chronic illness and intractable suffering, (3) symptoms that defy being categorized as primarily physical or primarily psychiatric, and (4) techniques that are potentially useful but that require at least some expert knowledge in such varied fields as psychology, physiology, biochemistry, anatomy, physics, and even electronics (for the biofeedback user).

A social worker whose graduate training has included electives that prepare him or her for a career in psychiatric social work or medical social work will be equipped with some, but not all, of the skills needed to treat patients' stress-related symptoms. The psychiatric social worker has typically received training in psychodynamics, psychopathology, and psychotherapy. The medical social worker has typically been trained in medical nomenclature, medical crisis intervention, health delivery systems, and hospitals' organizational structure. Both of these specialists have probably received some training in the problems and potentialities of the interdisciplinary team in health care, and both have probably been introduced to the concepts of psychosomatic medicine. Unfortunately, neither the psychiatric social worker nor the medical social worker has had full training in the other's specialty, and both typically lack technical backgrounds in behavioral learning theory, anatomy and physiology of the autonomic nervous system, pharmacology, and Ohm's Law. (Only the protagonist of a science fiction epic could have expertise in all these areas!) Hence, the real-life social worker who is a specialist in the treatment of stress-related symptoms must also be a generalist who has some working knowledge of the subject matter of several disciplines but who never misrepresents him- or herself as possessing the same qualifications as a physician, psychologist, or other practitioner. Clinical social workers who desire to develop skills in stress management and related techniques can obtain specialized postgraduate training from three primary sources: continuing education at work, workshops and classes, and personal reading and consultation.

Continuing Education. Continuing education for practice provides in-service training that may greatly enhance the clinician's understanding of the population served by the institution as well as give specialized training in techniques relevant to both supportive and symptomatic treatment of that population. Medical and psychiatric institutions often make available various training opportunities that teach employees valuable treatment skills. For example, in a cardiac rehabilitation center that is progressive, clinicians may enroll in continuing education classes geared to such objectives as (1) academic understanding of the anatomy and physiology of coronary artery disease, (2) comprehension of the role of nutrition in maintaining a healthy heart, and (3) appreciation of the effects of exercise on the physiology of the heart. A motivated social worker may often profit from continuing education classes provided primarily for another discipline such as nursing.

Workshops and Classes. Workshops and classes attended on social workers' own time (and usually expense) are almost always necessary in training clinicians to be proficient in treating the seriously ill. Specialized training in stress management and biofeedback is available in many communities. (The Biofeedback Society of America will provide information on programs leading to certification by state and national organizations of persons possessing biofeedback skills.) Specialized courses in autogenic training and other techniques are provided for interested clinicians by institutes and local practitioners, and such courses may greatly benefit the professional who seeks enhancement of current skills. These courses do not, however, provide the basis for a practice in the treatment of physical disease; they only augment the training of a qualified professional.

Reading and Consultation. Personal reading and consultation provide the final bases for specialized expertise in the treatment of the seriously ill patient. Knowledge of the scientific and professional literature relevant to stress management is invaluable for the practicing clinician, who must keep abreast of rapid developments in the field. Consultation and supervision are essential to ethical and competent provision of services to the chronically ill patient who invariably elicits strong, often negative feelings on the part of the treating professional. Effective consultation and supervision help the clinician remain therapeutic and useful with patients whose chronicity and intense human suffering have thwarted

the best efforts of other professionals to provide support and understanding, which are the foundations of any efforts to provide symptomatic
relief.

Research and Evaluation

Clinical observations indicate that patients at Huntington Memorial
Hospital learn to use stress-management techniques to become more
effective in recognizing stress and coping with it in everyday life. Moreover, many of these patients appear able to integrate the stress-management skills and knowledge they learn into their lifestyles and can even
modify aspects of their personalities that are endangering their health.

To obtain a more objective evaluation of the effectiveness of the program, however, the authors conducted surveys of patients' reported changes
in attitudes and life experiences. The surveys included follow-up questionnaires and interviews obtained from patients in the Cardiac Rehabilitation Program in 1978.[13] These cardiac patients were the first patients
to receive stress-management training in the program at Huntington
Memorial Hospital. The surveys were conducted at intervals of six months
and one year following the training.

The authors' evaluation of patients' reported changes was not a controlled outcome study, and the number of patients participating in the
study (twelve) was small; hence, the data should be interpreted cau-
tiously. Nonetheless, the majority of patients indicated improvement in
the following areas: social life, family life, work life, sleeping patterns,
feelings about self, feelings about lifestyle, recreational activities, and
adjustment to coronary artery disease. The technical limitations of the
authors' study notwithstanding, these preliminary findings supported their
clinical impression that stress-management training can contribute to the
successful rehabilitation of cardiac patients, not only with respect to physical recovery but also with respect to changes in lifestyle and attitudes.
Their expansion of stress management services to include patients outside
the Cardiac Rehabilitation Program was also clinically successful.

Conclusion

Social workers in hospitals are able to make a significant contribution
to a dramatic trend in health care: the active participation of patients in
the treatment process. Social workers who are able to translate the theories underlying stress management into practical clinical procedures join
with their patients in becoming active partners in reducing or eliminating
the patients' symptoms. A stress-management program in the context of
a multidisciplinary approach to hospital care can provide effective treat-

ment for psychophysiological symptoms related to the stress that is ubiquitous in this society. The pain and frustration of the patients—as well as the powerlessness felt by many physicians in dealing with stress-related symptoms—can be alleviated when health systems support such innovations by social workers and other health providers.

Notes and References

1. Kenneth Pelletier, *Mind As Healer Mind As Slayer* (New York: Delacorte Press, 1977).

2. Charles Stroebel, "Quieting Response Training" (New York: Guilford Publications, Biomonitoring Applications, 1978).

3. Donald Bakal, *Psychology and Medicine* (New York: Springer Publishing Co., 1979), p. 9.

4. Hans Selye, *Stress Without Distress* (Philadelphia: J. P. Lippincott Co., 1974).

5. Pelletier, op. cit.

6. Thomas Holmes and Richard Rahe, "Schedule of Recent Experience (SRE)" (Seattle: University of Washington School of Medicine, Department of Psychiatry, 1967).

7. Meyer Friedman and Ray Rosenman, *Type A Behavior and Your Heart* (New York: Alfred A. Knopf, 1974).

8. Ibid., p. 67.

9. Herbert Benson, *The Mind-Body Effect* (New York: Simon & Schuster, 1979); Bjoern Folkow and Eric Neil, *Circulation* (New York: Oxford University Press, 1971); and Richard A. Sternbach, *Principles of Psychophysiology* (New York: Academic Press, 1966).

10. Barbara Brown, *Stress and the Art of Biofeedback* (New York: Bantam Books, 1977).

11. George Fuller, *Biofeedback: Methods and Procedures in Clinical Practice* (San Francisco: Biofeedback Press, 1977).

12. Edmund Jacobson, *You Must Relax* (5th ed.; New York: McGraw-Hill Book Co., 1978); Johannes Schultz and Wolfgang Luthe, *Autogenic Training: A Psychophysiologic Approach in Psychotherapy* (New York: Grune & Stratton, 1959); and Stroebel, op. cit.

13. Cathey A. Graham and William H. Blau, "New Trends in Cardiac Rehabilitation Social Work: Risk Factor Modification in Stress, Diet, and Smoking Management, Biofeedback and Relaxation Training." Paper presented at the conference, Social Work and Health Care: Fission or Fusion? Seattle, University of Washington, August 13–15, 1979.

A Case Management Approach For Preventing Child Neglect

Julius R. Ballew
Barbara Ditzhazy

The Special Family Services Project of the Michigan Department of Social Services (MDSS) developed and tested a program and service delivery model for preventing child abuse and neglect. After early evaluation, the model was implemented in what is now the Preventive Services for Families program. The model is an integrated set of procedures and program elements that moves a case from intake to a successful conclusion. A case was considered to have such an outcome if a substantiated referral was not made to Children's Protective Services (CPS) and if, in the worker's judgment, the family had improved its functioning in areas associated with child abuse and neglect.

Planning for the project began in October 1979. It was conducted in nine counties in Michigan and involved seventeen front-line workers and eleven supervisors. The project received 741 referrals during its fourteen-month service delivery period from April 1980 through May 1981. Service was initiated for 524 families. A complete set of data is available for 430 of these families.

Prerequisites for the Model

After carefully considering the environment in which public social services are provided in Michigan and the anticipated needs of the target group, the planners of the special project established several conditions for the model. The broadest condition was that the model be designed to fill a gap in a continuum of public social services to families and children. At one end of the continuum were support services. These were short-term services for families who needed outside assistance but who were able to identify the problems they faced and the type of help needed. At the other end were the traditional public child welfare services of child protection, foster care, and adoption. These were often involuntary in nature and were designed for families who had problems that endangered their children and who were unable or unwilling to identify the problems and use help on their own. In between the two service areas was a preventive service for families whose children might be endangered if the families did not receive outside help. For a variety of reasons these families could not gain access to the informal or formal sources of help available to them. The preventive service not only engaged in outreach activities but also acknowledged and preserved the freedom and power of the family to make its own decisions.

Another condition was that the model be implemented with available staff resources. In Michigan this meant that the model had to be designed so that it could be used by public social service workers having little or no professional training. The planners believed that the families in the target group experienced multiple concurrent problems and that any single family might require services from a variety of providers. It was considered important, therefore, to maintain the preventive worker in the role of a *case manager* who would orchestrate the diverse resources that might be needed to assist such a family. The Preventive Services for Families program that is based on the model was funded under Title IV-B of the Social Security Act and met the requirements of the Adoption Assistance and Child Welfare Act of 1980.

The last condition was that the model have statewide applicability. Every program offered by MDSS is available through local offices in every county and therefore must be flexible enough to respond to special, local, and regional conditions. The remainder of this article describes the key elements of the model that were designed to meet the foregoing conditions. The model is innovative in the following areas: (1) it includes a procedure for defining and identifying a family at risk of abusing or neglecting children, and (2) it describes the appropriate balance between the direct services provided to the family by the case manager and the indirect services that the case manager provides in collaboration with other professionals, volunteers, and family friends.

Key Program Elements

Four program elements were considered essential to the successful implementation of the service delivery model: case finding, staffing, program evaluation, and staff training. *Case finding* was accomplished by depending on referrals from service workers in other programs both inside and outside MDSS. Although the preventive service had an outreach capacity, caseloads were filled with families already known to MDSS through its other service programs or known to other agencies. The project's planners agreed that referrals from the general community might be accepted in the future as the program grew.

To ensure that referrals were appropriate, preventive workers engaged in a considerable educational effort directed at their colleagues. This activity most often took the form of meetings between supervisors of related programs, presentations at staff meetings, and individual consultations between the prevention worker and the referring worker. It resulted in 741 referrals to the project, of which 578, or 78 percent, were considered appropriate. Of the 578, 15 percent were referred by CPS as families who had originally been referred to protective services but for whom abuse and neglect could not be substantiated. However, these families were still considered at risk of abusing and neglecting their children. Another 24 percent were families who had received protective or foster care services, whose cases had been closed, but who were thought to need follow-up services to prevent the future recurrence of abuse or neglect. About 37 percent of the referrals came from a family services program that had since been discontinued. The remainder came from miscellaneous sources. It can be seen, therefore, that the project was a secondary and tertiary prevention effort in that it sought to prevent the occurrence and recurrence of child neglect in an at-risk population.

Staffing was initially established at the ratio of one worker to thirty families. The project's field staff later indicated that when caseloads exceeded twenty-five families, it was impossible to maintain the contact needed to remain well informed about the circumstances of each family and thus to manage the case effectively. They recommended that in establishing new caseloads no more than five new cases should be carried by a worker at any given time and that four to six months should be allowed to complete the building of a new caseload. At the end of the project's service delivery period, 62.6 percent of the cases for which service was initiated were still open. The average case had received 7.9 months of service and the mode was 12 months. The duration of a typical preventive case is not known at this point. Other studies have suggested that from twelve to twenty-four months should be expected if positive outcomes are to be achieved.[1]

Ongoing *program evaluation* was integrated into the program's record-keeping and information system. The objectives of the program were to (1) improve family functioning and (2) reduce substantiated referrals and rereferrals to CPS. These objectives emphasized client outcome as well as measures of the program's effectiveness. The measurement of family functioning began with the initial assessment of the family, continued through the service delivery period at quarterly intervals, and concluded at the time of case closure. The use of standardized forms that evolved from the project permitted the collection of comparative data for each case and of aggregate data for the whole program. These forms included a case screening guide (CSG), a service plan format, quarterly reports that reflect evaluation and updating of the service plan, written client-worker agreements that contain a self-evaluation component, and a supervisor's referral log.

The logs were kept by the supervisor of each preventive service unit. The purpose of the log was to provide a written record of the source and disposition of every referral made to the prevention program. The log allowed program evaluators to track those cases that were originally unsubstantiated referrals to CPS or that were closed protective service or foster care cases. It could then be used to determine which of these cases received preventive services and of those, which were subsequently referred back to CPS. In aggregate, it established the percentage of preventive service clients who were subsequently referred to and accepted by CPS and so measured the second program objective.

Four *training and technical assistance* strategies were used by the project: formal workshops, written materials, cluster meetings, and case consultation. Eight days of formal workshops were provided on content related to the service delivery model, and written materials based on or related to workshop content were provided to field staff. Cluster meetings were small group discussions equally spaced between workshops. They were developed as a way of integrating material presented in the workshops with what actually happens in the field. Case consultation was offered twice per quarter as a way of providing a highly individualized type of assistance to each worker and supervisor in skill areas related to the project model.

Defining the Target Population

One of the difficult problems facing any prevention program is that of defining its target population. This problem is particularly taxing in the area of child abuse and neglect in which diverse opinions about what constitutes actual abuse or neglect exist and in which even less is known about incipient abuse and neglect.[2]

The project's approach to defining and identifying families at risk of abusing or neglecting their children started with the assumption that child abuse and neglect occur when families are subject to stress that exceeds their ability to cope. Stress may result from illness, unemployment, alcoholism, divorce, or the like. Poverty also causes stress, and it exacerbates the effects of all the preceding factors. Despite this stress, the vast majority of poor families do not abuse or neglect their children. When their own resources are exhausted, these families seem able to get the help they need from other sources. The other sources of help are often informal (for example, extended family, friends, or neighbors) and are occasionally formal (for instance, church groups and professionals). Some families, however, do not seem able to seek out and use help in this way. When stress mounts and the family does not get help, the situation sometimes deteriorates and child abuse and neglect can result.

The project developed a scale, CSG, that attempted to measure the stress both inside and outside a family that researchers or experienced practitioners indicated were associated with the maltreatment of children. The work of Berkley Planning Associates as reported by Cohn and the work of Wolock and Horowitz were used extensively in identifying problem areas associated with child abuse and neglect, as were the opinions of the project's advisory group and field staff.[3]

CSG was used by workers to determine whether problems existed in the following areas: (1) alcohol or drug use, (2) learning disability, (3) illness or handicap, (4) mental disturbance, (5) housing, (6) continuous, unwanted, or teenage childbearing, (7) emotional problems with self-esteem or anger, (8) health care of children, (9) education of children, (10) supervision of children, (11) social isolation, (12) money management, (13) marital relationship or "partner" relationship (that is, relationship between two people living together), (14) parent-child relationship, including affection, expectations, and discipline, (15) special child, and (16) previous substantiated maltreatment. Each of the sixteen items on CSG identifies a problem area and asks the worker whether the problem is present and, if present, to what degree. Each item was scored 0 (not evident or unknown), 1 (somewhat evident), 2 (evident), or 3 (strongly evident). The scores were then summed across all sixteen items, and the total score was used as an index of seriousness of the problems of a family.

In an initial attempt to establish the validity of the guide, the project's staff administered it to 292 cases of five types: active foster care, active protective service, family service cases that had received protective services, family service cases considered at risk of abusing and neglecting their children, and family service cases considered not at risk. It was hoped that the scores on the CSG would recreate these categories. The means, standard deviations, and ranges of scores in each category are displayed in Table 1. The means of the at-risk categories do not differ significantly. However, the combined mean of the at-risk categories differs significantly from that of the not-at-risk category. The table shows that CSG distinguishes adequately between the not-at-risk category and the various risk categories but does not distinguish well among different

Table 1. Univariate Summary Statistics by Type of Case

Category	Type of Case	Mean	SD	Range of Scores	N
Risk	Active foster care	19.84	10.12	3–46	56
	Active protective service	19.50	8.55	4–34	60
	Family service cases that had received protective services	19.21	6.90	7–39	52
	At-risk family service cases	16.30	6.65	2–30	63
Not at risk	Family service cases, not at risk	8.34	6.77	1–38	61

levels of risk. The distribution of scores suggested a natural cutoff score of 10 for distinguishing between risk and not at risk. Using this score as a cutoff point and grouping the first four categories yielded Table 2. It was concluded that CSG could be used to separate at-risk families from families not at risk but that some additional criteria would be required to distinguish among levels of risk.

The project considered at-risk families to be any family that was referred and scored 10 or above on the guide. If a family scored 19 or above, the staff referred it to CPS. If on investigation CPS could not substantiate actual abuse or neglect, the case was referred back to the project. Sixteen percent of the project's cases were of this type.

In future applications of the scale, expanding the interval from 19 to

Table 2. Discriminant Analysis of Scores on Case Screening Guide, by Risk and Nonrisk (*n* = 292)

Score	Cases at Risk		Cases Not at Risk	
	Number	Percentage	Number	Percentage
10 or greater	201	69 (At Risk)	19	7 (False Positives)
Less than 10	30	10 (False Negatives)	42	14 (Not at Risk)
Total	231	79	61	21

[a]83.22 percent of the cases (*n* = 243) were correctly assigned as at risk or not at risk of abusing or neglecting children, and 16.78 percent (*n* = 49) were incorrectly assigned.

21 would include 8 percent more of the families served by the project. Only 2 percent of the families served by the project scored below 10. Using intervals of 10 to 21 inclusive would have the effect of including 90 percent of the families who, both the guide and practice experience suggested, were in need of preventive services.

The reliability of CSG has thus far been examined only in terms of interrater reliability, that is, do different raters (workers) get similar results when they apply CSG to the same set of cases? Sixteen project workers, experienced with the guide, were asked to apply it to seven case vignettes. The seven cases were the same for each rater. The results were subjected to a two-way analysis of variance and are summarized in Table 3. They revealed a significant "case effect" that is desirable and a significant "rater effect" that is not desirable. The intensity of the CSG score depended on who the rater was, and thus interrater reliability was low. A large proportion of the interrater variance was attributable to the differences between the raters rather than to random fluctuations. Cases rated high by one rater tended to be rated high by other raters, but agreement did not necessarily occur on the rating of the magnitude of individual items contributing to a total high score. In summary, CSG needs further work, but in the interim it can be a useful field guide for uniformly identifying at-risk families when used in combination with workers' and supervisors' judgments.

Key Service Delivery Elements

In designing the service delivery elements, the project's planners anticipated that the target group would consist of families who experienced multiple, concurrent problems that would require services from a variety of helpers. In fact, 81 percent of the project's cases for which data are available (430 families) had six to ten problem areas indicated on CSG

Table 3. Case Screening Guide's Analysis of Variance Summary

Source of Variation	Sum of Squares	df	Mean Square
Rows (raters)	716.25	15	47.75
Columns (cases)	1,622.68	6	270.45
Residual (error)	526.75	90	5.85
Total	2,865.68	111	

$df\,(15, 90) = MS_r / MS_e = 8.16 \quad p < .01$

$df\,(6, 90) = MS_c / MS_e = 46.21 \quad p < .01$

$(MS_r - MS_e)/MS_r = .88$

at intake. Also, the cases had an average of 2.6 service providers per case in addition to the project worker. The multiplicity of problems and diversity of helpers seemed to require that the prevention worker act as case manager or organizer of a helping network for each case.

The term "case manager" conjures up a wide variety of notions and seems to cover activities as diverse as simple information and referral work to the most complex of direct interventions or advocacy strategies. There is agreement on one thing, however: the case manager must attempt to coordinate his or her own work and that of any other relevant service provider to achieve the goals that the case manager and client agree are desirable. Two questions then arise: When and to what extent should the case manager directly provide services to the client and when and to what extent should he or she coordinate the work of other service providers? The question of balance between direct and indirect services must be answered differently for each program context within which service is provided. The answer to this question is the focal point of the preventive services delivery model developed by the project.

The development of the case management element of the model began with a significant set of observations made by field staff. The key observation was that the clients, although superficially cooperative, were difficult to engage in a helping relationship and were difficult to pin down to a commitment to work on specific problems. Typically, the clients would accept the general idea of getting help but would acknowledge only the most superficial and obvious of problems and potential resolutions when pressed to make specific commitments. This characteristic was conceptualized as an inability to use help effectively. Generally, clients did not reject offers of help, but they showed many signs of being unable or unwilling to use the help once it was made available. The most common of these signs was the client's unwillingness to accept referrals for acknowledged problems or failure to follow through in getting help once an initial contact with a resource was made.

The goal of the preventive worker was to identify families at risk of abusing or neglecting their children and, then, to enable them to use help effectively. *Specifically, the worker's role was to identify the type of help needed and then to identify and overcome the barriers to the client's using this help effectively.* The worker then would provide direct service to overcome these barriers and direct and indirect services to connect the client to potential helpers and would maintain these connections until the problem was resolved. In carrying out this role, the worker followed a service delivery model that contained eight steps: (1) intake, (2) problem assessment, (3) resource assessment, (4) barrier assessment, (5) intervention, (6) connection, (7) maintenance, and (8) closure.

At the first step the workers used CSG to structure a decision about accepting a referral and getting in touch with the client. They completed the guide using information supplied by referring workers and contained in the case record if one existed. If the referral seemed generally appropriate, the preventive workers got in touch with the family and began the problem assessment.

The problem assessment enabled the worker to identify those aspects of the family's situation that contributed to the family's being at risk of abusing or neglecting its children. The worker developed a problem inventory and sometimes used CSG as an outline. Families varied in their ability to participate in this process. Often the family members acknowledged only those problems that were of a superficial and concrete nature. They tended to be slower to admit to problems in their relationships with others or in their feelings about themselves. The worker accepted these problems and began work on them immediately as a vehicle for building a relationship and eventually completing a more detailed problem assessment.

The next step was to assess the resources that were available for solving the family's problems with a view toward eventually connecting the family to them. The tool used at this step was the ecomap.[4] This device allowed the worker and family together to map the family's connections (or lack of them) to the major systems in its environment and displayed on a single page the types of resources needed and the problems that existed in connecting the family to them.

The next three steps were the heart of the worker's direct service activity. In barrier assessment the worker asked whether the family was aware of its problems, whether resources existed to help resolve them, and why the family had not already made use of the resources? The preventive service delivery model suggested that there are three types of barriers to getting and using help: external, inherent incapacities, and internal. *External barriers* are deficiencies in the family's environment that prevent the family from using the available resource. For example, a resource may exist but the family may not live in the right area to qualify for it, may have "burnt out" the resource, or may need information or transportation to gain access to it. *Inherent incapacities* are factors presumably outside a person's control that reduce or eliminate a person's ability to communicate effectively with potential helpers or to participate actively in the helping process. Mental retardation, psychosis, and incapacitating alcoholism are some examples. *Internal barriers* are beliefs, attitudes, or values held by the client that get in the way of the person seeking or accepting help when needed. People who think of themselves as so worthless that no one else could or would want to help are an example.

At the next step an intervention was designed to overcome each identified barrier. Broadly speaking, external barriers were addressed by traditional case management strategies of brokerage, mediation, and advocacy. Inherent incapacities were handled by obtaining expert consultation and then developing a support system even without the parent's active involvement. Internal barriers were overcome by a counseling approach that involved helping the client to gain access to personal resources that would assist him or her in getting and using help.

Moving with the client to the sixth step sometimes took many months of careful, patient work. Eventually, the worker began to connect the client to helping resources. During this process the worker's role also began to include supporting and sustaining the family in its work with other helpers. At this stage social work contracts and the task-implementation sequence were found to be useful tools.[5]

The worker considered closing the case when the problems were resolved or when the family demonstrated an ability to maintain connections with helpers on its own. It was useful to complete another CSG at this point as a way of structuring the judgment that family problems were resolved or that, at least, the family was no longer at risk. Therefore, in carrying out the role of case manager in preventive services, the worker had an assessment function in identifying problems and resources, a direct service function in overcoming barriers to the client's using help effectively, and an indirect service function in connecting the client to helping resources and maintaining those connections.

Program Effectiveness

Preliminary evaluations of the effectiveness of the program and service delivery model are encouraging but are not yet conclusive. The majority of cases continued to need service at the time that final project data were collected. An additional study will be required to be certain of the impact of the use of the model on the functioning of clients and the incidence of substantiated referrals and rereferrals to CPS.

The project did, however, collect data in four areas to get some early indications of program effectiveness. CSG was administered to all cases at closing or at the end of the service delivery period so that these scores could be compared with the CSG scores obtained at intake. The difference could be used as an index of change during the time services were provided. The results, shown in Table 4, indicated a significant drop in scores, which are taken to be a sign of lowered risk of child abuse and neglect. Workers were also asked to rate overall changes in family functioning on a six-point scale, moving from greatly improved to greatly deteriorated. The results are shown in Table 5. The probability of future

Table 4. Changes in Scores on Case Screening Guide from Intake to Closure or End of Project[a]

Measure	Scores at Intake	Scores at Closure
Mean	15.54	12.63
Median	14.57	11.48
Mode	13	10
Range	1–33	0–28
Standard Deviation	4.25	5.68
Number	430	430

[a]Findings are significant at the .005 level.

neglect was considered by asking workers to estimate the likelihood of a substantiated referral being made to CPS in the next twelve months. The results are shown in Table 6. These results tended to suggest that, in the workers' opinions, a majority of families experienced some improvement in areas associated with child abuse and neglect and were unlikely to be referred to CPS in the next year. Finally, the Supervisor's Referral Log was used to determine the number of cases that were referred to CPS after receiving preventive services. Of the project cases that had been closed at the end of the service delivery period (196 cases), only 12 percent (24 cases), or 4.6 percent of the total caseload, were referred to CPS. From this, it is concluded that at least for the duration of the project, 95.4 percent of the high-risk families for whom the project initiated service were not referred to CPS.

Table 5. Overall Improvement in Family Functioning ($n = 410$)[a]

Variable	Frequency	Percentage
Improved		
Greatly improved	31	7.6
Somewhat improved	94	21.9
Slightly improved	201	46.7
Total	326	
Deteriorated		
Slightly deteriorated	45	10.5
Somewhat deteriorated	25	5.8
Greatly deteriorated	14	3.3
Total	84	
Unreported information[b]	20	4.7

[a]For purposes of analysis the author has omitted zeros, which represent unreported information. For this reason, percentages are based on the number of cases for which information is available rather than the total number of cases.

[b]$N = 430$ cases.

Table 6. Probability of Abuse and Neglect (n = 423)[a]

Variable	Frequency	Percentage
Highly improbable	122	28.4
Slightly improbable	154	35.8
Total	276	
Slightly probable	89	20.7
Highly probable	58	13.5
Total	147	
Unreported information[b]	7	1.6

[a]For purposes of analysis the author has omitted zeros, which represent unreported information. For this reason, percentages are based on the number of cases for which information is available rather than the total number of cases.

[b]N = 430 cases.

Conclusions

The Special Family Services Project designed a model for developing services to families at risk of abusing and neglecting their children. As part of the model, it operationally defined at-risk families and developed a useful field guide for identifying such families. The model uniquely defines the role of a case manager in a preventive program and defines assessment, direct service, and indirect service elements in that role. It remains for future research to improve aspects of the model and to establish its long-term effectiveness.

Notes and References

1. A national study of protective services found that "the length of time a case was open was directly related to the degree of improvement seen. Families where little improvement was seen were those who were active for a year or less. Cases active over two years tended to have an increasingly higher proportion of families showing improvement." See Deborah Shapiro, *Parents and Protectors: A Study In Child Abuse and Neglect* (New York: Child Welfare League of America, 1979), p. 74. Another study related the duration of home-based services to the prevention of foster care placements and found that the longer the period of service, the greater was the likelihood service objectives would be achieved. The statistically significant cutoff point was between eleven and twelve months of service. See Edmund Sherman et al., *Service to Children in Their Own Homes: Its Nature and Outcome* (New York: Child Welfare League of America, 1973), p. 106.

2. See Norman Polansky, Carolyn Hally, and Nancy Polansky, *Profile of Neglect: A Survey of the State of Knowledge of Child Neglect* (Washington, D.C.: U.S. Department of Health, Education & Welfare, Social and Rehabilitation Services, Community Services Administration, 1975).

3. Anne Harris Cohn, "Effective Treatment of Child Abuse and Neglect," *Social Work*, 24 (November 1979), pp. 513–519; and Isabel Wolock and Bernard Horowitz, "Child Maltreatment and Material Deprivation Among AFDC Recipient Families," *Social Service Review*, 53 (June 1979), pp. 175–194.

4. Ann Hartman, "Diagrammatic Assessment of Family Relationships," *Social Casework*, 59 (October 1978), pp. 465–476.

5. Brett A. Seabury, "The Contract: Uses, Abuses, and Limitations," *Social Work*, 21 (January 1976), pp. 16–21; Seabury, "Negotiating Sound Contracts with Clients," *Public Welfare*, 37 (Spring 1979), pp. 33–38; and Dean H. Hepworth, "Early Removal of Resistance in Task-Centered Casework," *Social Work*, 24 (July 1979), pp. 317–323.

Genetics and Adoption:
A Challenge for Social Work

Rita Beck Black

Because of rapid advances, human genetics has become an important factor in the turbulent changes faced by society. New knowledge about the manner in which human characteristics are inherited joins with such technical advances in medical genetics as prenatal diagnosis and chromosome analysis to offer an often bewildering set of new choices.[1] These advances provide hope and reassurance for many; at the same time, all people are confronted, both personally and as members of professions and other groups, with the need to adapt to and cope with the very environmental changes that they themselves have created.[2] Social workers in the health field are being called on with increasing frequency to assist people who face genetic risks and reproductive uncertainties, and important progress has been made in identifying the psychosocial impact of genetic disorders, the service needs of clients who have these disorders, and roles for social workers that are related to genetic problems.[3]

Equal attention must now be given to the implications of genetic advances for other areas of social work practice. This article considers some of the critical issues that link genetics and problems involved in adoption. Four areas of the potential impact of genetics on adoption policies and practices are the implications of (1) genetic factors for the adoptive placement of children who are the product of incestuous matings, (2) situations involving the discovery in an adoptee or in one of the biological parents of a genetic problem that has major medical implications, (3) the issue of genetic heritage in placing adoptees whose family histories include psychiatric illness, alcoholism, or psychopathic behavior, and (4) the importance, broadly speaking, of one's biological and genetic heritage to the development of a sense of identity. A discussion of these four areas follows.

Children of Incestuous or Consanguineous Unions

The profession has made much progress in recent years in its willingness to discuss the once taboo subject of incest and in its development of clinical perspectives on the subject.[4] This is helpful, because sexual relationships between close relatives are far from uncommon, and sensitive support and understanding should be provided for all those involved.[5] Nevertheless, the genetic risks for the physical and mental development of these offspring cannot be ignored. Such risks become especially critical for the children who result from unions between first-degree relatives, that is, parent and child or sibling and sibling.

The main risk is that of autosomal recessive disease, and there is also an appreciable risk of disorders involving multiple factors (multifactorial disorders).[6] Autosomal recessive diseases commonly result from a situation in which parents are symptomless carriers of one copy of the same defective gene in a gene pair. If their offspring receive a copy of the defective gene from each parent, they will suffer from the effects of the disease. When parents are related to each other, the risks are greatly increased that they carry the same deleterious genes. Hence, the risks of autosomal recessive disease in their offspring also are increased. Specifically, first-degree relatives (parent and child, siblings) share half their genes, second-degree relatives (half-siblings; uncle and niece; aunt and nephew; double first cousins, which is the term used to describe the resulting offspring of sisters of one family paired with brothers of another family; grandparent and grandchild) share one-fourth of their genes, and third-degree relatives (first cousins) share one-eighth of their genes. Likewise, because close relatives have many of the same genes, they also are more likely to possess a genetic liability for the same multifactorial disorders.

Observational studies of the offspring of incestuous unions document the practical impact of these genetic risks. Reporting on a review of four studies of offspring of first-degree relatives, Bundey found marked increases in autosomal recessive diseases and mental retardation. Less than half the 215 studied were normal when followed into childhood or young adulthood.[7] Studies of the offspring of first cousins suggest risks of about 1 to 2 percent for autosomal recessive disorders, 1 to 2 percent for multifactorial malformations, and about 2 to 3 percent overall for severe mental retardation from any cause.[8] The genetic risks for offspring of second-degree relatives are less well defined but would fall between those for the offspring of first-degree and third-degree relatives. The risks for offspring of various consanguineous matings are compared to the general population risks in Table 1.

The adoption worker faces the question of what to do when a child is

Table 1. Observed Risks of Disease in the Western World

	Autosomal Recessive Disease	Polygenetic Malformation	Severe Mental Retardation
In the population	1 in 400	1 in 60	1 in 100
In the offspring of first cousins	1 in 50	1 in 60	1 in 40
In the offspring of second degree relatives	1 in 20	?	?
In the offspring of first degree relatives	1 in 7	1 in 8	1 in 4

SOURCE: S. Bundey, "The Child of an Incestuous Union," in S. Wolkind, ed., *Medical Aspects of Adoption and Foster Care* Clinics in Developmental Medicine Series, Vol. 74 (Philadelphia: J. B. Lippincott Co., London: Spastics International Medical Publications, 1980), p. 39.

known to be the product of an incestuous union, and those cases where incest is strongly suspected but cannot be proved may be even more problematic. In some cases, the child's disorder may be evident at birth (e.g., when malformations are present), but many other problems, such as mental retardation, may not be manifest until well into the first year, if not later. Social workers must work closely with geneticists in developing the best procedures for evaluating such children and planning for their placement. At least one genetics center has developed a detailed protocol for following these children during infancy, with the assumption that negative test results at the end of a year would give potential adoptive parents reassurance that the risks for future problems are slight.[9]

The policy of delaying an adoption until one year of age is far from an optimal solution in terms of the child's physical and emotional development; the decision of when to make a child available for adoption must be based on more than genetic risks for future health problems. Moreover, many adoptive parents may be willing to adopt a newborn even in the face of such uncertainties. Truly informed decision making on the part of the adoptive parents remains as the one absolute necessity in such situations. Complete information on the genetic risks should be made available to all parties, and potential adoptive parents should be involved in thorough and open discussions of these issues as a prelude to any decisions about adoption of such children.

Genetically Caused Health Problems

The second area of genetics that comes into play in adoption policies and practices concerns the possibility that the prospective adoptee or one of the biological parents is found to have a genetic disorder or to be the heterozygote carrier of a disorder that places relatives at risk. The individual who first comes to the attention of the geneticists may be an adoptee for whom information about biological relatives is needed to establish an important medical diagnosis. Alternatively, a person who has been diagnosed as having a genetic defect may reveal that he or she placed a child for adoption some years earlier. This child then becomes recognized as having a high risk for the newly diagnosed disorder.[10] An example of a disease that can result from such a genetic defect is Huntington's disease. Huntington's disease is a degenerative neurological disorder that is inherited in an autosomal dominant manner. Because the first symptoms usually do not appear until during adulthood, children and young adults who are at risk for the disorder can only be told that they have a 50 percent chance of developing symptoms later in life. There is no cure or treatment at the present time.[11] The following example, as reported by geneticists from a leading clinic, describes this situation:

> Huntington['s] disease. Three sisters whose mother had been affected with Huntington's disease came to the Genetics Clinic . . . for evaluation and counseling. Another sister had already died with the disease, as had six maternal siblings. Two of the sisters were clinically unaffected. The third (age 31) was found to be moderately severely affected. During an interview it was learned that six years previously the affected sister had given up a daughter for adoption in a neighboring state. In addition, because of behavioral changes that can now be attributed to Huntington's disease, this woman had been denied visitation rights to another daughter, then nine years old, living with the former husband. . . . The affected woman and her sisters urged that genetic counseling be provided to the adoptive family, so that it can be prepared, if necessary, to deal with the signs of Huntington['s] disease without the mother's long experience of misdiagnosis and mistreatment. After considerable discussion about the anxiety that would be caused and about the latent period and lack of useful treatment, we decided to try to locate the family before routes of contact might be lost. . . . The out-of-state adoption agency was contacted, and the social worker located the family, presented the literature, drew an immediate "shocked" reaction, but reported that the family "accepted the situation." There was no further contact. The ex-husband, who had the other daughter, was contacted by the family and has permitted the daughter to visit her mother. The Clinic was not permitted to make contact with the adoptors or the father.[12]

Another example of a disease that may be diagnosed after an adoption has been completed is Fabry's disease. Fabry's disease is an X-linked recessive disorder and thus affects mainly males. The defect involves an enzyme deficiency that leads to accumulation of certain lipids. The expression of the disorder varies greatly but can include progressive renal failure and serious central nervous system problems.[13]

> *Fabry['s] disease.* Two sisters whose father had died recently of Fabry disease came to the Genetics Clinic for diagnostic serum enzyme tests and counseling. [The tests] . . . confirmed that both were carriers, as expected. One of the sisters had borne a son who was adopted through a local adoption agency 10 years earlier. . . . the biological mother urged that we attempt to provide counseling to this child, as we were providing for her other children. . . . The adoption agency supervisor located and contacted the adoptors. According to the adoptors they were told only that "the child is affected with Fabry['s] disease, a serious genetic disease," which "scared the pants off the family." They called the emergency ward of the University Hospital and allegedly were told by a nurse coordinator that "this is a serious genetic disease affecting the blood vessels and nerves." Their family physician referred them to the Genetics Clinic, and the telephone discussion about the appointment itself was reassuring. The boy's general physical examination was normal, but changes consistent with Fabry's disease were detected. . . . The extremely variable expressivity of this disease was explained in detail. The parents were made aware of the possibility of fever, pain in the limbs, and gastrointestinal bleeding, so that unindicated diagnostic tests could be avoided should these symptoms occur. The pattern of transmission was outlined. They were greatly relieved by the general information, by the instructions that no limitation of activity or diet was necessary, and by the news that there is active research into the treatment of such lipid storage disorders.[14]

A perhaps less dramatic (but no less important) situation that can arise involves the otherwise healthy adult who discovers that he or she is the carrier of an autosomal recessive gene for a serious disorder. This discovery may occur as the result of specific carrier testing, although all too often the birth of an affected child is the first evidence of the parents' carrier status. If the newly ascertained carrier is an adoptee or the biological parent of a child given up for adoption in the past, the issue again arises regarding how and when to attempt a search for the biological relatives.

Although carriers of autosomal recessive disorders usually do not experience any medical problems, they have a 25 percent chance for bearing offspring with the disorder in question if their mate carries the same defective gene. Because most defective genes appear only once in thousands of people, the chances usually are quite low that two spouses or mates carry the same altered genes. However, the risks are appreciably higher when the partners are biologically related and also when they come from the same racial or ethnic group. For some disorders, definitive carrier testing may be an option for an adoptee who receives such information about his or her carrier status. In other cases, where no carrier testing is possible, just the knowledge that one has a significantly increased chance of being a carrier might be an important factor in making decisions about bearing children.

Examination of situations such as these makes it clear that the issues of confidentiality and the nature of the data to be obtained about biological families are closely related concerns. Although adoption records are generally sealed in order to ensure confidentiality, records can be obtained in most states by a petition showing "good cause" for opening the record. As indicated by the above cases, genetic defects have been among the good causes that have been accepted. Nevertheless, although confidentiality per se does not necessarily constitute an insurmountable barrier, it may create serious delays or contribute to the inability to locate biological relatives some time after the completion of formal adoption proceedings.

The nature of the data that should be collected on biological relatives is further complicated by issues of confidentiality because it is becoming evident that access to medical and genetic data should be available throughout the lifetimes of the major parties involved. It seems reasonable to expect that, with increased public awareness of genetic disorders and genetic counseling services, the need for such policies will become even more apparent. In Minnesota, for example, in the 13 months (June 1, 1977, to June 30, 1978) after the passage of a law that opened sealed birth certificates, fully 56 percent of the adopted adults who filed requests for birth certificates asked for information on their genetic histories.[15] In addition, 50 percent also asked for an updated report on their genetic backgrounds. Policies to enable such provision of information can easily be justified under existing regulations as an extension of the court's or the adoption agency's statutory obligations to provide full medical information.[16] Further support comes from the decision in *Tarasoff* v. *Regents of the University of California*, where the court held that when disclosure is necessary to prevent harm to others, the confidentiality of personal information must yield.[17]

Geneticists themselves are already beginning to grapple with these issues. Ball and Omenn have proposed the following approach to ensuring confidentiality and ensuring access to medical and genetic information prior to and after adoptive placement:

> First, information with regard to the adoptee's medical and genetic background should be carefully, routinely, and completely gathered during preplacement proceedings. That information should be placed in a report, separate from the adoption report, given to the adoptive parents at the time of the adoption and available to the adoptee later upon request. Any information that would allow identification of the birth parents should be deleted.

Second, provision should be made for addition to the adoption record and to the medical record of any significant relevant medical or genetic information obtained subsequent to the adoption.

Third, provision should be made to allow for contact with the appropriate persons (adoptee, adoptive parents, birth parents) by medical professionals in case significant relevant information were uncovered. [18]

Similar concerns also are appearing in relation to the use of anonymous sperm donors for artificial insemination. Annas has argued that current artificial insemination practices primarily protect the interests of practitioners and donors rather than the recipients and children. The children who are the products of artificial insemination not only do not know the origins of half of their genetic make-up, but also do not necessarily know that artificial insemination was utilized for their conceptions. Much controversy continues over whether and when the offspring of artificial insemination should be provided with such information. [19]

Attention also must be directed to the enormous task presented to the direct service workers who are called upon to conduct preplacement investigations and to contact relatives if critical genetic information arises later. Professional execution of such services requires basic knowledge of at least three areas in addition to a core foundation in social work and child welfare: (1) the basic principles of human genetics and modes of inheritance, (2) the nature of genetic counseling services and the procedures for referral to the closest genetics clinic, and (3) the major psychosocial tasks likely to be faced by individuals or families confronting genetic diagnoses.

In regard to the psychosocial impact of genetic disorders, the case examples only begin to hint at the turmoil into which the adoptive families were thrown when this unexpected and unsolicited genetic information was delivered to them. Unfortunately, the social workers in the examples are described as playing only the limited role of conveyors of genetic information. A much more extensive involvement clearly is indicated in order to help families cope with these unexpected crises.

The groundwork for developing and expanding the role for social workers in adoptions has been laid in the existing and growing literature on the social worker's role in genetic counseling. Social workers and other health professionals also have contributed much to our understanding of the impact of genetic disorders on families. Schild introduced the concept of the "shattered self-adequacy syndrome" to describe one of the dynamics operating in families with genetic disorders. [20] She went on to characterize a genetic diagnosis as precipitating both acute and chronic stress that may require a continuum of services over the life span of the individual or the family. [21] The general attributes of a genetic diagnosis, which describe a condition that is permanent, chronic, familial, complex, labeling, and threatening, help us to understand some of the difficulties experienced by affected persons and their families.[22] Social workers in adoptions now must begin to contribute to this literature in relation to those special situations created by the adoptive triangle, for example, when adoptive parents learn that their supposedly healthy child is at risk for a severe genetic disorder, or when an adoptee with a genetic disorder tracks down his or her biological siblings to inform them of their potential reproductive risks. Such cases may be especially troublesome, because one of the aspects of adoption that attracts some prospective adoptive parents and that may be reinforced by agency practices is the notion that, unlike biological parenthood, one "can ensure that the child is without serious defects."[23] The potential impact of negative information on relationships between adoptees and adoptive parents as well as on the adoptee him- or herself deserves systematic investigation by social workers who are involved in helping families cope with these difficult issues.

Placement of Adoptees at Risk for Developing Psychiatric Problems

Few people would be likely to argue against efforts such as those described in the preceeding section for providing critical medical information to the biological members of a family that has been separated through adoption. The situation becomes more ambiguous, however, when the genetic information that is available reveals a family history of psychiatric illness, alcoholism, or psychopathic behavior. The central issues involve, on the one hand, the rights of adoptive parents and adoptees to have full access to complete information (along with updated information should it become available) on the adoptees' medical and genetic histories. On the other hand, there is the equally compelling concern over the negative, deterministic effects of labels and for the rights of an individual to grow and develop without prejudgment.[24]

As noted by Kadushin, the general orientation of the adoption field has emphasized the view that genetic and constitutional factors are secondary and of limited importance in relation to the interpersonal environment of the adoptive home.[25] Efforts to understand an adoptee's behavior and the reasons for the success or failure of adoptive placements have focused on relationships between the adoptive parents and the child. As Kadushin says, "We have not, except on some occasions, considered the child's genetic constitutional factors."[26] Policies such as closed adoption records and efforts to match physical and religious backgrounds all attempt to create and perpetuate the illusion that the adopted child is in fact the offspring of the adoptive parents.[27] At least two of the recently published social work textbooks on child welfare make no mention of genetic influences on behavior.[28] Kadushin does mention briefly that the

evidence for genetic influences on behavior should be given more attention in the future.[29] However, one striking example that he cites dramatically underscores the view that has prevailed in the field of adoptions;
the case demonstrates some of the reasons an adoption agency might
decide to reject an applicant. It is presented by Kadushin as an example
of those situations in which agencies perform a helpful function by assisting applicants to reach, on their own, decisions that they are not ready
for adoption. An excerpt of this case follows:

> Mr. and Mrs. W came about the adoption of an infant. It had not been
> absolutely determined that they could not have their own child, although
> the chances were slim and Mrs. W felt that she did not want to wait any
> longer for a child. Mr. W brought out many questions about the effects
> of heredity on a child and how adopted children turn out. . . . The
> worker commented that *evidently* Mr. W was not sure he could feel
> comfortable about being a parent to a child strangers had borne. . . .
> [After further discussion] Mr. W seemed very relieved and Mrs. W
> agreed that they should withdraw their request for the present and ex-
> plore the possibilities of having their own baby [Italics added for empha-
> sis].[30]

Why are Mr. W's concerns so "evidently" an indication of his unread-
iness to adopt a child? Perhaps in Mr. W's case the social worker's assessment was correct, but when, if ever, would such concerns and questions
about the heredity of potential adoptees be considered appropriate for
applicants? Are such questions inappropriate if articulated as general fears
early in the preadoption process, as in the case of Mr. W, but appropriate
later in the process if specific background information is sought on a child
whose family history contains evidence of mental illness, alcoholism, or
similar problems? And equally to the point, how many social workers
would feel knowledgeable enough to answer Mr. W's questions and engage him in a discussion of the factual as well as the personal aspects of
his concerns?

These are difficult questions, but recent research on the influence of
genetics on behavior indicates that, at the very least, Mr. W's questions
cannot be dismissed lightly. As Kadushin concluded after an extensive
review of the studies in this area,

> Recent research [evidence] . . . may require reconsideration of our em-
> phasis and a more respectful consideration of the influence of genetic
> inheritance as a determinant of the adoptive child's development.[31]

A rather different reason for giving careful consideration to the evidence
both for and against genetic influences on behavior grows out of recognition of the potential impact of the so-called bad blood syndrome, in which
parents anticipate negative behavior in their adoptive children.[32] For example, a number of women have described the ways in which their

adoptive parents panicked when they reached adolescence. The parents feared that the adoptees' bad blood would come out in poor impulse control similar to that supposedly shown by their biological mothers.[33] It appears that, despite the attempt by those working with the problems of adoption to deny the possibility of the influence of genetics on behavior, many adoptive parents nevertheless have maintained at least some belief in such influences. Fortunately, in most cases their fears are likely to be highly exaggerated and far from true risks. Open discussion by adoption personnel, who are equipped with accurate information, will be needed if we are to prevent such self-fulfilling prophecies from developing.

An extensive review of the studies on the inheritance of various psychiatric problems is beyond the scope of the present discussion, but it should be pointed out that the accumulated evidence has repeatedly confirmed that an inherited predisposition to develop certain problems, ranging from schizophrenia and manic depressive illness to criminality and alcoholism, does appear among biological relatives of affected individuals.[34] The crucial point to keep in mind in discussion of this question, however, is that genetic influences have been found to be only one of many influences on the course of an individual's development. Equally compelling are the data that document the powerful impact that environmental factors have on complex characteristics, and the relatively low specific risk that exists for any given individual who has a family history of psychiatric problems.[35] In other words, although data on group rates indicate a significantly increased risk that the offspring of a parent with a disorder such as schizophrenia, alcoholism, or psychopathic personality will themselves develop that disorder, the overwhelming majority of these children will *not* develop such problems.[36]

Although the influential components of these environmental factors are not fully understood at this time, it is clear that all infants and parent figures bring more to the familial relationship than their at-risk genes. Of particular interest to the field of adoptions are results that have come out of the Rochester longitudinal study of schizophrenic mothers.[37] As part of a larger study, the researchers followed babies of schizophrenic mothers after the babies had been placed for adoption. The data indicated these babies were not representative of a random sample of offspring of all schizophrenic women. In contrast to infants who remained with their biological mothers, the adoptive group were more likely to be premature and to have developed more physical problems. Sameroff and Zax concluded that the adoptive infant of a schizophrenic mother

> may bring with him far more concrete evidence of his deviancy than his schizophrenic genes. He may bring also an underweight, tiny body which places extra caretaking demands on his new adoptive parents. These extra caretaking demands and deviant physical appearance have been demon-

strated to affect mother-infant interaction . . . and have the potential of beginning a negative chain of transactions which could produce a deviant outcome irrespective of whether the infant carried schizophrenic genes.[38]

Neither can we ignore the role that adoptive parents may play in the development of their child's mental illness. For example, Wynne and Toohey, in an assessment of communication disorders, found evidence of amorphous and fragmented communication patterns in both the biological and adoptive parents of children who became schizophrenic.[39] The adoptive parents of the normal children showed no such problems in communication. Although not refuting the possibility of a genetically based vulnerability in the offspring of individuals with schizophrenia, such data do suggest an environmental component in the etiology of schizophrenia. As Sameroff and Zax concluded,

> There is no evidence to suggest that schizophrenia will arise in the adoptive offspring of schizophrenics if the psychosocial environment in the adoptive home is a healthy one. The remaining task is for behavioral researchers to define what constitutes healthy psychosocial environments both in non-adoptive and adoptive homes.[40]

Social workers involved in adoption should give careful attention and study to both sides of the debate about the nature-nurture problem. In actuality, there is no true either/or answer but rather a complex interweaving of innate vulnerabilities and potentials that, in interaction with equally powerful environmental forces, influences the course of an individual's development.

Nonetheless, a clear understanding of these general principles still leaves unanswered such practical questions as the following: (1) To whom should information on psychiatric problems in a family history be given, that is, to the adoptive parents only or to the adoptee directly? (2) If the adoptee is to be told about his or her genetic vulnerabilities, at what age should this occur? Who should tell the adoptee, and what is the agency's role in following up with services in such cases? (3) Is it the responsibility of the social worker to point out the possibility of an increased risk for a psychiatric disorder in a child's family history if the prospective parents do not express any concerns about it? For example, if left uninformed, could those parents sue the social worker and the agency in the event that a psychiatric problem developed in their adopted child? Such questions serve to highlight some of the complex policy and practice decisions that social workers must make.

Genetic Heritage and the Development of a Personal Sense of Identity

Consideration of the importance of one's biological and genetic heritage for the development of a personal sense of identity provides the final area for discussion of the impact of genetic issues on the field of adoptions. Although Goldstein, Freud, and Solnit argued forcefully for the primary importance of the "psychological" parent, that is, the person who actually cares for the child, other visible trends point away from this position.[41] The current controversy over sealed adoption records, the organization of services to help adoptees search for their biological parents, and the increased interest of the general population in finding their roots all signal an increased recognition of the importance of one's biological heritage. In addition, social work professionals, drawing insight from an ecological perspective, are beginning to argue that sustaining connectedness to the biological family is a crucial imperative that should guide social work practice in child welfare.[42]

The accounts of adoptees searching for their biological parents offer moving portrayals of the importance of this quest for one's biological origins. Commenting on this literature, Laird has observed that

> the individual's sense of identity and continuity is formed not only by the significant attachments in his intimate environment but also is deeply rooted in the biological family—in the genetic link that reaches back into the past and ahead into the future.[43]

Fisher is one such adoptee whose experiences in searching for her biological mother have contributed to her observations on the importance of knowing one's genetic reality for the development of identity. She has written that the effort of adoptees to learn their biological histories

> provides a frame for their lives, and a continuity with their pasts. It confirms and solidifies their images of themselves . . . in a search to achieve a unity and persistence of personality.[44]

Situations that involve genetic disorders or uncertainty about future problems because of genetic risks may seem somewhat removed from these larger concerns with one's heritage and the development of a sense of identity. Yet, that assumption is far from accurate, because the impact of a genetic diagnosis has been found to strike at the very core of one's identity. Unlike many diseases, genetic disorders are not readily externalized.[45] They seem to be experienced internally more often than not. The genes and the chromosomes are located in every cell of the body, so that no part of the individual escapes the defect. This notion of our genes as somehow more closely bound up with our sense of self is underscored by Schild's description, noted earlier, of one dynamic that may operate in families having genetic disorders. She has called this dynamic the shattered self-adequacy syndrome because "the knowledge that one possesses a defective gene [may] cause a momentous insult to the ego structure of the affected individual. Self esteem is especially vulnerable: expressions of inadequacy [may] become very manifest. [And] intense feelings of stigma and shame [may be] evoked."[46]

For adoptees, their sense of identity and competency may be shaken not only by the loss of continuity with their biological families but also by concerns about specific genetic defects that are unknown to the adoptees. They fear passing these defects on to their offspring. Again, the observations of Fisher as she prepared for the birth of her first child eloquently describe those feelings:

> Who had I come from? What genes was I carrying? Were there abnormalities that might skip me but be passed onto my child? Or physical deformities? . . . why had I been given up for adoption? Was it because there was something wrong with my parents? . . . To give birth is to establish the heredity link. It forces you to think back about your own heritage—to think of the traits and talents, the shapes and size of ancestors whose genes you carry. The adoptee goes back only into himself. Beyond that there is a wall. And it is the fear of what is behind that wall—magnified a thousand rational and irrational times in one's imagination—that causes all the mischief.[47]

Our growing awareness of our biological selves helps to shed light on the profound impact that discovery of a genetic disorder can have on an individual or a family. Despite progress in understanding the nature of that impact, little is known about the unique circumstances involved in adoption cases—for example, cases where there are complex issues involving psychological versus biological parents—or where individuals are cut off from virtually all knowledge of their genetic heritage and then have this knowledge suddenly thrust upon them by a genetics clinic.

The dilemmas raised by this analysis of genetics and problems in adoption encompass an awesome range of concerns such as practical questions about information gathering and record keeping, and social work practice issues involved in providing services to clients facing genetic risks. Profound questions about the basic requirements for the development of a full sense of one's identity are also raised. Hope for future progress can be seen, however, in the current movement by adoptees, adoptive parents, and specialists in adoption services to open adoption records and provide adoption-related services throughout the lifetimes of the "adoption triangle"—adoptees, biological parents, and adoptive parents. This movement demonstrates a striking convergence with the suggestions of the geneticists described earlier. For example, following extensive research on the adoption triangle, Sorosky, Baran, and Pannor recommended the following:

> [1] Continuing commitments by adoption agencies to all members of the adoption triangle for as long as necessary, including the provision of viable, current information to any of these parties. This will involve the re-establishment and continuation of contact by the agency with the adoptive family and birth parents. . . .
> [2] The setting up of counseling services which recognize that adoption is a lifelong process for all involved.[48]

This recognition of adoption as a lifelong process is perhaps the most crucial conclusion to be derived from the preceding discussion. Whether the case at hand involves clear genetic risks for a major medical problem, insidious worries about bad blood appearing in an adoptive child, or the vaguely articulated fears of prospective adoptive parents, the challenge for social work is to develop a system of services that can address the need for accurate medical and genetic information as well as for the social work services that are critically necessary for preventing the misuse and distortion of that information.

Notes and References

1. R. B. Black, "Risk Taking Behavior: Decision Making in the Face of Genetic Uncertainty," *Social Work in Health Care,* 7 (Fall 1981), pp. 11–25.

2. C. Germain, ed., *Social Work Practice: People and Environments* (New York: Columbia University Press, 1979).

3. See, for example, R. B. Black, "The Effects of Diagnostic Uncertainty and Available Options on Perceptions of Risk," *Birth Defects: Original Article Series,* Vol. 15, No. 5C (New York: Alan R. Liss, Inc., 1979), pp. 341–354; Black, "Parents' Evaluations of Genetic Counseling," *Patient Counselling and Health Education,* 2, No. 3 (1980), pp. 142–146; Black, "Risk Taking Behavior;" M. L. Griffin, C. M. Kavanagh, and J. R. Sorenson, "Genetic Knowledge, Client Perspectives, and Genetic Counseling," *Social Work in Health Care,* 2 (Winter 1976–77), pp. 171–180; S. Kessler, ed., *Genetic Counseling: Psychological Dimensions* (New York: Academic Press, 1979); Sylvia Schild, "The Challenging Opportunity for Social Workers in Genetics," *Social Work,* 11 (April 1966), pp. 22–28; Schild, "Social Workers' Contribution to Genetic Counseling," *Social Casework,* 54 (July 1973), pp. 387–392; Schild, "Social Work with Genetic Problems," *Health and Social Work,* 2 (February 1977), pp. 58–77; Amelia L. Schultz, "The Impact of Genetic Disorders," *Social Work,* 11 (April 1966), pp. 29–34; and J. O. Weiss, "Social Work and Genetic Counseling," *Social Work in Health Care,* 2 (1976), pp. 5–12.

4. I. B. Weiner, "A Clinical Perspective on Incest," *American Journal of Diseases of Children,* 132 (February 1978), pp. 123–124.

5. Weiner, op. cit.; W. D. Weitzel, B. J. Powell, and E. C. Penick, "Clinical Management of Father-Daughter Incest," *American Journal of Diseases of Children,* 132 (February 1978), pp. 127–130.

6. S. Bundey, "The Child of an Incestuous Union," in S. Wolkind, ed., *Medical Aspects of Adoption and Foster Care,* Clinics in Developmental Medicine Series, Vol. 74 (Philadelphia: J. B. Lippincott Co.; London: Spastics International Medical Publications, 1980), pp. 36–41.

7. Ibid.

8. Ibid.

9. J. G. Hall, "Children of Incest: When to Suspect and How to Evaluate?" *American Journal of Diseases of Children,* 132 (October 1978), p. 1045.

10. G. S. Omenn, J. G. Hall, and K. D. Hansen, "Genetic Counseling for Adoptees at Risk for Specific Inherited Disorders," *American Journal of Medical Genetics,* 5 (1980), pp. 157–164.

11. See N. S. Wexler, "Genetic 'Russian Roulette': The Experience of Being 'At Risk' for Huntington's Disease," in Kessler, op. cit., pp. 199–220, for a sensitive analysis of the impact of Huntington's disease on individuals and families.

12. Omenn, Hall, and Hansen, op. cit., pp. 159–160.

13. See D. W. Smith, *Recognizable Patterns of Human Malformation* (2d ed.; Philadelphia: W. B. Saunders Co., 1976), p. 360.

14. Omenn, Hall, and Hansen, op. cit., pp. 160–161.

15. R. C. Weidell, "Unsealing Sealed Birth Certificates in Minnesota," *Child Welfare*, 59 (February 1980), pp. 113–119.

16. Omenn, Hall, and Hansen, op. cit.

17. J. R. Ball and G. S. Omenn, "Genetics, Adoption, and the Law," in A. Milunsky and G. J. Annas, eds., *Genetics and the Law II* (New York: Plenum Press, 1980), pp. 269–279.

18. Ibid., pp. 277–278.

19. For further discussion of this topic see G. Annas, "Fathers Anonymous: Beyond the Best Interests of the Sperm Donor," in Milunsky and Annas, eds., op. cit., pp. 331–340; Ball and Omenn, op. cit.; and A. D. Sorosky, A. Baran, and R. Pannor, *The Adoption Triangle* (Garden City, N.Y.: Doubleday & Co., Anchor Press, 1978).

20. Schild, "The Challenging Opportunity for Social Workers in Genetics."

21. Schild, "Social Workers' Contributions to Genetics Counseling."

22. Schild, "Social Work with Genetic Problems."

23. A. Kadushin, *Child Welfare Services* (3d ed.; New York: Macmillan Publishing Co., 1980), p. 455.

24. H. S. Becker, *Outsiders, Studies in the Sociology of Deviance* (2d ed.; New York: Free Press, 1973); E. M. Lemert, *Social Pathology* (New York: McGraw-Hill Book Co., 1951); and P. M. Rains, J. I. Kitsuse, T. Duster, and E. Friedson, "The Labeling Approach to Deviance," in N. Hobbs, ed., *Issues in the Classification of Children: A Sourcebook on Categories, Labels, and Their Consequences* (San Francisco: Jossey-Bass, 1975), pp. 88–100.

25. A. Kadushin, "Children in Adoptive Homes," in H. S. Maas, ed., *Social Service Research: Reviews of Studies* (Washington, D.C.: National Association of Social Workers, 1978), pp. 39–89.

26. Ibid., p. 74.

27. J. Laird, "An Ecological Approach to Child Welfare: Issues of Family Identity and Continuity," in Germain, op. cit., pp. 174–209.

28. L. B. Costin, *Child Welfare Policies and Practice*, (2d ed; New York: McGraw-Hill Book Co., 1979; and T. Stein, *Social Work Practice in Child Welfare* (Englewood Cliffs, N.J.: Prentice-Hall, 1981).

29. Kadushin, *Child Welfare Services*.

30. Ibid., p. 373.

31. Kadushin, "Children in Adoptive Homes," p. 74.

32. Sorosky, Baran, and Pannor, op. cit.

33. Ibid.

34. See, for example, M. Bohman, "Children of Psychopathic and Alcoholic Parents," in Wolkind, ed., op. cit., pp. 49–55; Kadushin, "Children in Adoptive Homes"; M. T. Tsuang, "Genetic Counseling for Psychiatric Patients and Their Families," *American Journal of Psychiatry*, 135 (1978), pp. 1465–1475; Tsuang, and R. Vandermey, *Genes and the Mind: Inheritance of Mental Illness* (New York: Oxford University Press, 1980).

35. M. Bloom, *Primary Prevention, The Possible Science* (Englewood Cliffs, N.J.: Prentice-Hall, 1981); Bohman, op. cit.; Kadushin, "Children in Adoptive Homes"; A. J. Sameroff and M. Zax, "The Child of Psychotic Parents"; and Wolkind, ed., op. cit., pp. 42–48.

36. Ibid.; and Tsuang, op. cit.

37. Sameroff and Zax, op. cit.

38. Ibid., p. 46.

39. L. C. Wynne and M. L. Toohey, "Communication of the Adoptive Parents of Schizophrenics," J. Jorstad and E. Ugelstad, eds., *Schizophrenia 1975: Psycho-Therapy, Family Therapy, Research* (Oslo, Norway: Scandinavian University Books, 1976).

40. Sameroff and Zax, op. cit., p. 47.

41. J. Goldstein, A. Freud, and A. J. Solnit, *Beyond the Best Interests of the Child* (New York: The Free Press, 1973).

42. Germain, op. cit.; and Laird, op. cit.

43. Laird, op. cit., p. 177.

44. F. Fisher, *The Search for Anna Fisher* (New York: Arthur Fields Books, 1973), p. 186.

45. Kessler, op. cit.

46. Schild, "The Challenging Opportunity for Social Workers in Genetics."

47. Fisher, op. cit., p. 52.

48. Sorosky, Baran, and Pannor, op. cit., p. 224.